2586 6-95

Trapped within Welfare

Titles in the Crisis Points series

Published

The Devil Makes Work: Leisure in Capitalist Britain
John Clarke and Chas Critcher

Schooling the Smash Street Kids
Paul Corrigan

Beyond Progressive Education
Ken Jones

Trapped within Welfare: surviving social work
Mike Simpkin

Forthcoming

Who Owns the Media?
Graham Murdock

Trapped within Welfare

Surviving Social Work

Mike Simpkin

SECOND EDITION

MACMILLAN

First edition 1979
Second edition 1983
Reprinted 1986

Published by
MACMILLAN EDUCATION LTD
Houndmills, Basingstoke, Hampshire RG21 2XS
and London
Companies and representatives
throughout the world

Printed in Hong Kong

ISBN 0-333-33956-8

Contents

Preface to the Second Edition

At the beginning of 1982 a BBC documentary series about the police achieved widespread publicity and notoriety, not least for the callous handling of a rape complaint. An opinion poll at the end of the series suggested that confidence in the police had, if anything, increased; top of viewers' priorities for institutions suitable for similar 'fly on the wall' treatment were Social Services Departments. In fact there had been a shorter and equally controversial series about social workers some months earlier. I have some doubts over the propriety of presenting intimate and emotional scenes from people's real lives as peak-time television viewing, though it may be possible to maintain adequate safeguards. But this poll confirmed how much more prominent a place social services now have in the public consciousness than in the mid-1970s when the first edition of this book was written. Much of the comment and of the depiction of social workers may still be ill-informed, but the interest is now there.

Why should there have been such a change? No doubt voyeurism plays a part, as, for the more fortunate, does relief at having avoided the fate of being a social work client. One young mother whom I visited after a psychiatric referral was at first offended because she had gained the impression from the television that social workers only visit 'grotty' homes. But this remark suggests another reason: expansion of services in the 1970s, combined with the effect of the recession presided over by the gurus of monetarism and the Tory Right, have brought many more people into the net of the social services than ever before. Forced increases in council rents and rates, in fuel prices and in regressive taxation have to be met out of diminishing incomes or by a social security system where many benefits have been made less flexible in addition to the loss of some of their real value. Social workers, housing authorities and the tottering National Health Service have all had to take account of massively increased personal debt as well as the social and emotional scars of large-scale unemployment.

Tory efforts to exploit anti-statist feeling as an ally in their assault upon public expenditure have, fortunately, been less successful than might have been expected. Generalised criticism of bureaucracy has not prevented people from rallying to the defence of services they regard as useful, though there has been no effective mass movement and the odds are often stacked against isolated defensive actions. Recognition of deficiencies, for instance in the NHS, has usually resulted in demands for improvements, rather than abolition; attempts to force social and health services to take a more residual role have met stiff resistance, though the Tories have done their best to encourage a burgeoning private sector, often parasitic on the state, which does present a serious threat to the principle of universal services. Perhaps surprisingly, in view of the fact that the structure of social work has altered little over the last few years, the major cutbacks have been in education and housing. Indeed, Labour has used the defence of social services as one of its major policies, though activists have quite rightly insisted that there should be increasing debate over issues of legitimacy and accountability. Areas of direct social work power are also coming under closer scrutiny: for instance, the much too ready use of section 3 of the 1980 Children's Act (formerly section 2 of the 1948 Act).

This politicisation of welfare issues is to be welcomed. Social workers have accepted the need to provide answers to questions of practice, if they are to win the battle for resources. As a result, the professional literature has become less cosy and more attuned to real political issues. Of course, much of the pressure has also come from within the social services: social workers' readiness in many instances to take an active part in defending services or facilities, and the experience of industrial organisation gained both in the strikes of 1978–9 and in subsequent actions, have enabled us to have a much stronger voice, even if this has alarmed the welfare establishment and created some new enemies. Dissident critiques of values and practice have emerged from both Left and Right, and although the latter have, because of the political atmosphere, had more influence than the quality of their criticism has deserved, the build up of both literature and experience on the radical and socialist side is beginning to lay some solid foundations for strategy, even if there is not as yet a fully agreed stance.

Developments on the Left which have affected radical social work have been on two fronts. Perhaps the most important has been the way in which a rising tide of disillusion with Left organisations coalesced with the increasing strength of socialist feminism in the support given to *Beyond the Fragments*, a collection of essays which repudiated much behaviour taken for granted on the Left, and helped to promote a much greater legitimation for the acceptance and exploration of personal issues as being necessarily political.[1] Although many orthodox socialists, mostly male, saw this as a retreat in the face of the Tory onslaught, using as evidence the failure of *Beyond the Fragments* to come up with any acceptable and effective organisational alternatives, there is no doubt that, at local levels at least, seeds have been sown for ideas and alliances that may have more widespread effect as the Tories falter.

Similar chords were struck by the collective which produced *In and Against the State*,[2] which stressed not only the contradictions facing state workers in all sectors, but also the importance of consumers' poor experience of state services; the administrative distance between resources and the people who needed them was suggested to be a significant hindrance in winning mass support against cutbacks. But once again, the proposals and the response were too diffuse to achieve successful united organisation.

On the academic side, the Marxist view of the state and welfare in capitalist society has received much more detailed consideration, mainly from the viewpoint of the Broad Left, which concedes most of the criticisms of welfare made by socialists who demand more revolutionary change, but none the less argues that socialists within the state have a quite legitimate role as guardians and propagators of working-class interests. Social workers have, not unnaturally, found this position more comforting than the rather bleaker revolutionary scenario which emphasises the controlling functions of the state and which can therefore seem both pessimistic and unduly limiting. But while it may be true that revolutionary socialists risk either being trapped in their own rhetoric or belatedly drifting towards reformism, the more conventional Left, with its belief in the possibility of transforming the state, stokes up enthusiasm for policies and projects only to be brought up short, amid accusations of betrayal, when the interests of capital demand retrenchment of state activities around a much more restricted and authoritarian role. The Broad Left argues that the state can be seen as 'an arena of class struggle' or as reflecting the balance of class forces.[3] This is the position of 'semi-autonomy' for the state which I criticise in Chapter 2. My own reaction is still one of suspicion. The fact that welfare is subject to the interplay of contradictory forces is one reason why over-simplistic analysis of the state as a crude instrument of social control is not really credible. But hard though it is to find single words that accurately reflect the complexity of the state as an institution, neutral terms like 'arena' foster dangerous illusions about the possibility of transforming state power and neglect its inextricable connection with the dominance of capital. Of course, the effectiveness of the state in ensuring conditions in which capital can accumulate depends on the balance of social forces at any given time. But it is equally important to recognise that even during periods when capital is on the retreat and needing to offer concessions, the state will, until some total change, always retain a structure through which the goal of accumulation can be achieved. However many benefits or services have been conceded, control of these benefits has never been surrendered, even when Labour has dominated the legislature. As Taylor-Gooby and Dale put it, the state cannot solve the relations of production because it is itself the product of those relations.[4] Thus when the authors of *Towards Socialist Welfare Work*[5] suggest that, in the absence of a vibrant and effective working-class movement, a strategic stand for democratisation is the most powerful option for socialists, they do so in the context of the belief that, in Leonard's words, 'the state can be transformed to benefit the working class'. Thereby they run the risk of substituting a democratisation which can never be fully effective for the building of that working-class movement without which there can be no effective socialist transformation. Analogies to this process may be found in the co-operative movement or by looking at the media; democratising the structure of one or more newspapers may make the paper more palatable for socialists and more rewarding for its workers. But the need to retain the goodwill of advertisers and the force of consensus values will still hold sway unless the structures of newspaper readership and of journalism are wholly changed.

There are no easy answers or options in this debate, which is discussed further in Chapter 8, but on its outcome hinges the general level of expectation for socialist change through welfare. The important thing to remember is that this will not be achieved in academic argument, but, as many of the Broad Left themselves recognise, only through active working-class struggle. I also consider it important that socialists do not confine themselves to broad issues of social policy and administration, but look in much more detail at the specific options in practical social work so that even at this individual level we can seek means of avoiding the reinforcement of dominant but oppressive cultural patterns and try to set up the possibility for progressive personal change.

The first edition of this book was commissioned as part of the Crisis Points series, and therefore written to a specific length with a brief to be provocative. At the time it was completed, there was still no extended account of radical social work, and my efforts to fill that gap meant that many topics got much less attention than they deserved. I was also unable to take advantage of some of the recent work which is now regarded as standard. However, most comment has suggested that the strengths of the book are in its flavour and use of experience, and therefore I have left the bulk of it unaltered except for a few minor corrections or updatings. I have rewritten the end of Chapter 2 and slightly altered some remarks on deskilling on page 95. I have, however, taken the opportunity of an expanded edition to recast the end of Chapter 7, including a personal account of the 1978–9 strikes, and considerably to enlarge the last chapter in order to offer some more positive direction. My debt to recent writers will be obvious. I should like to thank all those who responded positively to the original appearance of the book. For help with preparation of this edition, I should like once again to thank Carole Dale, and also Steven Kennedy of Macmillan for his enthusiasm and advice.

August 1982 MIKE SIMPKIN

Acknowledgements

Many people have contributed to the ideas expressed in this book, so I make no claims to originality. Particular thanks must go to the early members of the Editorial Collective of *Case Con*, who enabled me to see the value of a more radical perspective after my liberalism had been shredded by my post-Seebohm experience. I am also grateful to my present colleagues, especially Wally Reed, for their moral support, if not their total agreement, and to Paul Corrigan and Peter Leonard for allowing me to see advance proofs of their new book *Social Work Practice under Capitalism*. Ian Taylor suggested the book and his comments have saved me from at least some political and stylistic solecisms; Tim Fox at Macmillan was of great help at the copy-editing stage. My greatest debt is to Carole Dale, whose imagination and perseverance have not only ensured completion of the book, but also provided much of its inspiration. Needless to say, any mistakes are my responsibility.

1978 M. S.

Introduction

Social work: profession of the seven veils

I was recently asked by a senior colleague whether, when asked at a party what job I do, I am, like him, both reluctant and embarrassed to admit to being a social worker. He was much reassured to find that I shared his feelings; in fact I am certain the phenomenon is both widespread and characteristic except among those few social workers who profess complete certainty in the value of their work. Most people in controversial occupations are, of course, unwilling to rehearse too frequently the arguments which surround them, especially when they are supposed to be relaxing; in addition those in 'helping' professions often fear both the extra demands which may unexpectedly be made on them, and the air of virtue which their work endows. Yet the fact remains that for members of an occupation assertive of its own importance and frequently critical of other professions, we are, especially in private, curiously self-effacing and apologetic.

The reason, I suggest, is that social work is a fundamentally ambiguous and conflict-ridden activity which it is difficult to define or describe in a way which outsiders can easily understand. Eager to please, we are rarely able to satisfy one party, let alone all; we work in an emotional hothouse of guilt, blame and recrimination. Our material and methods are not quantifiable and we can rarely decisively control the factors which could lead our work to a successful outcome. Furthermore, the pressure we are under combines with the personal traits which have led many of us into social work anyway to make us highly defensive not only against outside criticism but even against each other – divisions which are reinforced by the highly individualistic tradition of our theory and practice. Our strongest defence is to concentrate upon 'client' behaviour. The very use of such a term suggests a realm worthy of detailed and separate attention, though I shall use 'client' throughout this book for convenience; alternatives are equally inaccurate and unilluminating. (It is the role which has to be changed; the terminology will follow.) By spending so much of our time purporting to understand clients, we are largely able to ignore our own actions and reactions, and the effect they have on all those who have to do with us, including each other. Our own behaviour appears to fall into some separate category. We talk about the use of self, but lack of self-awareness is common to all the helping professions; that too is a product of our role. Still the blatant social incompetence and insensitivity of many social workers and psychiatrists is astonishing among people who pretend to some expertise in relationships. I shall later explore some of the different and contradictory aspects of radicalism in social work, but fundamental to any radical approach must be a challenge to the artificial divisions which are made between social workers and clients, and the double standards which we operate. The essence of radicalism is to abolish the different levels of thought and action, and to recognise that to a large extent our fate is shared. An example may help to clarify the absurdities of not doing so.

Three months after becoming a trainee child care officer in a friendly and caring team I was asked to take over temporarily the caseload of someone who had fallen ill. By the time I started my second round of statutory visits, six or seven weeks later, clients were beginning to ask anxiously after my rather elderly predecessor's health and whether she was likely to return. I could not tell them because I did not know. Despite repeated requests for information it was not for another three weeks that I learnt that she had been admitted to a mental hospital with agitated depression. My point is not that she was not entitled to privacy; rather that the misfortune she had suffered was considered to transcend the boundaries of normality. While we were busy persuading our clients that nothing was as bad as it seemed, we were expected to apply a completely different standard to our colleague. By crossing the divide which separated us, she had placed her status in question, deserving no doubt our compassion and understanding, but apparently forfeiting our respect. In the last eight years we have become less falsely considerate, not least because more social workers have been driven near to breakdown; but, except among radicals, giving way to stress is still regarded as failure.

I will be writing here mainly about social workers, although I am aware that radicalism in social work has in general been associated with the advancement of client opinion. I make no apology for this. It is all too easy to write ourselves as social workers out of the script in the name of client self-determination only to take up the director's role. It is not that we do not try to understand ourselves. Much of our time is spent in bitter or regretful reworking of events and actions, but we fudge our answers by remaining confined within the double barriers of professional tradition and agency expectation, often ending up by feeding off our intraverted agonising almost to the level of indulgence. To work, as many social workers do, at a permanent level of emotional crisis is to labour perpetually under the illusion of facing up to important problems without ever being committed to particular solutions. Our responses have to be flexible but, without direction and perspective, they can be inconsistent and meaningless. In fact most social workers do have some perspective of their own but rarely dare to place it under detailed examination. We must be able to state and, if necessary, defend or modify the assumptions with which we work.

Social work is not in itself sufficient to attain its stated goals. We are working in a wider social context which delimits the possibilities open either to us or to clients. In order both to understand and to take effective action, we have to perceive and, if necessary, act outside the social work framework as well as within it. The way we are expected to act as social workers will not always coincide with our broader social perspectives or ideals – for instance, in dealing with truancy or mental disorder. We must, however, be ready to act simultaneously at both levels, even at the risk of appearing to contradict ourselves, and not be lured into concluding that our more immediate and small-scale actions are necessarily more real. Social work can achieve very little even on its own terms without attempting to move the world of which it is itself only a small part.

Even with such an understanding, social work is rarely much more than a profession of excuses and the provision of second-best substitutes. Without it, there is an irrevocable decline into dishonesty to our clients, to each other and to ourselves. In order to make any progress in our work, we have to deny, cover up, rationalise, reconcile, compromise and cheat. Failure to admit this or to examine the reasons why is a betrayal, but the consequences of examining the contradictions of the job are also ominous since they lead to a questioning of society itself. Taken to its logical conclusion social work is an inherently radicalising activity, but there is a built-in deterrent best expressed by C. Wright Mills as early as 1943:

> Present institutions train several kinds of persons – such as judges and social workers – to think in terms of 'situations'. Their activities and mental outlook are set within the existing norms of society: in their professional work they tend to have an occupationally trained incapacity to rise above 'cases'.[1]

Social workers, among others, have their heads (and hearts) so deeply buried in the forest of individual problems that they are often unable to gain any broader perspective at all, or to conceptualise about their work. Clients, by being isolated from each other, are less well equipped to distinguish the pressures which they have in common and to resist them. I shall examine some of the reasons for this individualisation in later chapters but we should meanwhile note that the need for a collective and conceptual approach is one of the most basic radical principles essential to change.

Professional myopia has another function. From the short-term gains which we can achieve in some cases, and the very few worthwhile long-term benefits we can secure, we derive an optimism sufficient to justify our labours elsewhere, even though the general terrain may look bleak to any examination. But while this badger-like behaviour may temporarily assist our survival, it is no more than an escape. We cannot thereby justify our seeming inability to give any meaningful account of ourselves which expresses the pressures, the frustrations or even the rewards of what we do. We communicate in a jargon which attempts to provide its own justification, but is merely bewildering to the uninitiated. Very few insiders have written revealingly about social work. Most ex-practitioners have adopted an academic style often less informative than the work of academic observers themselves. The struggle I have faced to produce this book, especially working to a deadline, has brought home to me how hard a task it is. Puzzled novelists and scriptwriters drift us social workers across their pages in highly stereotypical or caricatured roles. Politicians praise us or attack us at their convenience. Up to now it has made little difference; we are protected by the vagueness of our brief.

This is the heart of the matter. It is true that our work is neither unique nor anything very specialised. Many other occupations, from medicine to mining, can inflict greater stress and risk, both mental and physical. Many place their holders in what are at least as invidious positions and demand more unpleasant decisions. But none, with the possible exception of politics, leaves its practitioners so permanently vulnerable to everything except industrial injury, and I am surprised there is not more of that. We are neither protected by high social standing nor compensated with high salaries. Instead, despite all recent progress, we are still endowed with the vestiges of do-gooding, charity or welfare, which combine a variety of moral obligations with the aura of the Board of Guardians and the Town Hall. It is small wonder we have traditionally retreated into justifications and apparent rationalisations which conceal more than they explain and successfully divert attention from ourselves.

I have argued that our reluctance to be subjected to scrutiny and our concentration on client behaviour are inherent but unhealthy defences to the demands currently made upon social work. Radicals have to develop a position of clarity, based upon a rejection both of the arbitrary division between social worker and client and of an approach founded on individual case-analysis. Closer examination will show how deeply these are rooted not just in social work theory and practice but in our whole socio-economic structure, and that all social work of whatever form is essentially political. The ultimate target of radicalism has to be that structure.

I must, however, issue two caveats at this stage to prevent misunderstanding. First, the fact that I believe that change is now necessary on a revolutionary scale does not mean that I deny the value of past reforms or that I maintain that everything is just as bad as it has always been. That is clearly nonsense, but such denial poses fewer problems for radicals than is sometimes thought. Secondly, an emphasis on the political aspects of social work is not intended to detract from concern with human relationships, but rather to enhance them. The belief that human and political concern are separate is the product of a false dichotomy which has had grave consequences for both theory and practice, as I shall argue in Chapters 4 and 5.

One value of an underlying socio-political analysis is that it frees individuals (whether clients, social workers or neither) from accruing unnecessary blame and guilt to themselves, and thereby permits freer, more honest and more effective appraisal. For instance, it is becoming gradually clearer that the personal qualities of the social worker have much more effect on the nature and outcome of our work relationships than we have been prepared to admit because the implications for each of us could be devastating. We have tended to regard differences in personality as matters of style. This resistance has been backed by the ideals of therapeutic inscrutability, bureaucratic impersonality and objective technical ability, the respective endowments of psychoanalysis, local government tradition and the new professionalism. Radicals, too, have justifiably blocked attempts to focus on their own personalities, knowing they risk insidious attempts by tutors or supervisors to devalidate their opinions. Furthermore, personality is generally supposed to have to conform to some artificial therapeutic model based firmly on the prevailing conception of health. Not only do the values of such a paradigm have to be queried, but it has also to be asked whether it may not be that a social worker who recognises his or her own limitations and who conveys the possibility that they too might sometimes be unable to cope can contribute both more honestly and more lastingly than the social worker who appears publicly as a pillar of strength but collapses in the security or insecurity of their private life. Clients consistently ask for and value friendship, not perfection. A radical approach seeks to ensure the possibility of real personal encounters in which the contribution of the helped to the helper is also fully recognised.

In this book I shall attempt to suggest some of the ways this can be achieved, the implications of such an approach and the cul-de-sacs and barriers which block the way. After a short survey of recent developments in social work, including radicalism, I shall briefly describe the political and economic forces which shape the form and objects of social work and argue that no form of practice should fail to take these into account. In the second part, I shall ask who clients and their social workers are and suggest they are locked in an unbalanced but complementary symbiosis which reflects the inequality inherent in the structure of our society. In the third part I shall look critically at the different strategies which are on offer to social workers and press for the adoption of a radical strategy actively informed by Marxist theory and practice as the only way to make sense of what we are asked to do, and the only way to change it. The argument will necessarily be selective, the evidence incomplete and the prescriptions tentative. My priorities will reflect the conflicts and problems of my own experience, which may not all be relevant today. Nonetheless I hope they will at least succeed in renewing a more realistic conviction that radicalism in social work is not just possible but essential if we really mean to bring significant benefits and change to all our lives. No longer should we be able to upbraid clients for their inadequacies while we fail to tackle our own, and if we do face up, we shall find we have far more in common with them than our present sentimental lip service to 'caring' allows us to recognise.

Part I

Social Work and Social Policy

1

The pricking of the social work bubble

While preparing this book I went out to pay a second visit to the distraught mother of Susan L. Susan, a 20-year-old student, had just been compulsorily admitted for the second time to the mental hospital where I work after allegedly exhibiting manic and frightening behaviour. My initial call had been a few days after Susan's first admission, a month before; it had been a difficult interview, notable for the fact that Mrs L. was displaying far more overt symptoms of mental stress, mainly in the form of a paranoid hysteria, than we had any direct evidence of her daughter doing. It was Susan, however, who was lying in hospital – so heavily sedated that she could neither walk straight nor see clearly. At that time Mrs L.'s rejection of Susan had been so strong that she referred to her as 'that thing' and could explain Susan's uncharacteristic behaviour only through demonic possession (Susan had in fact played around with drugs and witchcraft). My task seemed to be to listen and reassure, to try and place the rejection in context, and to sow the seeds of alternative explanations for Mrs L. to consider as her immediate tension evaporated. To do this I had to try and obtain some sort of guide to the events leading up to this crisis. All of this falls firmly within the bounds of standard casework procedure. Inevitably it involved some disagreement as I cautiously attempted to limit her fears; she was especially indignant at any of my questions which had to do with the general atmosphere and history of the family. I had to tread a wary path between prejudging Susan and threatening the remnants of Mrs L.'s security.

The second time around, I knew Susan rather better and had no doubt that she was in deep personal anguish, although she could not trust anybody quite enough to express her pain. Her actions, though often exaggerated by others, were of a bizarre nature; most of the time she was quite rational but occasionally at home she would regress to being completely infantile. She denied any difficulties but we had, I thought, the beginnings of a *rapport*. Meanwhile I had had several long telephone conversations with Mrs L., who had regained some of her equilibrium and, while I had argued about her interpretations, was reassured by our agreement that Susan's behaviour was unusual, whatever the causes. This time, though still under strain, she was confident enough to tell me fairly early on how much she had hated and resented me before, to the extent, apparently, of having complained about me to all and sundry:

> When you came in, with your beard and anorak, I couldn't fail to be reminded of all the friends my sons had when they were at college. They just seemed to drop all their standards. They'd come and sleep on the floor like sardines, wearing funny Ho Chi Minh moustaches, and ready to pick up any banner without even looking to see what it said. They blamed everything on reactionary bourgeois parents, called me a fascist and a materialist, even though they knew that my husband and I know what it's like to be really poor; and, what's more, whatever degrees they were studying for, they just wanted to become social workers and save the world.

Among other things, Mrs L. was trying to enlist me as an ally, to apologise, and to probe my reactions; she knew I might be critical but now trusted me enough to go a little further. We were able to build up a discussion on the family and how its imperfections were not necessarily the fault of the parents, and why that was. Nor did I hesitate to tell her that I often went on demonstrations. She was surprised, as she had yet again to readjust her expectations, then interested as she tentatively explored one or two issues and, finally, obviously grateful that she was now in a position to evaluate my comments about her and Susan in relation to the views and assumptions which she now knew me to hold. I had, after all, previously been probing for the assumptions that *she* was working with.

For interest, I shall summarise the rest of the history, for I am not quoting it here as a model of radical work. Susan discharged herself from hospital, a little more stabilised and without medication – a move Mrs L. now agreed with. A fortnight later she quarrelled with her father and ran off to London, where she surfaced a few days later in hospital with one leg severely infected following lacerations when she put it through a glass door escaping someone's advances. I went to see her, and continued, as previously, to suggest ways of her attaining freedom, but pointing out some of the not wholly intended consequences of her actions. I thought it right that she should be away from home but told her that I had advised her mother not to send her any more money (Susan was wildly extravagant) because it was perpetuating her dependence. We talked about social security and possible jobs. With the help of the local social worker Susan found a hostel; she then took up a residential hotel job. After three weeks she decided she had had enough and came home. There were no problems and Susan has since found a better job as a nanny. Unfortunately, I still doubt whether she has really come to terms with the fears which were haunting her, and her obsession with adult/child relationships remains.

The material and the dilemmas presented in this case are familiar social work terrain: personal suffering, family and generation conflict, unusual and at times dangerous behaviour, drugs, psychedelic and psychotropic, detention in hospital, the general problem of self-determination. The social worker is involved but too remote to exert direct control; he has no choice but to intervene but has to tread a wary path between apparent indifference and infringing the rights of the different people involved. Facile dogmatism would have been of little help, yet at various moments the stance taken up by the social worker could have been crucial: it was important to Mrs L. that I was able to discuss the weaknesses of family structure without laying all the blame on her as a parent; it was important to Susan that I validated her reaction to the hospital, but did not thereby condone all of her actions; it was important to both of them that I was able to make the grounds of my judgement clear; and it was important to me not to have to deny my own beliefs. The encounter became more real because we were able to exchange expectations, and, as it happened, there was an explicitly political dimension; more often the political implications are implicit or hidden.

I shall return briefly to radicalism and casework in Chapter 8; I have mentioned this case here partly to establish my social work credentials and illustrate the problem area we have to discuss, and partly to make clear that I do not reject all forms of individual work, but chiefly to use Mrs L.'s striking statement on the stereotype of radical social workers as a springboard to look more closely at the genesis of radicalism and its recent history in relation to the general fate of the personal social services.

Social work as the universal provider

The latter part of the 1960s was dominated by the liberal optimism that universal welfare was at last attainable and a goal which could be promoted for its own worth, not as a spin-off from other successes. Under the Tories the nation had become conned about its own affluence; Labour would give prime place to the elimination of poverty. It was typical of the ethereal nature of such hopes that the economic tide was already beginning to turn against them, its ebb to be encouraged by the private profligacy and speculation permitted by the incoming Conservative government of 1970. But the reforming commitment of the Labour Party, the belief held by some Fabians that family support would minimise social dislocation, the growing pains of a social work profession beginning to burst the seams of its existing structure, and the idealism of many new social work recruits combined to thrust the social services forward as a cornerstone of a better future. Richard Crossman introduced Seebohm reorganisation to Parliament as 'the first action the state will be taking in building the second stage of the Welfare State'.[1] Inevitably such expectations would be disappointed, though few could imagine that the failure would be so gross that it encompassed not only inexperienced, chaotic and bureaucratic social services, but the threatened collapse of the foundation of the welfare state, the National Health Service itself. There can be no doubt that the social services have failed to deliver the goods which were promised on their behalf, though in our confusion we should not assume things to be worse than they really are. Blame has been cast on welfarism, bureaucrats, and even radicals; the coincidence of reorganisation with the implementation of wide-ranging legislation affecting children and the chronically sick or disabled has been proffered as an excuse. All of these have had some bearing on the current malaise of social work but the mistake is to see the problems of social work as arising out of internal organisational problems in the personal social services rather than in the broader developments arising out of the political economy itself – unemployment, immigration and the status of women being three important factors which have had a massive impact on the social work profession. We have to understand the processes at work as well as the needs these measures were intended to meet before we can either analyse the past or make the best choices for future action.

The Labour Party came to power in 1964 with a conviction firmly rooted in the thinking of Anthony Crosland's *The Future of Socialism*[2] that since the early 1950s economic interests had been subjugated to the political process and could be harnessed to provide the basis for a fair and egalitarian society. Labour's subsequent history, from Harold Wilson's first confrontation with the Governor of the Bank of England, who told him that raising pensions would start a run on the pound, to Crosland's death shortly after losing the battle to save the welfare state from the depredations of the International Monetary Fund, is that of a desperate attempt to maintain this belief of political supremacy in face of economic forces which Labour was in the end unable to control. The plans and promises which were made to improve the quality of life in every sphere have proved as empty and windswept as the residential and shopping megastructures erected after planners had been given the go-ahead to engage unilaterally in the wholesale reconstruction of urban environments. Everything was done on as large a scale as possible but most of it was on the cheap.

Seebohm reorganisation was typical of this process even though it was far from a straight product of Labour's ideology. From the start there was a profound contradiction between the nature of the reorganisation and the expectations put upon it, a contradiction which was the direct result of a political decision to make the Social Services Bill a simple measure of machinery by dropping the crucial recommendation that social service departments should have a general duty to *promote* welfare. Whether this was because of expense or the fear of producing too strong an independent pressure group is not clear; the fact remains that the propaganda surrounding the new departments, including Crossman's own introduction of them, and the coincidental legislation which was more a declaration of intent than effective reform placed a burden on social services which they were deliberately not equipped to bear.[3]

Until reorganisation gave social workers a significance they could not have previously imagined, the different 'specialisms' had all beavered away in their separate sectors with little appreciation of their role beyond the individual level: children's services were for the deprived, mental welfare for the ill and general welfare for the handicapped, homeless and elderly. These categories were rarely questioned. However, most people agreed that the existing structure was inefficient, unco-ordinated and in some cases duplicative; the bodies which represented the different sectors took advantage of this general agreement to promote the idea of a unified service which would identify and encapsulate the essence of social work, thus establishing an influence and status which had hitherto been conspicuously lacking. There were differences, of course; the more outspoken Association of Child Care Officers (A. C. C. O.) felt it might be silenced; the others resented the way child care officers tended to regard themselves as an élite; but the issues at stake were mainly of professional prestige rather than benefit to clients. Even A. C. C. O. was subject to this criticism; as Seed observes, the professional lobby was usually outdone in advancing client interests by the corresponding voluntary organisations, like the Child Poverty Action Group, Mind and Shelter.[4] The new British Association of Social Workers (B. A. S. W.) was and is little different and its early days were marked by empire-building among qualified social workers rather than by the organisation addressing itself to the issues which were really worrying social workers at large. B. A. S. W. did not make the political claims for social work that others did; it preferred to deny itself any political importance at all. But naïvety and professional self-interest reached their zenith at the 1972 B. A. S. W. conference in the standing ovation given to Barbara Castle as she intoned 'if you will build us a new Jerusalem, we will give you the bricks'. That the brick contractors were charlatans and the proposed builders mere chimney-sweeps appeared to escape notice.

Professionalism was, however, only one element in the changing character of social work. The explosion of sociology in the early 1960s proved to be as much a watershed as the 'psychiatric deluge' two decades earlier. Social workers were shaken from their seclusion. Not only did the newly popularised science quickly infiltrate the porous shell of social work theory, but its propagation proved to be linked with and the result of far wider political and economic movements. The sociologists' 'rediscovery' of poverty, the suspicion that Beveridge's Five Giants – Want, Disease, Ignorance, Squalor and, of course, Idleness – were still stalking the land brought those who had been dealing with and perhaps covering up the problems of low income, old age or homelessness into the central political arena for the first time. Despite much resistance the social, cultural, political and economic causes and consequences of social work became accepted, if suspiciously, as a proper topic for training, and social workers began to respond to the attacks made on them by developing an image of being prime instruments in the national redistribution of resources and opportunities. Though not welcome to all, this trend fitted neatly with the mood of the times, and was espoused, if briefly, by many radicals. But before surveying radicalism, it will be useful to look further at the values and goals of Seebohm.

The Seebohm compromise

This is not the place for history but since reorganisation has so distorted memory, it is worth recalling some of the assumptions on which it was based and its recommendations. The Seebohm Committee on Local Authority and Allied Personal Social Services was the final and most comprehensive of a series of enquiries into services for children and families, all of which were concerned with the failure to eradicate delinquency and 'problem families', which, for some inexplicable reason, were failing to take advantage of the good life which society offered. Prevention, it was argued, was better than cure, and could be achieved by enabling services to reach out to the deprived and catch them before they became institutionalised. A powerful Fabian lobby, influential within social work, attributed many social problems to family breakdown. Residential care not only failed to reform; it could be positively damaging. In addition, it was increasingly expensive. If social workers could prevent not only neglect but also crime by working with families in their own environment, the clinging permanence of deprivation might at last be torn away. This was to be achieved by making social work more relevant and effective. Although many child care officers had long recognised that many difficulties were caused or exacerbated by a lack of resources, and had won the right under Section 1 of the 1963 Children and Young Persons Act to aid clients in kind or cash to prevent the reception of children into care, the redistribution of wealth and income was not on the agenda. Material help was still seen as an aid to emotional stability rather than as an essential prerequisite. In practice it was often used to bind families to good behaviour.

The committee's own version of its origins confirms its originally limited scope. It arose out of 'a concern at the increase in officially recorded delinquency, the need to concentrate resources and a belief that preventive work with families was of cardinal importance'.[5] The eventual brief was for a well co-ordinated family service, with an emphasis on child care, which would make more effective use of existing resources and put them within the reach of all in need. In this way, the concept of prevention, which was the standard of the children's departments, was linked with community care and the priority of the welfare services. The use of community was to have more underhand implications.

Of all the issues raised by the report, including its general blandness over the possibility of conflicts of interest, I shall mention simply two, because of their relevance to our present situation. The first is its family orientation. The framing of the committee's terms of reference had itself been a matter of conflict. The original conception was of a family-based service but Professor Titmuss and others had argued strongly against such constriction; many needs were not essentially family needs and the service should be more universal. According to Hall,[6] Seebohm himself sympathised with this line, which is reflected in the introduction where the committee states that it could make sense of its task by considering not just families but 'everybody'. Nevertheless, despite pandering to the idea of universality, its final proposals were heavily biased towards a concentration on family support.

Secondly, social work with families was to be supplemented by help from the community, and here Seebohm latched on to the concept of community care – a system which would not just involve outsiders more in the care of the deprived and the handicapped, but would be essential if all needs were to be met. The committee appears to have understood that the question of resources was a crucial one but it hedged its answers, failed to think them through and failed totally to foresee the explosion of demand, although it must be said that some of the legislation which legitimated that demand post-dated the publication of the report, most notably the 1969 Children and Young Persons Act and the 1971 Chronically Sick and Disabled Act. The first responsibility of the new department would be 'to deploy existing resources more effectively'; in other words, if not to save money, at least to increase productivity. Even allowing for hindsight, this seems a naïve assumption, grossly underestimating organisational costs and placing too much reliance on the avoidance of duplication. The mistake was compounded when estimating the need for additional resources:

> Measured in manpower, buildings, training, intelligence and research, these will still not be large in relation to total local authority budgets; they will, however, in a disproportionate degree, prevent human deterioration, improve the lives of the most

vulnerable in our population and mobilise goodwill and voluntary effort within the community.[7]

Services were to decentralise (with the effect of increasing both access and supervision), enlist the maximum participation of individuals and groups, and become a focal point for the large numbers of volunteers which would be necessary. No state monolith was envisaged; instead self-help and voluntary assistance were to be the hallmarks of good citizenship. The committee was perhaps deliberately understating potential expenses, which might have jeopardised reorganisation altogether. Yet it is typical of the potential doublethink surrounding social policy that this call for a national regeneration of good fellowship should be led by a banker who had publicly admitted that 60 per cent of the problems with which social workers had to deal could be ascribed to poor living conditions.

The Seebohm factories

It is not my business to evaluate the reorganisation which followed the Seebohm report. It may never be possible, let alone useful, to disentangle all the disparate effects. In general, I have little doubt that the principle of unification was correct, not just because it removed anomalies but because it thrust social workers into the real world by breaking up the little niches in which different practices had become comfortable. By removing the labels which justified intervention, it became much easier to universalise the difficulties clients were facing. Similarly social workers who were now brought into close contact with each other found out what they had in common and had to face the implications of different practices. Child care officers, accustomed by and large to the personal needs and feelings of children received into care, were shocked at the way old people were despatched to homes without any thought of introduction; welfare workers found their standards challenged when they were faced with rebellious teenagers; both groups were alarmed at the cosy relationship of mental welfare officers with psychiatrists and hospitals, but terrified at the prospect of dealing with the mentally ill. There can be no denial of the turmoil and extra work caused when we were faced with unfamiliar demands, nor that standards in some areas dropped significantly. But those who look back nostalgically to previous practice are flouting history. Not only do they idealise the past; they totally misinterpret the present. Our present dissatisfactions have less to do with the principle of unification, or with the need for a common basis to all social work on which specialist experience may be built, than with the fact that most of the problems which are brought to social workers cannot be solved within the terms of our job.

Leaving aside the general question of resources, reorganisation seems to me to have introduced two major problem areas into social work. The first is the size of its organisation; bureaucracy, inflexibility and remoteness are criticisms frequently voiced by social workers and clients. Management is cumbersome with a structure based principally on the need to find senior officers jobs as the number of departments contracted from 377 in 1970 to 116 in 1974. The greater Leviathan grows, the more distorted are its responses. Decisions are taken at levels remote from those who have to live with their effects. But the causes of this remoteness are not just bureaucratic procedure or hierarchical structure. Both these phenomena have to be seen as defences against the second major result of unification, which was, for a time, the abolition of rationing. The plethora of demands made upon social services departments did not result simply from the raising of expectations or coincidental legislation, but from the fact that all demands for improvements in social policy were now channelled in one direction only, instead of being diverted piecemeal through different specialist bodies. The cross-referral between agencies in which social workers had previously been able to indulge in order to gain relief was no longer possible. The departments at all levels found themselves bombarded by individual need and pressure group promoting particular interests; there were not the resources even to process most of these, let alone meet them, and departments were ironically further weakened by the increased burden of children's work as expressed in the rising numbers of children committed to care for delinquency and mounting public concern about non-accidental injury to children. Bureaucracy and the need to carry out statutory measures of control and supervision became the new framework in which the rationing of social demand could take place.

The extent of demand did of course force additional financial allocation. In the five years from 1968 social spending increased by 68 per cent, much of it in capital growth as hitherto neglected sectors like the mentally handicapped began to have a rather greater proportion of their need met for the first time. The number of residential places available increased in all fields, as did the number of staff, but here the biggest jump was in the number of cheap and untrained welfare assistants, from 1118 to 2578 (130.6 per cent) and to a lesser degree in management and supervisory staff (44.6 per cent). Social workers increased by 36.8 per cent to 12 760.[8] Yet we were still only scratching the surface and, more significantly, were having little or no effect on what troubled officialdom most – the rise in delinquency.

The cumulative effect of reorganisation upon social workers was little dissimilar from the impact of the introduction of the assembly line by Henry Ford. Ford could hardly keep his workforce intact, let alone expand it. In 1913 his labour turnover was 380 per cent. By the end of the year, 'every time the company wanted to add 100 men to its factory personnel, it was necessary to hire 963'.[9] From being a craft, motor engineering had become the repetition of a detail operation and as long as alternatives were available workers took them freely; gradually they found that the same mode of organisation had encroached on every sphere of production; in the end jobs became less plentiful and workers were forced to settle for the employers' terms. Social workers, already dislocated by administrative changes, at first stood their ground, mainly for moral reasons; the next response was a rapid flitting from job to job, especially among the younger and more mobile workers who were flooding in to fill belatedly increased establishments and replace those who had opted for the apparent security of promotion. This process added to the depersonalisation of social work, which had been created by unmanageable caseloads. But despite this flux, the new conditions began to impose some solidarity among people who were traditionally individualists. We began to stand together both in support of client needs and to better our own conditions. Just as by 1915 unionisation had forced its way into Fords, so social workers, along with many other white-collar workers, began to develop a trade union consciousness informed both by our own plight and by that of our clients. Although this consciousness was partly shaped and given impulse by radical activity, the widespread acceptance of trade union values sprang from the conditions and needs we all shared, and its first major expression, in the withdrawals from emergency duty in 1971–2, was not, as Jordan would have it,[10] due to the demands for emergency funding made by clients who could not contact Social Security out of office hours, but to a refusal to allow any longer the extension of the intolerable conditions under which we were working, at nights and weekends particularly, for no worthwhile remuneration. Clients' demands for cash support constituted only a minute proportion of this pressure.

The advent of radical social workers

It would be foolish to deny that the character of social work was not only challenged but to some extent changed by the influx of new recruits. However, the radical movement was not at all coherent and its ideas would not have achieved such prominence and credibility, had people not been searching for alternatives. I shall discuss the different aspects of radicalism in more detail later on, but in order to give some perspective to the argument, it is necessary to summarise and disentangle the main influences which found their expression in radical social work.

The vigour and iconoclasm which radicals brought to social work was not, as Cypher has suggested, the result of the job being taken up by a larger number of men than before supplemented by 'women with masculine characteristics',[11] a remark which betrays the narrow limits of certain kinds of sociological categorisation. Though it is true that the proportion of men in what was traditionally considered to be a female occupation is now greater, social work has always tended to be a male-dominated profession in terms of position and policy. The change is one of values not of demography. In keeping with the trend towards making social work a central pillar of social policy, new entrants tended to be activists and community-oriented, with the belief that social work intervention could in some way be critical in promoting wider change. But though some were starry-eyed, the majority were conscious of the limitations of social work, both in theory and as it was practised. The last few years before Seebohm had seen growing criticism of apparently arbitrary, unconcerned or high-handed action by all types of social worker towards vulnerable groups, most notably the homeless. People who wanted to fight for change entered social work not so much because it was the ideal instrument, but because the increased availability of jobs was neatly geared to coincide with the glut of sociology graduates looking for ways of making a living which at worst would not involve too much compromise with their ideals and at best might enable their realisation. A generation already in revolt was to put its standards to the test; though some left in disappointment, others found their work experience radicalised them still further.

It is impossible here to analyse in detail the counter-cultural brew from which radical social work was distilled; it dates back to the faltering of capitalism in the 1950s after the post-war boom had lost momentum and the growing rejection of the market ideology led to a resurgence of alternative Marxist traditions (unfettered by any idealisation of the U. S. S. R.) and a broader popular protest which found its most powerful expression in C. N. D. The pacifist tradition had always contained a strong element of self-help and voluntarism, expressed, for instance, in the Family Service Units which were pacifist-inspired; this, when combined with sociologists' laments for the passing of old working-class communities, contributed to the regeneration of a communitarian socialism not seen since the nineteenth century. When it became clear that nuclear disarmament was not going to be achieved without major political change and C. N. D. split over the extent to which supporters were prepared to confront the government and the law, the Committee of 100 lent its experience of direct action to community protest. Anger at official hypocrisy over the atrocities in Vietnam helped to provoke a general attack on the violence of our culture and all its institutions, including the family. The counter-culture flourished briefly with tales of love, peace and togetherness to which few were completely immune, but the dream was fragile and brief. The powerlessness of the Labour Government to resist vested material and international interests produced a hardening of political attitudes. Nevertheless, the Seebohm committee, reporting in 1968, before the events of May in Paris, the student sit-ins and Labour's attempts to enforce an incomes policy, could still survey a scene of unprecedented community activity which they could indicate hopefully as the foundation of a new welfare society.

Criticism of social work centred around the issue of social control. Social workers, who liked to see themselves as being able to help people, were in fact merely encouraging them to adapt to prevailing conditions, to a sick society. Casework, with its emphasis on the individual's intra-psychic functioning and the primacy it allotted to the family, was the ideal tool for isolating and devalidating deviance. Furthermore, by focusing on alleged individual inadequacies, social workers blinded themselves to the basic material needs of their clients and encouraged them to tolerate the intolerable. To offer casework to a family in housing infested with rats was an insult; social workers' primary task should be to fight for them to be rehoused.

Most radicals adopted this or similar critiques, but offered differing solutions, which I think it is helpful to divide between libertarian and revolutionary. Those I call libertarians advocated self-help and community action, arguing that small-scale changes must precede wider revolution. They rejected authority of any sort and placed a premium on developing new forms of living and personal relationships. The community of the underprivileged was to be the milieu of action and change. As a result, libertarian social workers have often adopted more adventurous techniques than their revolutionary colleagues who, while not denying the need for personal change, took the broader Marxist view that relationships are ultimately fashioned by the needs of the production system, and it was this which had first to be overthrown. The revolutionary argument, best represented in *Case Con*, the first issue of which appeared in June 1970, was that social workers should reject their controlling functions, and assist their clients in any way possible to gain the material necessities they had a right to. However, this could not be achieved by grass-roots action alone since clients by and large had little economic power. The conditions for an adequate life for all could be obtained only by organised class struggle, and social workers should give priority to advancing that struggle.

Disillusion and retrenchment

In the period of time since reorganisation, the claim to which we responded but for which we were not responsible, that the social services could create a world worth living in, has been turned back on us with a vengeance. Social services departments were for a while successful in wringing some extra finance from local and central government, but to outsiders it seems as if these have been squandered on a bureaucratic army to staff our ever-hungry empire. Social workers have become the scapegoats for failure to meet quite impossible demands. The attack on welfare is mainly economic but the increasingly vociferous criticism of liberal social work ideology from magistrates, police and press indicates a shift in social priorities, despite the fact that much of it is ill-informed. When magistrates were complaining that adolescents committed to care were being allowed to go straight home, they were in part bitter at the apparent abuse of the power to send children straight to approved school which had been transferred from them to local authorities. But the fact is that more care orders were being made than before, that classifying and remand homes were overstretched, and that vacancies in children's homes were in short supply, especially since they could not cope with too sudden an influx of children who would previously have gone to approved school. In many cases brave decisions were made to keep children awaiting placement at home rather than send them to manifestly unsuitable institutions. But, as pressure was brought to bear, fewer children were left at home and more committed to prison-like remand centres under certificates of unruliness. Those decisions not to sacrifice a child's best interests to a shortage of resources were made in the best traditions of the child care service.

But what *was* new was a corporate readiness to defy official opinion, and it was this which enraged traditional upholders of the legal system, particularly as they saw responsibility in the hands of the young and often inexperienced. Radicals, of course, had much to do with this refusal, and our identification with aggressive community and client organisations, such as Claimants' Unions, provoked bitterness from officials who expected social workers to act responsibly and take their side. But such actions did not stem only from radicals, as more and more orthodox social workers, in attempting to assist their clients, shared their experience of rebuff, delay and injustice, which they felt impelled to resist on their clients' behalf, even if it meant defying the rules. All of us found that the attempt to apply professional values runs foul of the legal and administrative system. Geoffrey Pearson points out how widespread among social workers such rule-breaking, or tolerance of rule-breaking, is;[12] for instance, in social security claims, social workers will usually try not to let clients be penalised by regulations they consider unjust, like the cohabitation rule which stops a woman being allowed to claim if she has a man staying regularly overnight. Not only is the rule discriminatory; we do not consider that sexual intercourse needs to be legitimated by a financial exchange. The most general justification for such tolerance is that enforcement is not our business; we do draw the line at actively involving ourselves in false representations. Pearson calls such behaviour industrial deviance, suggesting it normally falls within the second and third of three categories used by Taylor and Walton to describe factory workers' personal reactions to the demands of their job: attempts to reduce frustration and tension, attempts to facilitate or ease the work process, and attempts to assert some control over the work process.[13] This is surely correct, except that social workers, as we shall see, are licensed to act in this way. But the fact that it is part of the job does not lessen its political significance or the effect it must have on our relationships with enforcement agencies and personnel.

The second major stand of criticism after Seebohm has come from within the profession, mounted not only by casework traditionalists but by a growing number of radical–liberals; the former point to what they describe as a dramatic fall in standards, especially in the more specialised fields, and the latter argue that the personal element has been removed from social services. Both these cases have some merit but, as I shall argue later, their diagnosis is incomplete, their view of the past is nostalgic and their solutions – respectively a return to specialisation and a separation of social work from service delivery – are misguided. Though it is important that the territory of social work should be more clearly delimited, such moves would have the effect of placing social work back into the service of official demand rather than moderating or controlling it. The crisis of social work is neither internal nor isolated; the problems of bureaucracy and large-scale organisations are peripheral. Our self-doubt is part of the wider crisis of a liberal and reforming ideology which has manifestly failed to deliver its promises; welfare can no longer straddle the back of the economic tiger; it is in the process of being devoured. The political polarisation of the last ten years has produced an increasing shift to the right in official and consensus opinion. Social services are enjoined to become more selective, and to concentrate on the real business of helping those deprived through no fault of their own and controlling those who have transgressed the law. As juvenile crime increases we are forced back to the old business of combating delinquency without any control over its causes; as defiance of the state increases, our reins are checked and we are marshalled back to order. Now is not the time to retreat from the political stage; our role is, if anything, more important than before.

Radicals have also reassessed their positions since 1970. The initial coalition around *Case Con* diminished as radicals divided between those who became drawn more and more into trade union rather than client-based activity, and those who focused mainly on community work, practised a permissive non-intervention or campaigned for welfare rights. Thus radicals risked a dangerous dishonesty of their own; libertarians tended to deny they were social workers or controlling agents at all, revolutionaries continued to practise a profession whose value they appeared totally to reject. The contradictions have been painful and rarely resolved. Some important victories were won: fewer heady claims were made for casework, active interventions to secure welfare rights were sanctioned, and social action, if not encouraged, was accepted as a legitimate technique which could win important concessions. Yet all this was achieved at the cost of dulling the edge of radical protest; a process of repressive tolerance was under way. Meanwhile the weaknesses of part of the radical case became apparent: material help was not always sufficient, authority had sometimes to be used, not all professional skills were irrelevant or necessarily oppressive, and community work could secure only small-scale improvements; the Home Office Community Development Projects were forced to take on financial and industrial giants, including local government, as the ultimate arbiters of a community's conditions of life, and were wound up as a result. For a time radicalism seemed an increasingly nebulous phenomenon; it did not, however, lose its importance. As libertarians licked their wounds and were forced to recognise that their tactics were too limited to achieve any measurable social change, revolutionaries have been beginning to use their experience to try to integrate political principles more closely with practice. The economic attack on the welfare state has not only forced us all back on to common ground, it has radicalised many orthodox social workers and openly politicised much of our work with clients.

The significance of the cuts in public expenditure is twofold. In the short term they have made life more difficult and expensive for our clients as facilities like day-centres or nurseries are removed or cancelled, rehousing is slowed and charges for services are raised, as well as increasing unemployment. Meanwhile our own job has become even more frustrating and our workload increases as vacancies remain unfilled and redundancies bite in services like Social Security. Even more of our time is spent on refusing clients' requests, absurd systems of priorities are worked out, and new anomalies arise as small and isolated cuts begin to grow into a virus-like attack. In the year preceding March 1977, there was a 3.7 per cent drop in social work services in Scotland (0.8 per cent in England) excluding reductions in capital expenditure.[14] This was only the start.

But the crucial long-term effect is the realisation which is being steadily borne in to all those involved with welfare that our society's priorities lie in industrial enrichment and public order. To meet those ends we are asked not only to sacrifice our own living standards but to police the casualties of unemployment, redundancy, inflation, wage-control and economic neglect. In order to understand how this comes about and what we can do to resist it, we must examine social work in relation to the state.

2

Social work, the state and social control

One measure of the change in social work is that nobody can now embark on a general discussion of it, however brief, without at least a token acceptance of the role of social workers as agents of social control. Once the battering ram of radical criticism and a source of shock and horror for traditionalists, the idea has now passed into commonplace discourse, almost to the point of being irrelevant. Yet it is on our analysis of this particular function that our approach to social work must turn, because it highlights the standards by which we work and poses the question of our ultimate loyalties.

The background for this sluggish but steady absorption of the control concept has been the increasingly explicit use of social work as an instrument of social policy. This aspect did exist in the creation and development of children's departments but was never so obvious because of the restricted nature of their field. But now that social workers are the medium through which a goodly proportion of social policy reaches the public, we have little escape. Indeed Crossman, continuing his speech to Parliament about reorganisation from which I have already quoted (on p. 12), went almost so far as to state the goals of social work itself, at any rate as far as he was concerned. The primary objective of the personal social services, he announced, was 'to strengthen the capacity of the family to create for its members a concept of support within the home for those unable to look after themselves'. His words are notable for their neglect of any of the principles to which caseworkers are accustomed to refer, like acceptance or self-determination. It is a short-sighted goal framed by economic priorities and was ignored because it was inappropriate; yet as justifications are sought for cutbacks, it is increasingly reiterated.

Goals apart, the role of social services as executors of policy has meant that social workers have become far more entangled with the administration and bureaucracy not just of local government but of the welfare state as a whole. One of the most rapidly increasing areas of our work has been the distribution and rationing of resources. Some benefits, like access to residential or day care, or the allocation of telephones and bus passes to the elderly and disabled, are completely controlled by social workers and our administrators. If the required resource is available, the recommendation of the social worker is paramount and the client must present his or her case accordingly. If, as is much more usual, it is in short supply or non-existent, the process is more arbitrary, for the success of an application may depend on how well the social worker has learnt to use the bureaucratic codes in which the recommendation must be phrased. Some, quite fortuitously, are much better at this than others. If the application is rejected or delayed, the social worker's job, quite explicitly, is to placate the client and even offer supportive casework, an expensive, unsatisfactory and even dishonest substitute. Even casework is rationed, though, as we have to make more and more decisions about priorities, and these decisions are taken on the basis of pressure rather than felt need. Vulnerability is now the official criterion, but children are always said to be more vulnerable than the elderly or mentally ill.

Rationing is not confined to the direct distribution of benefits, for social workers have become the fail-safe mechanism of the welfare state. At first this was limited to being the last recourse of families in dire need, but pressure on social workers justifiably anxious to ensure that poverty should not be the cause of family break-up or individual deprivation, led them to exploit Section 1 of the 1963 Children and Young Persons Act, which permitted emergency grants in cash or kind to prevent the reception of children into care. The use made of this power varied between authorities and budgets were often strictly limited. Nevertheless, this new facility began to be abused by social security departments which would often merely refer claimants on to social services when their claims should in fact have been directly met. It took vigorous action from the Claimants' Unions to persuade liberal-minded social workers that they were recreating charity grants, and that if they became involved at all, it should be as advocates to social security on the claimants' behalf. But now even this function has been administratively absorbed, so that certain concessions, most notably over fuel debts, have become conditional on social work intervention and recommendation, though even this is not always sufficient to prevent disconnection. It is social workers who have to maintain the casualties of the new requirement that the Gas and Electricity Boards should run at a profit, by turning debtors into clients, but as prices soar more and more of us are running into danger of debt ourselves.

Rationing is the newest aspect of control and there are some critics who place much of the blame for our present plight on its introduction. But control is much more fundamental to our work than access to resources. Its most obvious manifestation, again in enactment of social policy, is the use of statutory powers which social workers have over members of the public – for instance, those which allow, in consultation with or at the request of other authorities, the removal of children and sometimes old people into residential homes against their wishes and of adults of any age into mental hospital. Although we cannot so act in isolation, we are usually landed either with supervising or personally effecting such removal. Furthermore, we have to prepare court reports for criminal, adoption and divorce proceedings, undertake the compulsory supervision of children and mental patients on licence, and initiate court proceedings. All this implies a power of inspection and a requirement on clients to maintain our approval, particularly as they are no longer able to rely on the division of powers between different specialisms.[1] Many social workers find this authority distasteful and seek to avoid its exercise either by evading decisions or by interpreting rules as liberally as possible. But in general this leads to confusion on all sides; the social worker remains uneasy, law-enforcement agencies grow more critical, and clients retain all their suspicions and reserve.

The overt control which social workers are expected to exercise is supplemented by very definite values about the ways in which people should behave and relate to each other, informed, as Jordan says,[2] by the need for family responsibility, the work ethic and the preservation of law and order. The liberalism which is most prevalent in social work usually disguises the extent to which they influence social work activity. Behind an ideology which stresses the somewhat troublesome concept of client self-determination lies a positive affirmation of the united nuclear family as the deepest source of human emotional satisfaction, and a tendency to judge people's emotional capacity by their ability to adapt to family life. Theoretically, some forms of conflict are recognised as inevitable and even useful but, in practice, mediation is the social worker's role. The principle of individuality allows variation to the point of eccentricity, as long as nobody rocks the boat. Behaviour must never appear to be out of hand. Despite a traditional sympathy for the offender, liberalism demands that all action should be responsibie and expects that everybody ought to be able to see every side of the story; inaction is the usual result. Commitment is regarded with suspicion. Concessions may be made to the short-term constructiveness of rebellion, but social work's view of authority is static and parental: persistent defiance is attributed to individual problems. Outside the family, work is the chief source of virtue. Degrading labour for little reward is seen as more worthwhile than not working at all. In sum, the social worker's world is a soggy web of reciprocal obligations and damp responses which is founded more on respect for institutions than a realistic appraisal of personal need.

But control does not always mean preserving the *status quo*. The forces which lead to change must also be harnessed and guided in acceptable directions. As social work has begun to understand its place in society, there has been at least a partial recognition that it operates at flashpoints where different groups are in conflict over resources, influence or power. We have been forced to pay more than lip-service to the legitimacy of conflict although our role is still one of arbitration and conciliation, and where these are ruled out by the intensity of difference we have to choose between taking sides and perhaps alienating the opposing faction, and standing apart and confirming our irrelevance. Advocacy and community action are permitted but only within limits. Certain institutions must not be challenged. Harry Specht, arguing against over-commitment to radicalism, states these bounds quite clearly:

> A professional may give his *personal* commitment to rebellion; but it is outside his professed area of competence. . . . Social work operates in a framework of democratic decision-making and if one decides that framework is no longer viable, then there is no profession of social work to be practised.[3]

Social workers do have some freedom because of our peculiar position as mediators between state and public, and our conflicting loyalties achieve official recognition. But we must not bite too hard at the hands which pay us, we cannot challenge spheres of interest outside the immediate welfare arena and we have to operate within that type of democracy which our state allows. We may recognise the extent to which we are expected to exert control; we have also to understand from where it emanates and in whose interest it is exercised.

Pluralism: the state disguised

Discounting the fascist idea of the state as a quasi-mystical unifier of the race, there are two major views of the state in current political thought. The Marxist view, which I adopt, is that the state is the most powerful instrument of the ruling class, though some Marxists believe it has attained some degree of autonomy. I shall develop these arguments in the following sections. On the other hand, liberals, of whatever hue, tend to play down its power and influence; and because theirs is the dominant ideology, every use of the phrase 'the state' makes people wince and suspect exaggeration. Liberals propagate a pluralist view of society in which power is divided among competing interest groups whose activities are controlled by a set of rules, the law, which acts as independent arbitrator. Through the law and its officers the state is represented as the guardian of the 'public interest' and of individual rights; the degree to which the rights of particular groups or classes of individuals are safeguarded depends on how well they are doing in the competition. Those who fall out of the game may need the help of a social worker to direct them back to the starting point. The state thus appears, in Engels' phrase, 'to stand above society' and to become an extra-historical entity expressing, in its essence, values which are permanent and essential to any well-ordered civilisation. The state is not to be confused with the government or the political system; its legal, administrative and executive machinery, theoretically at the call of whichever party is in control, in practice imposes checks on their activity, thus maintaining stability and consensus. Democracy is understood as the right to express criticism and periodically to confirm or replace the members of the legislature by direct or indirect election. Politics is limited to the competition between parties for the privilege of controlling the legislature, and their actions when elected.

Because the representative system has made politics a career, the advancement of ideology has also become associated with personal advantage. Such naked pursuit of self-interest and power is not to British taste; we prefer self-interest to be clothed in nobler motives and it ill befits the myth of pluralism. Individual gain, private profit and electioneering are permitted because they are essential, but they are licensed. Most activities of citizens should be non-political in that they do not appear to advance the interests of any party. Groups which are not overtly dedicated to the winning of legislative power may function more freely, unless the interests which they advance may be fulfilled only by a change in the distribution of power. In this case, by a neat device, they are seen as part of the political process, limited in their activity, and smeared with the dye of personal gain.

Such a conception of the state is essential to a competitive society since it maintains order while apparently permitting the possibility of change. The appearance of choice is essential and is preferably maintained by a two-party system; more parties either form permanent coalitions and dominate the legislature or create a dangerous flux. Indeed in one country, Colombia, where elections were usually marked by extreme public violence, the two parties agreed simply to alternate power every four years. However, when the dynamic of competition falters and power is concentrated in monopolies outside and independent of the government, the political system becomes increasingly weak and irrelevant as the limits of practical choice sharply narrow. In order to retain at least the appearance of democratic control, state machinery is brought more overtly into use, in an attempt to avert both the excesses of power and its worst effects; if this is not sufficient to maintain consensus, then more repressive powers are invoked to curb dissent. But the more the state intervenes, the more likely that it will lose the appearance of neutrality and earn discredit for both its commitment and its inevitable failures. The concentration of capital and technological power which characterises and determines the economy in which we live makes it more crucial than ever before to define the source of ultimate control. It is not only legitimate but essential for social workers to take up a clear stand on this question, both because, as state employees, we are intimately involved and because the answer will determine how far we can expect our clients' interests to be served. Moreover, the traditional values and practice of social work are inextricably entwined in the pluralist framework. If pluralism has been superseded, or if it is in fact a myth, then the character of social work will undergo a radical alteration.

The state as the instrument of class

Ralph Miliband, the outstanding English contributor on this topic, has commented that the deficiencies of pluralism can be shown only in empirical terms.[4] Admittedly he does so in the context of a debate with the French structuralist, Poulantzas, and perhaps underplays the value of theory. Nevertheless, it is not so much the intrinsic beauty of Marxism which has recommended it to a growing number of social workers as the increasing evidence of the economy's incapacity to meet real need, the government's inability to redirect it, and the consequent use of welfare not just to regulate demand but to divert and control the inevitable dissatisfaction and deviance. Marxist theory offers not just the only alternative explanation of why this is happening but a strategy for procuring change.

Marxists are often their own worst enemies, for while the basic elements of Marxism are attractively uncomplicated, they lend themselves to oversimplification. On the other hand, simplicity sometimes creates suspicion in the minds of those accustomed to the sophisticated apologetics of bourgeois commentators. Fortunately, I am spared the necessity of laying out the detailed principles, of Marxist theory to illustrate their relevance to social work; that task has been admirably begun by Paul Corrigan and Peter Leonard.[5] I do not totally agree with their exposition or with some of their conclusions but they have at least supplied a framework and vocabulary in which more detailed discussion can follow. In this book I shall have to take some knowledge of that framework for granted.

In contrast to the pluralist view of the state as a mediator between classes competing on more or less equal terms, the most long-standing Marxist tradition asserts that the interaction between classes has to be analysed not as competition but as a fundamental conflict over power. As Lenin wrote in *State and Revolution*, 'the state is a product and a manifestation of the *irreconcilability* of class antagonisms'; the state exists so that the classes do not consume themselves in fruitless struggle, but it is 'an organ of class *rule*, an organ for the *oppression* of one class by another; it is the creation of 'order', which legalises and perpetuates this oppression by moderating the conflict between the classes'.[6] George and Wilding summarise the reasons which Marxists have proffered for the survival of capitalism, as the economic strength of the ruling class, its domination of the state apparatus and the creation of a national ideology to reflect its interests.[7] To these they might have added the lack of a properly organised, flexible and powerful workers' movement, but economic power is the pivot of domination. Capitalism, except *in extremis*, has the muscle and flexibility to fall back, change direction, transfer resources, or simply buy off trouble, and the size of modern corporations enables them to transcend national boundaries. But as class conflict grows more intense, so capitalism is increasingly forced to rely on the public power of the state, a process ironically reinforced by national rivalry. The state, in other words, is a coercive instrument designed to hold the working class in subordination and loyalty.

Many socialists find it hard to swallow the hard and uncompromising nature of this analysis. Faced with the possibility of gaining at least some share in state power, some, like the Mensheviks, abandoned the analysis altogether and adopted the pluralist strategy of reconciliation. Others, starting with Kautsky and the German Social Democrats, have argued that it is possible simply to take over the existing state apparatus and use it finally to liberate the working class. This position has formed the basis of social democratic ideology ever since and has now been more or less adopted by the Western communist parties. Further plausibility has been added by the observation that the organisation of the state now reflects the massive gains and reforms won by the working-class movement over the last hundred years. The ruling class, it is said, has legislated away much of its power; the state, rather than a coercive instrument, is in fact a semi-autonomous body representing the balance of class struggle at any given time.

The attractions of such a view are obvious. It offers a framework in which the contradictions of progress can be readily expressed, it avoids the manifest absurdity of appearing to hold that every legislative act, however beneficial to workers, is manipulative and conspiratorial against them, and it holds out the very real possibility of a peaceful and dignified transition to socialism. However, I believe that by glossing over the vital distinctions between the government, the ruling class and the state apparatus, both their similarities and differences become blurred, leading to the optimistic hope that mastery of one will lead to mastery of the others. Furthermore, by underestimating capitalism's powers of resistance, it is fundamentally disarming and minimises the need for workers to organise themselves for their own freedom. The political consequences of such a position are either tragedy (as in Chile) or an increasing accommodation with the Right, the 'historic compromise'.

It was Kautsky himself who wrote that 'the capitalist class rules but does not govern, it contents itself with ruling the government'.[8] Though not invariably true, in that capitalists do sometimes rule directly, Kautsky's observation contains an important principle: that domination is in the long term more effective if it is not openly exercised. Government must at least appear to act in the general rather than in sectional interest, a tradition which tends to fetter socialist rather than capitalist parties. Sometimes capitalists may not approve or enjoy the advent of a self-styled socialist government but are ready to make concessions, confident of their long-term control. Furthermore, such parties are usually insecure in power, often inheriting financial crises which they are then forced to solve in capitalist terms in order to retain 'public confidence'. Indeed, capitalists are often eager to enlist social-democratic support to bale themselves out in order to neutralise their most dangerous opposition. The nationalisation of risky enterprises, like steel in the 1950s, can even enrich them at the expense of public coffers. In any case, the concentration of capital has forced employers and the government to work in far closer cohesion than ever before, whatever their political complexions. But control remains firmly in capitalist hands, because of their economic power and because of the entrenched system of the state.

The state safeguards the prevailing order both by its tradition and by the make-up of its personnel. Although in theory the state apparatus exists to serve the government, its primary function is to administer regulations and institutions which play an essential part in keeping the system in operation. Some of these institutions may be legitimately occupied in promoting change, but only within fairly well-defined limits; two examples illustrate the extremes: the Community Development Projects transgressed their boundaries and were wound up; the Equal Opportunities Commission, set up to advance women's rights, has been toothless and irrelevant and so continues in existence. Moreover, as Miliband points out,[9] the legal system, already in its corpus designed to protect and reinforce property rights, public order and the *status quo*, serves also to protect individuals and groups against political interference. The hindering effect of the legislative process with or without such institutions as the House of Lords adds further immobilisation to reform. Parliament is quick to react if its own interests are threatened; otherwise it is a palace of obstruction. Traditionally the state has to appear independent, but this guise serves only to promote a consensual respect, particularly towards its coercive arms, the police and the armed services, whose actions in times of crisis betrays no doubt about the focus of their loyalties. The actual or threatened use of troops by both Labour and Tories to replace striking dustmen, firemen or tanker drivers is an obvious example.

The second safeguard is the close link between state officials and business and other élites. It is not simply a matter of birth or public-school education; in some ways these are incidental. The key lies in the professional culture of the civil, legal and military services, the interchange of personnel with industry, the links produced by the joint problems of management and contractual negotiations (even local government is now big business) and the inevitable financial rewards of privilege which tie both officials and representatives into the business system. At junior levels radical dissent may be permitted, but promotion is contingent upon security and responsibility. Again, in crisis, radicals may be weeded out at all levels. The infamous *Berufsverbot* in West Germany prevents anyone entering or remaining in public service, including lecturing, teaching and social work, if they show the least sign of disloyalty to the state, even by attending quite ordinary demonstrations.

My argument is that, although in times of security and plenty the ruling class displays tolerance and liberalism, it tightens ranks when under threat. The machinery of the state was set up to service the ruling class, which will not hesitate to use that machinery to repress opposition. This view does not entail that every enactment of the state is *ipso facto* repressive; thus Stanley Cohen, who is inclined to reject Marxism as a useful tool for social workers, grossly misinterprets *Case Con* when he writes that it uses 'the standard polemics about a world in which every government measure, down to obscure clauses in the Mental Health or Children's Acts, is an attack on the working class'.[10] Two points need to be made in reply. First, capitalism is inherently crisis-prone and at present permanently crisis-ridden. While it is true that parts of the Left have tended too eagerly to overestimate the seriousness of particular events, and that the vocabulary of revolutionaries sometimes seems limited and shrill, we cannot but recognise that capitalism has entered a crucial phase in which it may change considerably. Not every crisis is a revolutionary situation, but each one brings the possibility of revolution nearer. Secondly, it is nonsense to suggest that all legislation is a class attack. On the other hand, if a class analysis of society is correct, then one must examine all legal measures to see whose interests they serve.[11] Every new power granted to the state can potentially be used against the working class. That is not necessarily a reason for opposing such powers, but we have to be on our guard.

How then do we come to terms with the existence of welfare and other progressive legislation? Corrigan and Leonard argue that radicals who adopt the coercive view of the state are unable satisfactorily to justify their own positions as state employees except perhaps by sabotage, and are caught in a contradiction which is untenable, especially when they fight to save the welfare state from being dismantled.[12] However, despite the difficulties involved in this, as any other Marxist view of welfare, neither argument is as cogent as they suggest. The state system does embody gains won by the working class and concessions made by the rulers, buying either time or stability. These have both to be defended and to be pushed further. Of course capitalists themselves benefit from the existence of welfare. They even use it occasionally. As we shall see in the next chapter, it costs them less than it costs the workers; it provides them with a healthy enough and appropriately educated workforce, provides a modicum of control, and legitimates them by its apparent benevolence and generosity. But workers benefit too: their conditions are better than they would otherwise have been and they have greater freedom. Only the most Machiavellian of revolutionaries would seek to provoke acute repression for its own sake, and Lenin himself wrote that while a democratic republic is the best shell for capitalism, it is also 'the best form of state for the proletariat under capitalism' because despite being subject to 'wage slavery', workers can organise and make inroads into the interests of capital.[13] Two questions are crucial: will workers be content with their gains or with half-measures which perpetuate their exploitation? And, whether this is initially so or not, will capitalism be able to continue providing a sufficiently high standard for all to perpetuate its own dominance? Marxists must answer in the negative. We defend the welfare state as a basic protection for workers and we refuse to permit its erosion by a transfer of resources back directly into capital. But the existence of welfare provision, however far-reaching, does not make state machinery 'semi-autonomous' of capital: a dangerous illusion.

The same can be said of the law, whose alleged independence is dedicated to the same end as that of state officials – to keep the machinery ticking over, regulate conflict and prevent disputes getting out of hand. It is true that some laws serve individuals more or less equally, and that socialists can sometimes turn the law to their advantage. But the fact that workers have won some modicum of legal protection does not mean they have the law on their side; in fact it is biased in the opposite direction. At a local level the Community Development Projects have documented how laws favour business rather than its victims.[14] The industrial dispute at Grunwick's shows how allowing only minimal picketing serves to make it ineffective. The 1977 Criminal Law Act will control radical activity much more closely and exact greater penalties. Meanwhile judicial decisions are reported which allow the police to break the law with impunity by searching without warrant. Individual deviance is hounded; corporate offences are excused or punished disproportionately lightly. The history of Britain, and especially Northern Ireland, is studded with patently oppressive legislation. To obtain rights and redress by legal process is a lengthy, uncertain and expensive affair. Delay works in favour of vested interests and success often depends upon resources; often there is little freedom of manoeuvre. Almost all major social changes have involved agitation which broke the law.

Defiance of the law is associated with violent behaviour. Social workers rightly prefer reason, but we are not above using the violence of the law against disruption. State coercion is endemic but disguised; the person struggling to break free always appears to be more violent than he who has the grip. To this coercion is added the structural violence with which our sensitivity and consciousness are continually bombarded. When considering personal violence, social workers should never ignore the factors to which it is a response.

Ideology: the permeative stabiliser

The portrayal and public definition of violence is one example of the way ideology shapes our perceptions. The media continue to pump out news and views which reinforce the ideology of capitalism and the state, lending just enough support or encouragement to radicals to give the illusion of balance, occasionally even splashing particularly newsworthy causes, but in the long term providing an unremitting diet of conventional opinion. Crusades against individual cases of ill-treatment are outweighed by the general feeling that these are exceptions, and are totally cancelled out by unscrupulous campaigns against alleged scroungers or muggers. Meanwhile we are cajoled by advertising to conform to ever more desirable stereotypes.

The assumptions of social work are another way of conveying ideology. As a background there is the general illusion we purvey that ours is a caring society, supplemented by the general framework of liberal pluralism which I have already criticised; I shall have more to say about social work and caring in Part II. However, there are certain other key pillars of capitalist ideology which play a crucial role in influencing much of what social workers do. Three of them I shall also discuss in Part II: the predominance of individualism, the enthroning of the family as the indispensable collective unit on which society must be based, and the oppression of women, which is in part consequential on our valuing of the family and in whose perpetuation we are customarily enrolled. But perhaps even more fundamental is the pessimistic view of human nature to which capitalism is committed.

Are we trapped by original sin?

The prospects for a changed society depend almost totally on whether we believe that human nature as we perceive it is a given and unalterable entity or that the human race is variable enough to develop and grow. Most cultures have some perception of man as being flawed; in Western thought, the Platonic tradition has had most emphasis, exalting mind at the expense of body with its animal passions, dirt and decay. Our material world tends to underplay this aspect, but we are equally accustomed to offer 'human nature' to excuse ourselves and others for a multitude of failings of which selfishness is the most prevalent. 'There'll always be somebody who'll take advantage', people say. Social workers are caught in a particularly schizophrenic attitude. On the one hand, our ideals are based upon the possibility at least of individual change; on the other, we continually condition ourselves to expect the worst.

It is significant that selfishness, the vice which causes us the most concern, should be that whose operation is essential to our economy, which is based on the individual pursuit of gain. It is small wonder that what should be so virtuous in one context should reappear in others as less than appropriate. From this phenomenon, the system makes a secondary gain because, while self-interest can now be vindicated, it needs to be limited. Not only will deviance or political argument be inevitably ascribed to self-interest, thus evading any more telling reasons, but a control structure can be justified. As many other observers have pointed out, an excess of self-interest seems almost always to emanate from the working class, not from their capitalist masters. Perhaps it is only given to some of us to supersede our natures.

The issue cannot be argued out here. It is a similarly interminable debate to that between posing genetic or environmental factors as predominant in human development. There is ample evidence that different societies and cultures demand distinct qualities from their members. Even in the West, individualism was never so deeply rooted as it is now. Yet, by gathering workers together in unity to sell their labour and engage in production, capitalism itself sows the seeds of something different, for while the capitalists continue competition, whether open or restricted, workers learn the pleasure and power of unity. It is from our collective experience as workers that change will spring. Radicals must reject the capitalist principle that human nature will not alter and instead assert, with Marx, that 'it is not the consciousness of men which determines their being but, on the contrary, their social being which determines their consciousness'.[15]

Radical dilemmas

The project of achieving sufficient liberation for the human race collectively to change what is understood by our nature faces a formidable array of obstacles. One reason for stressing the controlling aspects of the state, in its economic and ideological roles, as well as its repressive function, is that the state represents the institutionalisation of wide-ranging conservative assumptions; these dominate more progressive ideas, often by a process of 'repressive tolerance', and play an important part in containing and reinforcing our conception of our potential and our limits; they also form the official (if sometimes unspoken) ground-rules for the area in which social workers operate and over whose application and content we have some influence.

To say this is not to accept Leonard's view of the state as an arena of class struggle (discussed in the Preface); but it does acknowledge the contribution of both Leonard and other authors in Macmillan's *Critical Texts in Social Work and the Welfare State* series in re-emphasising the force of dialectic, not just in debate over the nature of the state, but to help us encompass much of the ambiguity and paradox of human life and history. By returning to the original and dynamic concept of Marxism and the basic contradiction between the forces of production and the social relations of production, they have helped to steer Marxist argument away from the crude functionalism so well charted by John Clarke[16] and towards a much more detailed appreciation of how the economic and ideological conflicts which created and dwell within the structure of our work derive from that basic contradiction and are the source not just of limitations but of the energy for change. This remains true even in quite limited fields: see, for example, the chapter on child-care decisions in Bolger *et al.*'s *Towards Socialist Welfare Work*. But the basic philosophy of dialectic, the central contradiction in the nature of thought, history and all things which, as they come into being, produce their own negation, may also provide the roots of a Marxist psychology; it is here that we can begin to grasp the space within which we must manoeuvre, by instinct as much as by intellectual principle. In my view dialectic is the root, not, as some would have it, of Marxist determinism, but of our ability to choose. By recognising this contradictory process, we may find some of our dilemmas less insoluble, not least because we may be able to avoid drifting into falsely exclusive positions, especially in the small-scale work which is necessary to underpin any broader strategy. We therefore need not to be afraid of the constraints within which we are placed, but rather to exploit them.

One example of the need to pick our way carefully between contradictory ideas is the relationship between care and control, which are often presented, especially by the libertarian Left, only in the most extreme form of irreconcilable opposites. But both at the individual and societal levels the relationship is both close and dynamic: control is not in itself an evil concept, nor is caring (which is discussed from another angle in Chapter 5) easily separable from it. Sometimes the only way to care is by control; sometimes it is only possible to control by caring. But we cannot sensibly discuss care and control in the abstract without asking who is offering, attempting, threatening or managing to control whom, by what means, in whose interests and after what choices have been put forward. I have tried to show how the principal but not the only function of the state is to act as the agent of the dominant class and that social workers play some part in maintaining such control. I have argued that this does not necessarily mean that welfare is oppressive: even some of our control functions, though initially restraining upon individuals, can be both essential and beneficial; we may still be unhappy about such situations, but we cannot repudiate control entirely unless we follow through all the implications of such a position. Not all control, still less discipline, favours the interests of capital. It is, however, essential for socialists to unmask the official ideology of a humane and caring capitalism, not only to reveal the extent of empty rhetoric (for example, over the elderly) but also to reveal the extent to which both rhetoric and practice, both good and bad, are used to appease working-class demands and legitimate the dominance of capital. But even a demystification which avoids a lurch into functionalism is still far from being a complete description. It is necessary, for instance, to recognise how the controlling aspects of our caring stem not just from being state employees, but from the social content of caring itself, particularly as expressed in social work under whatever auspices. Pearson writes brilliantly of how the nineteenth-century origin of social work stemmed from fear of the mob, and how Chadwick, hailed as one of the great Victorian reformers, justified social reform in the same terms as the introduction of urban sewerage.[17] While the actions of caring and controlling may be simultaneous, and may indeed have the same end, they are frequently justified in quite different language and with reference to distinct sets of facts and values. It is therefore possible, by counterposing these, to explore how each is socially realised. This is the first step towards dismantling the ideological scaffolding of welfare with a view to developing practices and justifications, not from state policy, professional jargon or well-meaning benevolence, but in the terms, languages and priorities of the subordinate classes whose interests we are trying to advance; for it is only by so doing that we can assert our positions in welfare to be in any way progressive, let alone radical. Our structural location at the frontiers of social 'caring' does to a considerable degree both legitimate and necessitate such action.

Our practical dilemmas over priorities are rendered no easier to resolve by the fact that, precisely because of our socialist ideology, we cannot refuse the welfare which capital needs to lubricate the reproduction of labour-power; welfare is, after all, part of our moral self-justification. From conception to old age, difficulties of all sorts crowd in on a population increasingly isolated from one another and thus forced into contact with the welfare network. Help is requested; improvements are demanded. The social worker is expected and needed to act as a mediator among individuals or between individuals or groups and private or state institutions, the more so at a time of recession. We are criticised if we do not advocate reforms. We cannot expect clients to wait, watch and work for a revolutionary change before their needs are met, at least in part, or their pain relieved. Often we can obtain resources like benefits, housing or holidays, which would otherwise have been out of reach. But the consequences of individual relief can be dire. Because resources are generally scarce, one person's gain may be another's loss. We may thus not only be legitimating the system for those who get help, but dividing the class of potential clients against one another. The price we pay for access to resources is not infrequently an unwelcome involvement in oppressive statutory machinery, which calls on us to make assessments and decisions which may profoundly alter people's lives. We can condone this only if we find adequate ways of working against the system as we work within it, and of using every opportunity to transfer power to those who lack it, even if this is often possible only at an individual level.

In and against the state

The collective who coined this title summarise the problems for those who use or work in state services in the succinct phrase: 'Resources we need, involve us in relations we don't';[18] a comment which is true for workers within capitalism generally, but acquires a special poignancy in areas of work where relationships are thought to be important. They distinguish between the state apparatus, a network of institutional rules and controls, and state form, the oppressive form of social relations. This latter, they argue, can be challenged while remaining within the state, and they hope that such challenges will eventually shatter the hollow and brittle apparatus. Whether this theoretical distinction is wholly adequate seems doubtful to me; after all, social relations, as feminists would surely be the first to point out, are in a crucial way part of the apparatus.

But there are at least some sectors of the state, especially within welfare, where the relevant ideological demands possess their own contradictions even when they emanate solely from the dominant class: for instance, between meeting need and rationing resources. Here state workers can push the structure towards and possibly beyond its limits. There is room not only to exert an important industrial role both with other workers and within the state bureaucracy, but, in at least some spheres, to develop work practice which defends the oppressed and minimises control. Even within the police force, where there is no room for Left politics, there can be debate about the development of a policing which reflects or acknowledges developing tensions within society. Education, though still subject to state control, offers important opportunities for dissent. But social work is perhaps exceptional in that it has developed a peculiar and privileged role in the state system; not unlike the court jester, we are licensed to criticise; we are the institutionalised conscience of society. Social work faces both ways, to client and society, and because of its contact with the casualties of the economic system is in part enjoined to feed back understanding of why such casualties have occurred. As long as welfare forms a central objective of government (and Mrs Thatcher's regime has shown that we cannot take such centrality for granted) we fail our clients, ourselves and the working class as a whole if we do not find ways of expressing its shortcomings as forcefully as we can. Obviously there will be different ideas about what constitutes acceptable criticism or action: court jesters had a limited life expectancy. Nevertheless, as long as we can justify ourselves as acting in clients' interests and more especially if we can win their active support (or vice versa), we are in a strong position. We should not exaggerate our independence, nor underestimate our potential room for manoeuvre.

In this chapter I have reapproached social work from the outside, and attempted to measure it against political principles. A number of important questions of ethics and practice have been raised, many of which have been staples of social work discussion for years. In the next part of the book I shall argue that an essential preliminary to resolving them and to achieving a real understanding of our work is the unravelling of the moral superiority conferred on us by the existence of clients.

Part II

The Welfare Trap

3

Not clients but workers

One of the most pernicious legacies of Freudianism to social work has been the treatment of individual and society as if they were unrelated abstractions. The conceptual difficulties caused by this dichotomy are not peculiar to social work but take on a special significance because of our traditionally emphatic espousal of human subjectivity. One of the main themes of this part of the book will be the way in which this bias towards the individual lies at the root of much that is wrong with social work and that our capacity to understand and maintain relationships depends upon a comprehension of people not as individuals but as social beings.

In order to grasp the complex way in which individual and social forces intermesh, we need what Raymond Williams calls 'mediating' descriptions, terms which accurately reflect the social groups and processes which express collective pressure but from within which people discover and preserve their individual identities.[1] Williams approvingly refers to Fromm's development of the term 'social character' to describe the positive and varied process by which social behaviour becomes part of the individual personality. However, established concepts tend to get pulled in one or the other direction. 'Family', for instance, though acting as the principal agent for producing a desired social character, is more often conceived as an entrenched protection for its constituent individuals against the outside world. Psychoanalytic thought has been particularly responsible for reinforcing the view of the family as the only significant unit. 'Community' and 'class' on the other hand appear, says Williams, to be unremitting agents of society, biased towards the reinforcement of social norms.

Social workers have finally learnt to treat the individual as an active family member, though it has taken us a long time to develop a relevant practice. Despite being enjoined to focus on family support, we still find that the networks, experience and expectations of the families we work with are often quite remote from our own. They are difficult to comprehend and almost impossible to influence. We are even now groping towards understanding the dynamics of community, though this amorphous term is subject to a host of differing interpretations.

But because we are trained to think in terms of cases, we have an inherent tendency to separate those we work with from those who do not call upon our help. We begin almost to think of clients as a separate homogeneous group, about whom myths are constructed which often prevent us from seeing them as real people. We build up images of how clients talk, dress and behave, even become adept at recognising client types in public places, creating the illusion of a culture of poverty by defining those people solely in relation to our professional selves. 'Client' thus becomes a mediating term with connotations of inadequacy and deviance.

We forget that 'client' is descriptive not of a person but of a relationship. Being or becoming a client is quite different from simply needing help. Client status depends on the services offered, the number of people to convey them, and on the extent of behaviour which is considered offensive enough to warrant punishment or supervision. The more services and social workers that exist, the greater will be the number of our clients. Clients are created by political priority as much as by objective or felt need for social work services. The people who receive the greatest proportion of our attention are families with young children, whose purses and patience are stretched to the utmost because they have not the opportunity to gain the resources and rest which they need. Yet our financial provision for them is grudging and niggardly; we offer supervision instead. The state manifests concern about children, whom it portrays as weak and vulnerable. So are old people. But children become the focus of a social policy whose form suggests that it is not their vulnerability that is being protected but ours. If they sense neglect, they may become uncontrollable and dangerous. Additionally, as Pinker observes, we hope ourselves to reap the fruits of the attention we bestow on them;[2] in other words, the state needs those children to be reliable producers. Yet, when they grow up, they will apply the same arguments in favour of their own children, and we who have become elderly will be neglected.

People who become burdened with problems and resort to being clients may superficially display different social characteristics to other people from the same economic background. Yet their major concerns are the same; the existence of clients merely betrays the extent of the problems which other people repress from public view. The resultant isolation feeds clients' alienation and leads them to bitter self-accusation or hostility against the nearest scapegoats – for instance, black people. In this chapter I want to reject any notion that clients form any sort of separate group in our society, or even a claimant class. Class, however, does seem to me to be the most useful mediating description from which to start considering client status, not only because it renders the underlying economic and social causes of personal problems much more comprehensible, but also because instead of dividing us from each other, we can use class to perceive our clients, other workers and ourselves as different sectors of the modern proletariat. This will enable us to achieve a better understanding of our own position as well as suggesting an honest way to relate to clients both directly and indirectly. Class itself is of course too broad a concept to explain everything that happens to people, and I shall try not to overextend its determination of events. However, client status is intimately linked with the effects of economic exploitation. Class is not the only such indicator; women, for instance, form a group whose exploitation transcends class boundaries and underlies far more of social work than most of us dare to admit. Their role will be discussed a little later.

Social-working the working class

Nobody to my knowledge has ever *proved* that most of our clients are from the working class. It is, however, a widespread assumption which experience appears to bear out.[3] When I used to work in the Home Counties, naïve acquaintances would sometimes evince surprise. 'You don't mean to say they need social workers there', they would say. 'Aren't they all stockbrokers?', as if half the population did not exist. The assumption also underlies the widespread critique of social work that it is practised by the middle on the lower classes. Unlike the Health Service, which is still patronised, if reluctantly, by a reasonable cross-section of society, social work is limited to the less wealthy except for its most specialised fields. Of course sometimes the stockbrokers did come my way, especially if there was a black sheep in the family whose delinquency or mental stress became a really unmanageable habit. And we heard of more than was referred to us;

G. P.s often suggest that the most callous cruelty exists behind suburban shutters. But most of my visits to the better-off would be in connection with subjects like adoption, which we discussed over a glass of sherry.

However, when social workers think about class, it is usually in terms of culture and values, not as an economic and political category. Although an increasing awareness of cultural difference finally forced a re-examination of social work assumptions and practice, it became easier to characterise the poor as a separate group in society. By categorising both our clients and ourselves as being objectively part of the proletariat, I want to make the political point that we stand in a similar relationship to capital. Some are exploited more directly and to a greater degree than others; some are more privileged. (I shall elaborate on the 'proletarianisation' of social work in Chapter 5.) But being a member of the same class does not of itself guarantee equality for workers any more than for capitalists. Our work tends to focus on the strata of the working class where exploitation is at its most acute, or where resistance is at its weakest. But a fully developed class analysis enables us to identify our weakest clients much more closely with other workers including ourselves as political allies for each other. It also means that we can root the phenomena that we often blame for client suffering within the workings of the system, rather than treating them as floating and coincidental signs of the times. The people who become our clients occupy those sectors of the economy where stress is heaviest and compensations most lacking, where opportunities are fewest and life is at its most alienating. It is characteristic of these sectors that resource systems, both social and personal, often function fully stretched and are manipulated with great ingenuity. However, there is little margin for accident, error, handicap or mistake, and should any of these occur, the effect is often cumulative.

For example, in her study of children's departments published in 1969, Jean Packman found that wealthier areas had more children in care than poorer authorities. She offered two explanations: that traditional working-class areas fostered more self-help and solidarity than those subject to social mobility; and that deviance was most likely to be conspicuous where the standard of living was higher. However 'the lower social classes and particularly manual workers, were heavily over-represented among the parents of children in care'. She went on to suggest that this was mainly because they needed help with emergencies – for instance, when mother was ill – whereas other classes had alternative resources available.[4] Davies, Barton and Macmillan found similar variations which they called 'territorial injustice'.[5] Although the numbers of children in care depended partly on the facilities available (larger authorities being able to provide greater variety and specialisation) a high degree of social disorganisation was associated with the take-up of services, reinforcing Packman's remarks about the influence of social mobility. Davies, Barton and Macmillan also found some association between bad social conditions, high use of approved schools and a low propensity to receive children into care. This suggests that voluntary use of the service in such areas was affected by the stigma of control.

It is dangerous to make too much of statistics like these because the factors involved are so complex, and one can derive a number of conclusions without much certainty attaching to any of them. Nevertheless I believe they are an important indicator of the weight of use of our services. Bill Jordan, in *Poor Parents*, argues strongly against too great an emphasis on any supposed link between poverty or deprivation and 'maladjustment', and casts doubt on some of the evidence about social disorganisation.[6] He is, of course, quite correct to refute any necessary connection between poverty and emotional deprivation, as well as the idea that real need is manifested only by a small and self-perpetuating social group; as he cogently points out, it is selective social work attention which is more likely to perpetuate dependence. But in arguing for a decent living for all, Jordan fails to take full account of the structural nature of deprivation. Even social disorganisation, whatever its effect on demands for help, is the product of the requirements of capital; the scaling down of the family unit, the need for the workforce to move according to the convenience of employers, and having to put up with poor-quality housing blocks, whose design has been dictated by cheapness or speculation, are but three examples.

Crushed by conventional simplicity

One of the most revealing and beautifully written books about social work to have been published recently is a novel by George Konrad, *The Caseworker*.[7] It describes a day in the life of the Hungarian equivalent of a child care officer, who goes to arrange for the care of a mongol child whose parents have, after long years of despair, committed suicide. The heart of the book describes how he finds the child still penned in the flat, and while he sits with it trying to decide what to do, he fantasises his own metamorphosis into that parental role, imagining his reactions, his struggle, the bewildered visits he would receive from those who have taken his place, finally concluding that the parents' suicides were 'just as foreseeable as the falling of a distended drop from a telephone wire'.

I have seen references to *The Caseworker* by liberal or Right-wing social workers who seek to use it as proof of the social and economic backwardness of Hungary, of the pervasiveness of individual problems, and even of the iniquity of socialism. Certainly Konrad's function is more akin to that of detective or examining magistrate, and is much more tightly integrated into the state control system. Nor is all his experience easily transferable. It would be my argument that the contradictions he describes are dictated by requirements similar to our own, except that the movement of capital is controlled by a central bureaucracy; nevertheless, economic controversy aside, what makes Konrad's book remarkable are his devastating insights into the social work process. This is how, near the beginning, he describes a typical encounter with a client:

> In my official capacity I am informed of his job, habits, and previous blunders; this allows me to estimate how much freedom of action he has. Of course, what I see isn't the man himself, but only the envelope in which he moves about. Yet, reluctantly, I identify my client with all these odds and ends, and feel sorry for him because so many obstacles have impeded his development. It would be commendable if his relations with his environment were somewhat more complex, if the rules he chose to live by were a little less conventional. But his system is depressingly lacking in complexity, his income wretched, his physical surroundings dreary, his vision blurred, his burden heavy. His freedom of action is below average, his drives, which are without direction, conflict and sometimes collide head on. When this happens, the traffic jams up, and official intervention is needed to start it moving again. Since my job is to protect children and safeguard the interests of the state, the most I can do is reconcile him with his circumstances and oppose his propensity for suffering. I do what the law and my fumbling judgement permit; then I look on, mesmerized, as the system crushes him.

Compare this account with that given me by Elaine, a young mother, living without electricity because her husband has broken open the meter, who, in desperation, went to the children's department for help.

> The Electric came for money so I went to the Welfare with my mum. I expected them to do the world: we'll see to this and we'll see to that. But in the end I walked out. They offered me W. V. S. clothes but I didn't want them, though I took them in the end. It was horrible, I came out in tears. It was only a young girl trying to be nice, but everything was on top of me. I couldn't talk, she couldn't accept me, so I didn't listen. They said they'd 'phone but they didn't. I don't know why. She said she would help and then she didn't. We hadn't any light for a fortnight so I threatened to abandon the children, but it made no difference. I don't talk well for myself; you've got to be cheeky to get on. I didn't push the threat. I just thought they're bound to help, though I had a friend who just plonked her baby in the outer office. They say, 'It's your responsibility to look after your children'. I say, 'Why do you think I've come here?' They could have shown a bit more sympathy. It's not me who's been in trouble. Every time he's been off work, the Assistance thought it was my fault. I couldn't do any more.[8]

The social worker involved hesitantly expressed to me her own despair at the extreme and demanding nature of Elaine's request. She admitted that her attention had been diverted from the pressing problem of electricity to ways of calming Elaine and getting her to accept the Electricity Board's decision. Elaine had called later on to get some clothes, but meanwhile her husband illegally reconnected the supply, for which he was later heavily fined.

What Konrad is getting at, and Elaine graphically illustrates, is that clients reach us more or less at the end of the road, when they have exhausted whatever limited possibilities were available to them. Sometimes there are alternatives which they have missed or of which they could not have been aware. More often, we are the last resort; we do not perceive the effort which has preceded our encounter, and whatever weaknesses of personality they have are compounded by their desperation. As we look for the causes of their plight, it is those individual quirks which strike us first, and on those foundations social work has traditionally built its theoretical castles. But though these weaknesses are expressed by the individual, and it is the individual person whom we must reach, they are not essentially *of* the individual. The form they take and the extent to which they can be overcome is determined by their class. Clients' most crucial need is freedom of action, and the extent of their freedom is bounded not just by their personality but by their condition – being a woman, a single mother, being unemployed or badly paid, living in surroundings which grate upon the consciousness and pulverise imagination. Even at the most personal level, whatever degree of skilfulness or versatility exists is either eroded or distorted by consistent deprivation; if the consequent frustration is characterised by high emotion, our attitude is to allow 'ventilation', an evaporation of the pent-up energy, after which we can help mould the most convenient and untroublesome response.

In talking of limitations, I do not mean inherent restrictions of the kind associated with the ideas of Basil Bernstein about language;[9] I mean restricted opportunity, restricted relaxation and, above all, the restriction of rules which were not intended to work to the advantage of those who most risk becoming clients. The rules of our society are made to favour those with access to capital, upon whose service positional or financial rewards are usually contingent. But those who are not content with the meagre and dependent living which is left to them, can, unless they are lucky, do better only by breaking the rules or taking full advantage of them. In business, such action, if discreet, is praiseworthy. To exploit the Inland Revenue or company law shows initiative and common sense. If you play it right, you need pay little if any tax; even petrol can be free of V. A. T. If you hit trouble your friends may not be able to afford to let you go under. When Mr Jim Slater resigned from Slater Walker Securities, personally owing nearly £1 million, he found that he did not have to change his life style to any great extent.[10] But if the only system you are in a position to exploit is the Welfare, even if you remain within the law, you get labelled manipulative, a trouble-maker or a scrounger, and if you are forced to approach the social services, the price you pay is an abrogation of rights and permission for somebody to interfere without your having any knowledge of the consequences or redress in case of dissatisfaction, still less any guarantee of success. What is more, the very fact that people are willing to pay such a price is taken as yet another indication of inadequacy.

Client accumulation

One of the major originators of dynamic psychiatry, Pierre Janet, once said that many a neurotic or borderline schizophrenic could manage very well if only they could pay for the efforts of others which they could not make themselves.[11] Money may not buy a perfect personality, but it certainly compensates. Conversely, as we shall see in general terms, stress, uncertainty and poverty frequently provoke the need for specialised or in-patient treatment.

It would be easy for me to use such a case as a further illustration, but there are already many examples, documented most frequently by campaigning organisations. However, many social workers remain unconvinced that such examples accurately represent the 'meat' of the job, and I have therefore chosen a family where the parents can, at least in the conventional sense, be shown to have made some contribution to their problems.

Bob was a long-distance lorry-driver in Yorkshire, but moved with his wife and two sons to the West Country on obtaining a better contract which would give him more time at home. He was not, however, a 'family man', but impulsive, independent and popular in the pub. He had a high ideal of himself but either did not put in the effort or was not able to live up to it. A daughter was born, but his wife began an affair with the landlord. When Bob found out, the marriage broke up; leaving his wife to move in with the landlord and look after the boys, he returned to his home town with their daughter. There he met Rita, mother of two teenage girls, and they began living together, at first in very poor conditions; later they were rehoused. However, shortly afterwards, the little girl, now four, was run over and killed while playing in the road. Bob became almost inconsolably depressed and only recovered after the birth of a son to Rita.

Two years later, Bob's wife died. Bob had had little or nothing to do with her or the boys since leaving, but retained an idealised version of what his sons were like. Appalled to hear that they had been received into care, he immediately went to fetch them back to Yorkshire, giving them little preparation or time to adjust. The boys had had a fairly unsatisfactory life with their mother, and were already disturbed. Once home, they began truanting, stealing and running away. Bob was unable to cope with this, became depressed, and had to ask for them to be received into care again; guilt, however, led him to get them back home; this sequence occurred twice. Bob continued to be moody and depressed; it began to affect his work. His failure to understand the boys finally caused him to vent his frustration by beating them, particularly the older one, who was his namesake. Finally, Bob junior was placed under a care order for a minor offence; again Bob's guilt was so severe that he was unable to bring himself to visit his son.

The general air of despondency and defeat took its toll on both Bob and Rita; Bob's wages dropped but he drank more heavily, leaving Rita less and less to manage on. The contributions towards the children's maintenance in care were never made and the social services department repeatedly threatened him with imprisonment. Meanwhile the middle boy, Barry, now eleven, had been sickening for a while and was finally found to have Perthes' disease, an erosion of the hip-joint normally diagnosed in the first few years of life, and cured by seven or eight. For several months he had to remain at home in traction. Bob and Rita were worried about his condition, having little faith in the consultant, and asked for a second specialist opinion. Because of their troubled record, their G. P. refused to make the necessary referral. When Barry was able to get around he was refused readmission to school because of his splint and became the subject of dispute between the protagonists of integrating handicapped children into ordinary schools and headmasters who felt it inappropriate. Despite his parents' concern, he was not given home tuition; it was eight months altogether before he was able to return to school, where he was teased by the other children for being a cripple. However, in the intervening period, two days' absence from school by Peter, Bob and Rita's son, elicited an immediate visit from the education welfare officer to ensure his attendance. Rita took Barry to his consultant for a routine check-up, and in order to reassure her, he showed her an X-ray which proved the trouble had cleared up. Unknown to him, Rita is a trained nurse and was able to point out that he was showing her the wrong leg.

Meanwhile Bob lost his job. To keep up his image he insisted on retaining adequate spending money, leaving Rita to cope with the soaring price of food and the debts. Rent arrears began to mount, electricity and gas were cut off and, with winter approaching and no hope of reconnection, the electricity supply was illegally reconnected. Bob junior started coming home for weekends, which went well, but because of the non-payment of contributions, no allowance was paid to cover his stays. During this period Bob insisted that Rita did not reveal the extent of their financial problems to the social worker. Nor did Rita dare tell her that she was pregnant again. In January of the severest winter for some years, the Electricity Board discovered the illegal supply and disconnected it at 8p.m. Peter had bronchitis and Rita put him to bed, intending to get him some medicine. The house was pitch black and she fell right down the stairs. Next day she lost the baby. The social services committee, under pressure because of the cuts, refused a loan to have power reconnected, suggesting a reapplication in six months, and the family had to resort to paraffin heaters and bottled gas, which infringed local fire regulations. After a struggle, the family cleared its rent arrears but did not have anything left to reduce the electricity bill. In desperation, and despite warnings from her social worker to look at the small print, Rita approached a private finance company. After five weeks she realised that they were charging 25 per cent interest and terminated the agreement at a total loss of about £30. Meanwhile she had been taken to court and placed on probation for having the electricity reconnected.

This case raises a number of interesting issues, some of which I shall refer to elsewhere. It does not fit easily into any glib category. Nevertheless, I believe there are two fundamentally different approaches. The traditional social work view would be to interpret the history as stemming from the weaknesses of Bob's personality and that of his wife. Rita was foolish to get involved with him. Every effort should be made to ameliorate the situation and to get the couple to face up to their responsibilities. Radicals, on the other hand, have to begin by understanding the impact of social demands and expectations, both in forming and in reinforcing what appear as weaknesses simply of personality. We also have to take account of the limited and diminishing opportunities for escape. Only in this way can we hope to lift sufficient of the burden of guilt and inadequacy for the individuals concerned to be free enough to reassess both their performance and their opportunities, and to understand how blame and responsibility must really be distributed, what sorts of change will be necessary and how they can be achieved. This is a preliminary to individual work, not a replacement for it. Meanwhile there are three aspects which deserve notice.

The first, and in some ways most basic in this case, is gender. Bob brims over with a totally unrealistic masculine ideal, one side of which is exemplified in his social life with 'the lads' and his occupation, the other in his general abandonment of domestic affairs to Rita. He sees himself as an old-fashioned hero, rushing each time to the rescue, and cannot cope with his failure. He worries about being soft, and will not let Rita out to work, allegedly because it is not right when there are children but actually because he is afraid of her independence: he will not even let her wear make-up. So Rita gets lumbered every time. She falls downstairs, goes to court, runs up the debts; it is all part of being the wife and mother. He has the traditional right to control her life and enjoy its fruits. Woman's lot, as one notoriously clumsy registrar in my hospital said to his grimacing patient while taking blood, is to suffer and endure. It is all too easy to concentrate on Rita as the presenting client; that is why social workers have so much more to do with women; the men are secure in their freedom however much they may be targets for abuse. Yet it is Bob who will have to change. All of this can be expressed in quite orthodox Freudian language; analysis of gender roles is nothing new. But challenging and changing them is something else. The pattern of Bob and Rita's relationship can only partially alter on its own; it is a distortion, but a quite recognisable one, of behaviour which is generally accepted, and even encouraged by the media and advertising. To focus on Bob and Rita simply as individuals, because the other factors are beyond our influence, is to betray them.

Secondly, there is the question of income, education and job requirements. Although Bob has a slightly less routine job than many others, it is lonely, heavy and tiring. Nor does it pay as well as myth suggests. Whatever Bob's mistakes, more money could have lessened their impact or bought him out of trouble entirely, though he would not thereby necessarily have acquired happiness. In the West Country, he might have had a mortgage and a better house; the same could have applied back in Yorkshire; there might have been a garden or more indoor play-space, lessening the risk of an accident to his daughter. The children's schools would have been better. He could have taken on a housekeeper or au pair. While the boys were with their mother, he could have laid on visits more easily. More acceptable distractions could have been found to keep them out of trouble; in any case, they would have had more in life to look forward to. Bob might have been able to control his own hours better, and to have been educated to find other relaxations than drink. Most important of all, he would have had access to cheap credit. The more debts which accumulated, the less likely he was to pay them; yet they were not on a scale where he could go bankrupt. Welfare or money-lending sharks were his only choices. Of course things go badly wrong in middle-class families, but not many of them become clients; they have the assurance and reserves to cope somehow, for they have not been socialised into deference.

Finally, once the dam of independence is breached, the family has no way out; it sinks slowly into a morass of debt and permanent client status. Money to help is eked out and carefully supervised. The family becomes publicly demeaned by the education department; Rita, being more available, becomes the major client of the partnership.

She is held in contempt by the consultant. Finally her client status is legally defined by being put on probation. The family's living standards and nutrition deteriorate. Social work support achieves little or nothing; it certainly does not alleviate matters for Rita. Ultimately Bob seeks refuge in dreams of a driving job in Saudi Arabia. Rita begins to lay the blame elsewhere but in the wrong direction; her brother is standing as a candidate for the National Front.

Individualisation: the easier answer

Another shorter example makes a similar point in a more dramatic way. Brian's parents split up when he was a child. He did not get on with his stepfather and left home at 17 to join the Parachute Regiment. On his first day he was put into a boxing ring with his best friend; the burly sergeant-instructor let them spar a little then called them apart. Removing their gloves he took each of them aside and told them: 'Right. I want you to kill that bastard before he gets you. And if you hang back you'll have me to reckon with.' At Aldershot he learnt about women, who were slags to be used in whatever way he wanted. Once again to hang back was cowardice. He was posted to Ulster, where he took part in routine beatings of civilians. He came under fire himself and he shot people, including, he said, a child. Every time he showed any grief or sympathy it was disciplined out of him. Finally the strain grew too great, he took to drink and was discharged. When he returned to England he became engaged to a 'decent' girl. But his violence got out of control. Whenever he got upset he beat her. Afterwards he was full of remorse. He grew more and more depressed, got into trouble at work, took an overdose and was admitted to hospital. The consultant was reluctant to admit that he could have been brutalised by his experiences. 'Thousands of people go through the same experience', he said, 'then they come back and live normal lives. Whatever's wrong with Brian happened long before he went into the army. People like him continually demand affection which they cannot cope with.'

The consultant in question is a conservative but humane psychiatrist who takes more account than many of environmental factors. His comments would command widespread agreement but neglect the significance of Brian's condition. Even if Brian was vulnerable before he joined up, the army capitalised on his weaknesses. The fact that he was too frail to withstand the pressures was used to evade the question of whether they should have been applied and what their purpose was. The content and desirability of the 'normal' lives which other veterans are supposed to lead is equally open to challenge. Brian himself was no radical; he was too self-obsessed and indoctrinated seriously to consider the military role in Ulster. But the individualisation of his diagnosis not only absolves society from blame, making military training a subject of distaste rather than censure; it also fragments any possible dissent. Brian was pessimistic about his own fate. The hope of decent living which his girlfriend represented vied with the pressure from his former regimental companions to become a mercenary. Brian hardly disguised his knowledge that to accept such a contract would merely be one brutal step towards fulfilment of his death wish.

The extent of inequality

One of the radicalising factors in social work is the realisation of how limited are the opportunities open to those with whom we come in contact. A general look at how socio-economic position affects the personal lives and resources of the population illustrates how far-reaching such limitation remains. Unsurprisingly, in fields like health, housing and finance, the greatest pressure tends to fall on those least equipped to bear it, however ingeniously they adapt. The strain is not even, nor is it necessarily associated simply with poverty. Nevertheless on any broad analysis the facts are clear: exploitation takes a heavy toll.

Health

Despite an uneven distribution of facilities, the impoverished N. H. S. has eased treatment for the less well-off, but has done little to alleviate class differences. Among the bourgeoisie, serious ill health remains a deviant phenomenon. For workers it is often the norm. These differences can be largely accounted for by nutrition, lifestyle and occupational hazards. They are particularly acute at either extreme, but their distribution corresponds to class gradations. They begin before independent life. Evidence assembled by Reid shows that social class (anomalously of the father) 'is related to the length of gestation, birth weight, and chances of survival at and just following birth'. The rate of post neo-natal death per 1000 for social class I is half that of classes III and IV and one-fifth that of class V.

Up to 55, the death-rate of class I is half that of class V and 'the chances of surviving through adulthood into old age are similar to those of surviving birth'.[12] Moreover, these differences are *increasing*. By the age of 65, 10 per cent of all workers are already retired through ill health. The old saying that disease knows no barrier of class has perhaps a grain of truth in respect of infection and contagion, but is otherwise quite implausible. Unskilled workers are 63 per cent more likely than average to die of stomach cancer, professionals 51 per cent less likely and managers 37 per cent less likely. T. B., bronchitis and lung cancer show similar distributions, as do the diseases often associated with lush managerial living – for instance, coronary disease and duodenal ulcers.[13] These figures cannot be closely related to occupation because they refer to both men and women; diet is, however, of obvious importance. The poor have to spend a far higher proportion of their income on necessities but, even so, the most nutritious foods are often well outside price brackets accessible on an average income. The recent doubling of food prices at a time of compulsory wage-restraint will hardly have improved matters.

Occupational hazards are a frightening source of inequality and stress.[14] Recent public concern has focused on contact with dangerous materials like plutonium, coal and chemicals. The varieties of pneumonoconiosis are just one example of crippling industrial disease which has wiped out whole workforces before their time, but whose existence has been only recently and reluctantly admitted by employers. Asbestosis was not officially recognised as a ground for compensation until 1970, when the Central Asbestos Company was found guilty of persistent breaches of regulations. Such diseases are slow to manifest their effects, and it is not always possible to pinpoint causes with sufficient accuracy to satisfy the law. It is a long battle to secure compensation; even then its amount may be trifling; Lord Ryder, on the other hand, finds it 'a logical reward' to be offered a £49,000 gratuity after eleven years' service with a prosperous company.[15]

Hazards are not limited to materials: the normal environment for shop-floor workers places them at perpetual risk. Noise, vibration, dust, and temperature are all accepted as an ordinary part of working life, but all cause disabilities, frequently at a severe level. The possibility of accident or even death is built into industry. About fifty miners are killed each year. In industry as a whole there are about 500 fatal accidents each year. One in 500 building workers dies in a site accident; about half of these deaths are attributable to a breach of law by the employer.[16] Machines and other equipment are rarely designed with operational safety as a prime factor, and regulations or procedures are often circumvented. There is a myth that accidents at work are due to carelessness, but a survey of 2000 accidents found that risk was built into industry, and carelessness was only a minor factor.[17] Sometimes whole communities suffer when safety is skimped, as after the chemical explosions at Flixborough and Seveso or the asbestos poisoning at Hebden Bridge. One might expect nationalised industries to set a higher standard, but the economisation which is demanded can lead to disaster. The explosion of a British Steel Corporation blast furnace in 1975 which killed eleven men was officially attributed to 'deficiencies in plant design, maintenance and personal protection for employees'. In the view of the Factory Inspectorate, 'senior management had not implemented the declared safety policy of the B. S. C.'.[18] Because the cuts in public expenditure had forced the postponement of a planned burns unit, there was no appropriate treatment facility within fifty miles. In September 1975, shortly before the disaster, nearly 5 per cent of the workforce in the Scunthorpe and Lancashire group of the British Steel Corporation had to take three or more days off work because of accidents. As social workers we pay far too little attention to the impact of people's work conditions on their ability to manage and improve their domestic lives.

Psychological breakdown and social class

It has long been known that certain common mental disorders are significantly associated with social class. But while hardly a year goes by without some usually spurious claim being made for the discovery of a biochemical basis for mental illness, social researchers are forced to be more modest and their findings tend to be regarded as being without clinical application.

The incidence of most psychoses, and especially schizophrenia, is inversely related to class, and the Psychiatric Rehabilitation Association has concluded that 'it is now possible to calculate, with 95% accuracy, the numbers of schizophrenic patients to be found in urban communities according to the degree of poverty that prevails'.[19] The P. R. A. suggests that there are three types of explanation for this association: downward drift, differential diagnosis and stress.

Downward social drift has some plausibility and with its connotations of undeservingness and individual failure is the most widely accepted theory among doctors for the high incidence of schizophrenia among the working class. However, the evidence is not entirely consistent and in any case does not apply to other psychoses.[20] Whatever the extent of social drift, it remains quite clear that people with schizophrenic symptoms do not do well in a class society.

The second hypothesis is that the differential diagnoses and treatments meted out to patients from different classes tend to reflect doctors' expectations and prejudices rather than any genuine syndrome and this argument is relevant to most or all medical conditions. How rife prejudice can be is illustrated by the following summary of a research finding in a standard psychiatric textbook. Lower socio-economic groups contained a relatively high percentage of 'organic types, psychotic types, psychosomatic problems, character disorders, alcoholism, dissocial behaviour, hypochondriasis, passivity, dependency, and schizophrenia. Higher groups were twice as often free of symptoms, with a high incidence of aggressiveness, while lower groups scored high in immaturity, rigidity, suspicion and frustration'.[21] Recent research in Britain has indicated the importance of accent in diagnosis. Descriptions of symptoms set in exactly the same words but spoken in three different accents, – urban regional, rural regional and received (B. B. C.) pronunciation – led final-year medical students not only to different diagnoses but to widely differing judgements on the intentions, abilities, common sense, vocabulary and syntax of the speaker, the most derogatory judgements being reserved for the urban regional accent.[22]

In Boston, Hollingshead and Redlich[23] found, for instance, that symptoms which would be diagnosed as hysterical in class I became schizophrenia in class V. Differential treatment then confirmed prejudice and prolonged class division. Upper-class patients were sent to analytic psychiatrists; others were referred to more drug-oriented practitioners who were authoritarian and tended to use compulsory methods. The authors commented that the need and value of insight-therapy is not appreciated by lower-class patients 'who seek material help in the form of pills and needles, obscure rays and rituals'. Only some of these patients, they thought, were actually seeking support and sympathy. It is of course a commonplace that workers 'do not appreciate psychotherapy'. From this assumption it is deduced that workers are either incapable of talking about their problems or unwilling to do so. In addition, rapid treatment is essential as few can afford to be off work too long; nor can the economy afford the increasing number of days being lost as a result of mental illness. Treatment is therefore organised more and more along production lines in order to achieve a quick turnover. The smaller units which result mean fewer overheads. Bed efficiency is justified in the name of community care and an attitude of bemused deference is encouraged. Thus working-class people, whose upbringing has been mainly non-verbal and authoritarian (though none the less affectionate), are not only educated to their place in society, and cajoled into a mystifying respect for technology, but find that the disadvantages which perpetuate their passivity are used to deny their human potential. For their part, they know enough to recognise that mere words will change nothing at all.

Even recovery is harder for workers, as Myers and Bean found, following up the Boston patients ten years later.[24] Once admitted to hospital, they were more likely to remain, and when discharged, they had a harder time readjusting. Employment opportunity was an important factor in their difficulties, since the jobs available to them needed stable workers with regular work habits. (Contrarily, Goldberg and Morrison suggest that routine work which offers structure and security is eminently suitable for schizophrenics.[25]) In the more upper-class occupations, personal variations were accepted much more readily and paid sick leave was usually available.

The third hypothesis for the association of mental illness with class is stress. The different stresses felt in differing class positions provoke different conditions; the greater incidence of stress in working-class life provokes a greater incidence of illness. The part played by stress in mental illness is so obvious that it is often underemphasised. For example, senile dementia is taken for granted as an inevitable condition to such a degree that many lay people attribute any unusual behaviour in elderly people to a dementing process. Yet evidence exists to suggest not only that social factors can precipitate dementia (for instance, when old-age pensions were doubled in Denmark, psychiatric admissions dramatically dropped) but that in a high proportion of cases its onset can be linked with particular stresses in earlier life.[26]

Also of great importance is the work of G. W. Brown and his associates at the Maudsley Institute of Psychiatry. They have attempted in detail to relate psychiatric breakdown to the occurrence of isolated or serial life events.[27] After a series of reports they conclude that a case can be made for showing that loss conceptualised in different ways 'plays a vital role both in bringing about depression and in determining its severity and form'. Brown goes on to relate loss to class position: working-class women, especially with young children at home, showed a much higher rate of depression than average, rising to five times as great when they had experienced a severe event or major difficulty. Brown identifies four 'vulnerable factors', which

> increase the chances of developing a psychiatric disorder in the presence of an event or difficulty, but which have no effect in their absence. They are: loss of mother before the age of 11; presence at home of three or more children aged less than 14; lack of a confiding relationship with a husband; and lack of full or part-time employment. The first three are more common in the working class and between them largely explain the class difference in incidence of psychiatric disorder.

Stated in isolation these conclusions might be used to bolster the image of feckless women with large families, but Brown goes on further. He suggests that the ability to accomplish the psychoanalytic task of 'grief-work' depends on a cognitive scheme which is founded on a sense of identity and purpose separate from the bereavement. He places more weight on

> a second aetiological mechanism whereby a person deprived of important sources of value can develop a feeling of hopelessness . . . this may form a central feature of the depressive disorder itself. We believe that what is crucial . . . is a person's ongoing self-esteem, their sense of their ability to control the world and thus to repair damage, their confidence that in the end alternative sources of value will become available. . . . Of course an appraisal of hopelessness is often entirely realistic; the future for many women is bleak. But given a particular event or difficulty, ongoing low self-esteem will increase the chance of such an interpretation. . . . Therefore for the second aetiological mechanism, loss as such is not central; hopelessness and not grief is the crucial element.

We shall return to consider this question of vulnerability, particularly as it affects women. Meanwhile, whatever different interpretations there may be, it is quite clear that being working class renders one more likely to breakdown, to be treated on a purely mechanical level, and to have less chance of recovery.

Housing

It is probably fair to estimate that well over one-third of initial enquiries at social services departments include worries about housing. The housing problem is itself a microcosm of the chaos caused by half-hearted attempts at reform. As private tenancies dwindle because legislation to protect tenants has reduced profit to an unacceptable level, so council rents have soared, particularly in the newly-built estates which gathered high interest rates; in 1974, before these hit their peak, 60.9 per cent of all income from rents and subsidies went on the repayment of interest alone.[28] The cheap schemes which councils have been forced to adopt have often produced unacceptable living conditions; meanwhile the tenants of the 28 per cent of housing stock which is council-owned subsidise owner–occupiers through the latter's favourable tax position. To correct the balance they are forced to claim rebates which signal entry into the poverty trap and divide neighbour against neighbour. Although councils owe tenants a greater obligation than does the private landlord, their rules and actions are often arbitrary and incomprehensible and tenants find it hard to gain redress. For instance, it is common practice for councils to threaten a court case for arrears and charge for costs even if full settlement is made before any hearing. It is no surprise that tenants should have become disillusioned with municipalised housing, particularly since the expense and difficulty of obtaining mortgages in less respectable areas has further defined municipalisation as the compulsory but uncomfortable second choice for the less well-off.

At the root of it all: money and wealth

I have left income and wealth as the last of the factors of inequality which I want to consider so as to avoid appearing to harp on financial poverty as the sole source of underprivilege. Nevertheless, ultimately money determines opportunity. The myth which has been fostered by social democrats is that it is possible to achieve redistribution by progressive taxation, rising wages and the welfare state. A second belief is that reform has encouraged equal opportunity and wide-ranging social mobility. On this second question Westergaard and Resler concluded in 1976 that while there is a good deal of movement, upward mobility is restricted by the lack of downward drift and is often only a statistical illusion; white-collar occupations no longer contain either as much skill or prestige as before and the extremes of class division are little affected.[29]

Evidence on income and wealth does confirm that some of the worst excrescences at top and bottom of the class divide have been curbed but otherwise suggests that redistribution is as fictitious now as it has ever been.[30] The greatest redistribution this century took place between 1938 and 1949; nowadays, even after direct taxation, the top fifth of the population receive nearly six times as much as the lowest fifth (39.4 per cent against 6.8 per cent of the national income). The top 10 per cent receive 23.6 per cent of post-tax income. One should also note that manual workers have to put in far more hours to gain their share because of low basic wage-rates. Distribution of wealth is similarly skewed. If wealth is considered to include only marketable assets, and it is these which confer freedom of action in emergencies, half the adult population in 1973 had no wealth at all. In 1972, 82.4 per cent of disposable wealth was owned by the top fifth of the population. On methods of redistribution like taxation and welfare the Royal Commission on the Distribution of Income and Wealth came to the unequivocal conclusion that 'indirect taxes have a regressive effect which can be shown as broadly offsetting the redistributive effects of benefits in kind'.[31] The Commission did consider the combination of benefits and transfer payments with taxation to be redistributive but did not ask between whom such redistribution was taking place. In fact, from a socialist point of view, the greater proportion of public finance still operates regressively.

Welfare: from workers' privilege to workers' burden

In 1970 those below income tax threshold returned 25 per cent of their income to the state, but those in the highest tax bracket returned only 38 per cent. The introduction of V. A. T., the current moves to reduce income tax and increased charges for welfare services have probably reduced the difference still further. Flat-rate National Insurance contributions bear heavily on the lower paid; the graduated pension scheme merely subsidises existing pensioners and it is officially recognised that employers' contributions are passed directly on to the consumer as an indirect tax. The net result is that public health and welfare services are funded largely from individual wage packets and most redistribution occurs not between classes but within them, 'between households at different stages of life rather than households of markedly different levels of income'.[32]

The political pay-off is subtle. As public services are impoverished, the skills which they have nourished begin to subsidise a parasitic private sector. A growing emphasis on selectivity creates a stigma which has been condoned by both Labour and Tory governments seeking to cut expenditure. To the extent that benefits do improve, recipients find themselves the target of resentment from wage-earners who do not receive similar 'privileges'. The consequence is that members of the working class become still further divided from each other at their own financial cost.

Vulnerability

I have presented some of the most important factors determining working-class life and opportunity which I believe are fundamental to any real understanding of our clients' plight. I have done so not out of moral indignation at the continued existence of inequality but because so much of social work practice depends upon ignoring it. But it is not sufficient simply to describe inequality, for two ripostes are possible. The weaker is that even if all this is true, we can do nothing immediate to affect it, and therefore we should concentrate on individual support and amelioration. Such a position is, I believe, dishonest and evasive; individual helping is used to mask need and delay more global improvement; we have to try and make helping a force for change not against it. More cogent is the argument mentioned above that talk of working-class exploitation is all very well, but not all members of the working class become clients; the minority who do are individually unfortunate or inadequate, and therefore must be diagnosed and treated as individuals or a small group, but certainly not simply as working-class.

In answering such criticism radicals must avoid being drawn too far either into the individual-class/society dichotomy or into reinforcing the divisions within the class. Class experience is mediated through the individual and his or her empirically unique variations on that experience. Similarly individual social experience and identity are mediated through class, the individual and collective relationship to the process of production. And in practice, whatever allegiance to individual worth and value social workers may profess, our advice and actions are conditioned by class realities and our perception of them. We cannot, however, speak of the working class as a homogeneous body. Even among industrial workers, the uneven development of different industries has led to some degree of stratification, in income, experience and ambition. There are cultural and even moral differences between localities and between the sexes. The very fact that some workers have been forced to seek outside assistance has put a premium on self-reliance. It would be difficult these days to unearth any group that was truly representative of the class, let alone claiming such status for our clients. But if they are not typical as people, their problems are both representative and symbolic of the deprivations faced by the class as a whole, even though their experience may be somewhat distorted; and this I think gives us the cue for an integration of social work with political action. As social workers our job is to try and build up our clients' personal and financial resources; this in itself is a political task. But we have to make clear that the problems which cause most difficulty can be solved only by overtly political manoeuvre.

Given this distinction between resources and problems, we can begin to answer the question of who becomes a client by looking at the sectors whose problems are the greatest and resources the most stretched.

At-risk populations

I have argued that the basic criterion of vulnerability is an insecure relationship to capital. This insecurity is shared not just by the traditional working class, but by all those groups which are at risk because they are either heavily exploited or marginal to the economy, including women at home, the unemployed and the disabled. None of them have much or any ultimate control of their destinies, and to challenge their status is to risk perpetual confirmation as a deviant. Women have been taught that equality is a reasonable demand, liberation is not. The person who sees the streets lit up and decorated with other people's marks, their buildings, their cars, their advertisements, and leaves his own mark as a slogan on the wall is branded as a criminal. The brevity with which I shall have to enumerate these populations risks doing injustice to their causes; if so, I hope it will be pardoned.

A majority of social work clients are women, even if this is sometimes only because the husband or father is unobtainable. We have already observed this process at work with Bob and Rita. Women are deprived and oppressed in their work, in their personal lives and as consumers. Apart from their chameleonic obligations as mothers and as the butts of sexual aggression, whose caring is a perpetual lubrication of the wheels of production, they now form the greater part of what Marx called 'the industrial reserve army', whose role varies according to economic need. In times of boom, or during war, they are rushed to the factories, day-nurseries are provided for children, and they are encouraged to some sort of independence. But when production falters, work is scarce and the dole-queue long, the media are full of talk about the family and the glories of motherhood in order to persuade women back to the hearth. They service industry as cheap, disorganised part-time labour. Despite legislation, their pay is often less than men's. Women are always the first to be laid off. Working-class women do at least have one advantage over their middle-class counterparts: necessity has forced the recognition of their right to work; marriage is not as much a specialised career as for the middle-class housewife, whose husband thinks it a slur on his earning capacity if she has to work, and is therefore limited to coffee mornings and charitable activity. She has no independent status, no wage and is in fact a recipient of her husband's charity in return for services rendered. This is a major cause of the breakdowns such women frequently experience. Nonetheless Brown's work, quoted earlier, has highlighted how lack of income compounds this deprivation and puts the greatest stress on the young working-class mother. One of the saddest features of women's oppression is that because they are saddled with the responsibility of keeping society going, and because they are so vulnerable, many, especially in the working class, have internalised its standards much more rigidly than their menfolk. They are more judgemental and especially critical of failure. It is thus doubly important that whenever possible we link the plight of women clients with the demands and activities of the women's movement, to release them from the plight of unmerited blame.

Black people, who share with gays the distinction of being the most openly oppressed groups in our society, often manage to avoid calling on welfare help, because they run their own resource networks and because attributes of weakness or dependence like old age do not exclude their bearers from the community, as they do in Western urban culture. It has been estimated that although blacks pay equal taxes and perform low-paid labour for the state, each white person receives at least 30 per cent more from the state than each black.[33] (This is only partly because of the different age structure of the black population.) The degree of self-help is breath-taking, given that black people are so deeply underprivileged; they tend to live in the worst-housing, pay high rents, receive poor education for their children and scattered welfare services, work the worst shifts and be most liable for unemployment. Despite strenuous efforts to maintain themselves, blacks face rejection in almost every sphere. It is hardly surprising that apart from a few culture-specific problems, their major contact with the machinery of the state should be in the courts rather than in helping agencies. Some liberals see black rebellion and state harassment purely in terms of racial prejudice, and some blacks respond by seeking to build up a powerful racial identity. But the problems they face are not purely racial, any more than those of clients are purely a result of inadequacy; they are symbolic of what is happening to the working class as a whole; black people, like women, are the earliest to suffer from economic crisis and other workers must resist the sacrificial offering of black workers as appeasement. If they do not, they will be the next to become unwanted and the fate of blacks and the other unemployed will be used as precedents against them. Social workers faced with prejudice from their white clients have continually to make the links between different experiences and resist the false divisions which prejudice encourages.

Perhaps most demeaning of all is being a claimant of any sort, because one's life becomes subject to arbitrary power and official whim. In 1975, 8.1 per cent of the population were dependent upon supplementary benefit.[34] The case of Bob and Rita illustrated how easy the progression downwards is. Instead of being guaranteed a reasonable subsistence, insecurity becomes a condition of life. Earnings, sexual life and budgeting all become subject to official inspection. There are no public standards for determining what may be classed as an exceptional need. Mistakes in administration are frequent. A delayed letter can mean going hungry. It is not a condition of choice. Yet claimants have also to live with the stigma of scrounging, when survey after survey shows that most claimants have little alternative. In 1971 two-thirds of those living at or below supplementary benefit level were elderly, sick, disabled or single parents.[35] The structurally unemployed face an even greater burden of public derision.

Being a woman, being black, even being a claimant much more often than not, is a condition which one cannot help, but which is not in the least abnormal. Many people are willing to accept that the stigma and discrimination they suffer is unjust and unnecessary. A radical approach may succeed in removing them from the ambit of social work. But what of people who cannot or will not help themselves? Even radicals have felt their case to be limited in such instances.

What about the losers?

The fact that some people do need help much more consistently than others is less of a justification for such an artificial method of helping as social work than an indication of a need for a society in which mutual help and respect are spontaneously and consistently available. Social work help, though sometimes a necessary crutch, has the effect of marking out individuals, families or groups as being in some way outside the normal functioning of society, when the effort should in fact be towards integration. There are two general categories involved: those like the aged or the handicapped who are already burdened by some obvious incapacity; and those whose alleged inadequacy or criminality makes them a focus for attention, support or seclusion. But provided the distinction between resources and problems is adhered to, the need for support is not at all inconsistent with the radical case. In fact to consider their difficulties separately from the operation of capital is to perpetuate exactly the same tidying away which has been the object of much welfare policy.

Sometimes the dependence of people in the first category is directly attributable to capitalism, through industrial accidents and diseases, pollution, or corporate negligence, the effects of asbestosis and thalidomide being among the more horrifying examples. The burden of close dependence is increased by the strain which modern living imposes on all families and by the lack of real communal support resulting from the social disorganisation which the economy demands. Finally, liberal pressure to find activity for the disabled has so far tended to result in their becoming a source of extremely cheap and easily disciplined contract labour to the profit and advantage of those enlightened enough to employ them. Disabled people who resent this find it hard to express their feelings, not least because they are supposed to feel grateful. Of course one cannot lay most handicaps, still less aging, directly at the door of capitalism; it would, however, appear to be one of the contradictions of capitalist progress that some people should be enabled to live and most people enabled to live longer in an era when those who cannot play an active part in the productive process are valued less and less. It is small wonder that individuals should have been tempted to regard their dependent relatives as a disposable burden.

As far as the second category is concerned, I hope I have already said enough to show how individual weaknesses are exaggerated by a disadvantaged social position, and social workers who attempt to introduce some perception of worth into such lives are often labouring against odds so heavy as to be alterable only by a more global change than any social work intervention. The functioning of supposedly recalcitrant families has improved overnight when they have become involved in squatting or community campaigns. Obviously potential for development will partly depend on the extent of damage to the personality, and the libertarian fancy that there is never any need for some kind of seclusion is totally unrealistic, at least in our brutalised society. But to judge people by their ability to respond to the confusing messages and inconsistent measures of social work, which is what most of our opinions and reports are based on, is to collude with depersonalisation and the removal of their rights.

Alienation and dependence

The word 'alienation' has passed into common language to represent not the process which is the central pivot of capitalist production, but an experience whose major forms Seeman has characterised as powerlessness, meaninglessness, normlessness, isolation and self-estrangement.[36] It includes both lack of control and lack of identity. Our clients display such characteristics to a frightening degree, often enabling social workers to consider the experience of clients as being separate from that of the rest of us. Dependence is analysed in terms of the welfare apparatus, the social work relationship and particular handicaps from which a client may suffer, when it is in fact the prevalent mode of general experience.

Dividing off what our clients undergo not only serves to class their experience as exceptional but also enables us to conceal the fact that our own occupational identity is contingent on their existence, and that whatever sense of purpose or integrity we feel is founded upon the alienation of others. The individual structure of social work functions to preserve this divide, but the demands which capitalist society makes upon us are now forcing us to recognise that our traditional identity is shaky and our predicament not dissimilar. No analysis of clients is complete without a similar examination of social workers.

4

Blinkered self-denial

Just as some people are unable to find any more passable way of resolving their problems than by becoming clients, others tackle the ordinary problems of living by becoming social workers in the belief that it is satisfying, respectable, relatively autonomous and even remunerative. It is, however, a limited and parasitic resolution of life's contradictions. A world full of social workers would be quite unbearable. Nevertheless, the fact that we set ourselves up as purveyors not just of survival but even sometimes of fulfilment suggests the possession of some secret understanding which is protected, as Geoffrey Pearson puts it, by an arcane professional culture, designed to persuade both our clients and ourselves of its potency. The result is a serious loss of reality and perspective.[1]

The purpose of this chapter is to set the scene for a fuller examination of social work strategies by attempting to clear away some preliminary sources of misunderstanding, in particular in the unnecessarily convoluted subject of motivation, describing how a bankrupt ideology supplements the bureaucratic control of our activities, and suggesting some of the reasons for the process by which we develop from being beneficiaries of the welfare state (as its employees) to displaying an increasing number of the symptoms we expect from our clientele; we conceal these as if they were the first signs of leprosy. Three of the most important conditions which we hold in common are isolation, alienation and helplessness.

A constant theme throughout this chapter and the succeeding one is the way in which our inability to think beyond individual perceptions distorts and obscures the issues at hand, diverts our attention and often results in some kind of moral blackmail. Within our departments actions tend to be judged by their manifestation of personal loyalty or the lack of it; disagreement easily develops into personal attack.

The history of a team I once worked with provides a perfect example of the sort of confusion social workers can get into. We were a new and non-homogeneous team, relatively experienced but with minimal training, under the leadership of an utterly dedicated former child care officer. All of us were under great stress from the volume of referrals of different types, many of which we did not know how to cope with, and grew increasingly dissatisfied with our leader's performance; she was under strain herself, particularly as she was trying to protect us, and could not control her edginess. She tried to develop teamwork but could not gain our trust. Meeting after meeting went by in simmering discontent. Some of us tried to raise the problem during supervision but individual complaints were met either by vigorous personal attacks, some less justified than others, or by criticism of other team-members. More tentative attempts to raise the problem in the group, including one by the leader, failed because most members were too inhibited to take them up. Privately, people in the team said they did not want to hurt her; nobody admitted not wanting to risk being hurt themselves. The leader herself gave the same reasons for not forcing the issue into the open. Finally, in desperation, I suggested that the team meet without the leader and we did so in somebody's house at lunchtime. The discussion was helpful and constructive; we did not all agree but for the first time everyone participated openly. We all began to feel better and arranged an informal support system. Yet the major problem was avoided because most people were so riddled with guilt that they did not want the leader to know they had met. In fact, she herself sensed an easing of the atmosphere. She was hurt because she did not understand why and felt even more isolated.

I have no reason to think that this sort of situation is unique; it displays many typical features of social work of which the most prominent are a fear of open conflict, the slow development of any sense of the legitimacy of collectivity, the power available to superiors to break up subordinate groups, and, above all, an almost total failure to see the situation in any terms other than those of personality. Some of these I shall comment on elsewhere; the most fundamental, however, is the isolated concentration on personal capacity and performance which begins at the moment of entry into the profession.

I, social worker

Pearson rightly suggests that the choice of a social work career is a public statement not just about internal drives but about a desired relationship with the world, one's perception of reality and the opportunities it offers. Entry into the profession is often accompanied by a revulsion at existing social priorities and a desire to work for change. However, the individual focus of traditional social work ideology and training sabotages that desire by eradicating the social context and purpose of its expression. This loss or relegation of social context is the first step towards subjection to professional culture and control.[2]

Concentration on the individual may have a functional effect in lessening the attention given to action on social issues, but equally serious is the consequent removal of any brakes to prevent the process of individual scrutiny from culminating in examination of the psyche for its own sake. When liberal social work does attempt social understanding, it adopts a conservative functionalist approach which places a premium on emotional and social equilibrium, is patronising towards conflicts and offers no suggestions for how to overcome those with which we are faced. The logic of our stress on the individual responsibility of clients for their failure or success means that our own failures have to be ascribed to individual inadequacy as well, as we oscillate uneasily between complaining about clients and directly expressing our own guilt. This mordant self-questioning leads to a stagnant practice whose private face is an introspective indulgence laced with bitter complaint.

It is not surprising that this bias towards masochism should have produced a reaction in the opposite direction. Both Seebohm reorganisation and society at large were used by traditionalists and radicals alike as universal scapegoats for what was going wrong. Some radicals, in an effort to avoid being undermined, particularly during training, seemed to reject the need for self-examination as predatory and irrelevant, a rejection parallelled on one flank by that of casework and on the other by the general educational refusal to allow teachers to be the sole arbiters of relevant fields of study. This reaction was both healthy and necessary, despite occasional overemphasis. However, what needed attacking was not the need for constructive self-examination but its exploitation to personalise issues, devalidate disagreement and distract from social concern. We not only need to understand our capacities for relationship and their distortion by the forms and priorities of our society, but to be able to use this awareness constructively. More than other helpers whose skills may be more capable of definition and whose setting is more clinical, we have to know and modulate our personalities, often under intense pressure. We need to learn to survive in unwelcome situations without losing our spontaneity or resorting to crude control. Though such problems are exaggerated and distorted by the nature of social work, they are in essence the same as in any human relationship. Radicals have to find ways of supporting each other in developing awareness without disengaging from political reality. We cannot allow thinking on personal life to be monopolised by the guardians of professional and bureaucratic health.

The last few years have seen a considerable diminution of traditional assumptions about social work, but we have made little progress in integrating the personal, social and political dimensions. Most practitioners are fairly ribald about orthodox theory, but in times of crisis and in confrontation with radicals it is wheeled out like a portable guillotine from a museum simply because there is nothing else. It is therefore necessary to spend a little time in trying to clear a way through orthodoxy's misconceptions.

Disentangling motives

There are, I think, three separate but overlapping categories of motive for social work political, occupational and personal – which vary in importance according to individual priorities at any moment in time, developing and shifting during the progress of a career. Blau reported that while experience increased social workers' ability to help clients, it decreased their interest in doing so. The first three years were often marked by great enthusiasm which gradually became replaced by an emphasis on service delivery at the expense of emotional involvement. Familiarity with the demands of client and agency breeds cynicism; stress produces weariness.[3]

By political motives, I mean not the common and perverse limitation of politics to party activity, but those which relate to the world-view of the person concerned. I include the desires to help change the world and relieve suffering, and also the ideal of service. Even at its simplest, the ideal of dedication of one's life to others has political consequences since it assumes that such work is both necessary and possible. Furthermore, it contrasts with the activities of the majority, who are presumed to be self-seeking. I do not want to disparage the personal ideal of giving, but public giving always has political effect, which, in a class society, is peculiarly perverse. Herschel Prins implicitly recognises one aspect of this when he writes that underlying Judaic teaching about personal affairs 'is an emphasis on orderliness and the prevention of chaos'.[4] The aristocratic and bourgeois ideals of service are based on the belief that those who have done well out of life should contribute to the less fortunate, bridging the class divide by compassion and tolerance. But the provision of moral example, kept within proper bounds, is used as a licence for self-seeking in other spheres, and its support subtly confirms social advantage; voluntary sacrifice produces prestige, subordination and obligation; philanthropy both mitigates and justifies the insolence of rank.[5] It is an offering against Nemesis whose kinship to ritual sacrifice is made more poignant by the sexual division of labour which characterises philanthropy as opposed to more educated forms of service like the Church or the law; while men continue in the business of exploitation, with or without a touch of paternalism, they leave it to their wives and daughters to represent the altruistic portions of their souls. It is ironic that the most vulnerable sector of the population should be largely ministered to by 'trusties' of their own kind, appearing to represent an escape from oppression but in reality engaged in its reinforcement. Thus even if political considerations do not dominate, the choice of social work and the approach adopted to it reflect and are in part determined by assumptions about the kind of society which exists, the needs it creates and the relationships necessary to meet them. The political effect is no less significant if it contributes to order, not to change.

Occupational motives have received more attention from sociologists than social work writers, although they are becoming more openly expressed among all grades of practitioner. Welfare offers the prospect of secure employment which offers more intrinsic satisfaction than the alienating rat-race in search of profit. The rising demand for adequate public services has gone hand in hand with an expansion of the labour market, both in terms of school-leavers and of women wanting properly constituted employment. For middle-class youth, welfare work offers the possibility of a professional career requiring less specialisation and technical skill than medicine; middle-class women have welcomed economic recognition of their traditional labour. But social work is no longer the province of those with bourgeois origins; the benevolent volunteer has now joined forces with the workhouse official; both are state employees engaged in a similar task. For those from working-class backgrounds, there are not only the gains of interest and security, but of upward mobility and social advancement. There are few other occupations within easy access which offer social status and reasonably favourable working conditions but which require little more than a basic academic ability, a receptive personality and a stable temperament. This type of motivation is now common and has always been linked with a relatively conservative approach. A similar syndrome has occurred in new careers programmes for offenders and in community organisation, where 'leaders' are identified, quickly sucked from their milieux and resocialised into the professional and planning networks. However, experience shows that occupational motivation may play a significant part in the struggle for better working conditions. Some use this to castigate such motivation as mercenary, and it is often said that the major beneficiaries of welfare organisations are their employees. There is enough truth in this to pose serious moral and theoretical problems for those seeking to improve conditions, yet occupational resistance to the public exploitation of moral dedication may ultimately prove the most secure base for a radicalised service. It has been suggested that generous remuneration for foster parents is as effective in ensuring a successful placement as an initial altruistic love. There is no reason why our own ability to serve should be polluted by ensuring that we have a decent wage, at least until we have a society where wages have been superseded.

Personal motives are less easy to describe simply; they may be open or covert. In open form, the most prominent are creative self-expression and the personal satisfaction that derives from any human contact which breaks down isolation. Social work above all offers the opportunity 'to work with people', to offer directly one's personal talents and capacity to love, to subject oneself to a human perspective and appreciation, to contribute to the relief of suffering. Job satisfaction consists in the constant working at and confirming of one's own identity. The list is brief; we do not talk about it much. The reason, however, is neither just embarrassment, nor the fear of base associations, nor the wish to deny reward, but the fact that we cannot bring ourselves to admit the sheer unreality of our expectations, especially since the ideology of love presupposes its own validity. Where love exists it must be given or at least giveable whatever the circumstances. Our sentimental faith in the human potential of social work is too fundamental to be shaken.

To our covert motives we tend to pay an often joking lip-service because while we admit their existence we do not know what to make of them. Once again we are trapped between belief in unadulterated human goodness and pessimism about the human condition. In a profession which continually strives to lay bare motivation, social workers can never be certain that faith does not have its origin in much baser and more animal passions. For instance, Halmos quotes a psychoanalyst who claims that sexual curiosity is a motive drive in many people's work, but soothes any worries by asserting that its infantile characteristics can be purged by analysis, so that it becomes adult and benevolent.[6] Halmos is rightly sceptical about the mechanism and success of this transformation, and the Freudian emphasis of the sexual drive is also open to challenge. But the attention which is paid to such speculation is based on the safeguarding of social workers' own illusions and the enforcement of professional conformity, thus precluding any honest examination of motives which would deleteriously affect clients. It is ridiculous to pretend that the association of commitment or even caring with other more sordid motives necessarily defiles them; they are merely two sides of the same coin. 'Fair and foul are near of kin, and fair needs foul', cried Yeats' Crazy Jane, adding pungently:

> But Love has pitched his mansion in
> The place of excrement.
> For nothing can be sole or whole
> That has not been rent.[7]

These associations are part of our whole experience; we need to accept them, not to eliminate or dwell on them.

Sexuality is in some ways less relevant than three apparently more innocent types of need and satisfaction so common to social workers that attention must be drawn to them because they are among the principal determinants of our attitude to clients. The first is indeed curiosity, not so much of the sexual kind but the compulsive sort which leads people to cluster around road accidents or rivets them to soap operas. Social workers have the opportunity to be gorged with events more real than those at Peyton Place, but still without full personal commitment. As bit-players we have a more intimate view than the spectating public and the intensity of our gratification is correspondingly increased. The reasons for this are not just individual; we are all continually encouraged to substitionism, watching others engage in activities we wish we could accomplish. But whereas spectators may identify with public heroes, and the products which they endorse, the satisfaction gained from watching clients' lives is not simply vicarious pleasure but a feeling of 'thank goodness I'm not like that' – not recognition but separation. As in horror films, the effect is cathartic. Curiosity, however, is not evil in itself; it is a natural and constructive quality. When my first supervisor used to tell me, 'You do see life in this job', her curiosity was innocent rather than morbid; it was, however, tinged with relief and its effect is to confirm clients as different sorts of person.

The second satisfaction arises from the need to give, the extreme of which Prins calls 'The Great Mother Complex', an overwhelming giving which is no more than an oppressive infliction of self. Such pap is easy to recognise though hard to deal with. Much more common, and ironic in these times of social-worker-bashing, is the open need to be liked and loved, again a universal attribute but one which is particularly associated with giving. This yearning is prominent in social work, and apart from producing distortions and delays in both judgement and action, it means that social workers continuously avoid the possibility of conflict, or go about it surreptitiously. Meanwhile criticism is deflected by the virtue inherent in the gift. Radicals are better able to deal with conflict but our own difficulty here arises when we have to take action against clients by removing them from home or otherwise controlling them – so that many of the criticisms they may be making of our action and the institutions which may be involved are perfectly correct. Yet somctimes we have no option but to act and radicals need to be as conscious of the seductive and mistaken desire to please as any other social worker.

The third covert motive is the propensity to work out or avoid one's own problems at the expense of others. Thanks to the psychoanalytic theories of transference and counter-transference, this phenomenon is widely recognised and its individual excesses curbed. It is natural that different problem areas should interest different people, for whatever personal reason, and we all have to avoid the accepted danger of imposing our own feelings or solutions on vulnerable individuals. But what is denied is as important as what is imposed, and we return here to the parasitism of social work. A well-known Mackie cartoon depicts a bedraggled woman social worker donning her mask in the morning, using it to hector or exude sympathy during the day, and finally getting home, hanging it up again and collapsing amid the dirty dishes.[8] Social workers frequently allow themselves to be sucked into other people's lives as a substitute for their own but for which they do not have to take full responsibility. It is a predictable occupational hazard but one whose implications we are reluctant to face. The result is that we return to our colleagues and our private lives spent and exhausted. As a result the last people to provide genuine help to social workers are usually their co-workers and the problems of colleagues in administrative jobs go unnoticed. This neglect is a microcosm of our failure to confront the difficulties we all share, and, as I shall argue in the next chapter, arises directly from social workers' confusion of the mass-produced individually gift-wrapped nutrient which they purvey, with real caring.

If we stare too hard at altruism, it disappears like a mirage. What should concern us is not the worth of its origin so much as its manifestation and its social effects. In a study of foster-parent motivation, Neil Kay concluded that one major component in fostering was guilt arising from some form of deprivation and that the success of placements depended on how far foster-parents had been able to master their feelings so that they could constructively adapt their experiences to the world.[9] Social work training attempts to assist students to such mastery, but whereas fostering is a specific task, social workers find their whole existence under clumsy, half-hearted and misdirected review. Most learn not self-awareness but how to defend themselves.

Putting up the shutters

All social workers are aware that helping can attract damaged or disturbed people; the hidden returns on giving tend to draw those who are insecure, dependent and even in some way starved of human contact, looking to establish more real relationships with the help of professional cover. At a broader level social workers, to be successful, need to have sensitive emotional antennae and to be able to summon up an extra emotional charge to cross or break down barriers of communication and mistrust: by conventional standards most of us are highly neurotic. We are, however, terrified of believing this seriously, of having the same labels applied to us as to our clients, and operate a peculiar verbal defence system. While the liberals among us at any rate are generally careful not to apply technical terms like 'psychopathic' too freely to our clients, we bandy them around about each other. The fact that 'paranoid' or even 'neurotic' itself are not being used in their full technical sense reassures us that they are not being seriously applied.[10] By teasing each other about our madness, we convince ourselves of our sanity. On the other hand, our jokes and gossip about clients, though not necessarily unconfidential or malicious, reinforce our image of them as a separate and irresponsible group.

Our natural weaknesses are exacerbated by the personal stress of the job, forcing us to develop ever-stronger defences in order to resist our heightened vulnerability and insecurity. One major source of stress is the nature of the job itself and by this I mean not just the responsibility and occasional unpleasant decision but the burdens which clients place on us. We are like sea-anchors thrown into the storms, buffeting our clients' lives in order to hold them head-to-wind and stable until the waves subside. Sometimes clients will unload all their emotional upset on to us and walk out much easier in their own minds, but leaving us feeling miserable and depressed.[11] A second source of stress is sheer helplessness in the face of the problems which clients have to battle with, a despair we have to confront but cannot always admit to. Another general cause of stress is our mediating position between the increasing volume of demand and the pressures of our organisation. William Whyte once conducted a study of restaurants which included trying to discover what made waitresses cry, and he concluded, perhaps obviously enough, that it was when the crossfire of demand between customers and kitchen reached an unbearable intensity.[12] Our experience is no different, and it is repeated right up the management hierarchy. The result is an ever-increasing personal retreat which often culminates in conduct of gross insensitivity.

The siege mentality

The problems of residential work are a microcosm of those which affect social services as a whole. Residential workers are the infantry of the social work army. For years they were among the most isolated and exploited sectors of the working community;[13] they had little bargaining power and their skills were undervalued in the general move away from institutions. Although Seebohm has brought a considerable improvement in both standards and conditions, their traditional mistrust remains. All that I have said about social workers applies to residential work, which also offers a certain institutional security. In some ways the stress is less intense; demand is more easily contained, there is some rhythm to the day, and the closer contact which staff in homes can have with residents often makes working with them much more rewarding than the sporadic visits of fieldworkers can ever be.

On the other hand, staff find themselves under pressure from the administrators who control their resources, the fieldworkers who have ultimate authority in a case and, most of all, from residents themselves. Because contact with residents is more intimate, the temptation is to make the barriers more defined. Institutional routine encourages a hardening into role-performance. Many residential staff display uncertainty as to how far their residents can be trusted. Many would like to be able to relinquish their power and share their responsibility with residents, but most believe that residents are incapable of adequate performance. The suppressed anxiety which staff feel was illustrated for me at a conference for which a game was devised in which the participants took the role of residents in different types of home affected by reductions in spending. It did not take long for the purpose of the game (identifying different strategies) to be forgotten. The staff began to act out the crudest caricatures of how they thought their residents would behave, and one or two had to be forcibly restrained from severe physical violence. Obviously some of the tension was created by the atmosphere of the game itself, and afterwards some people felt bitter and manipulated. Nevertheless, after a long discussion the next evening many of the participants admitted both the value of the game and some of its more disturbing implications.

This underlying insecurity tends to reinforce the mechanisms of control both over residents and over junior staff. The principals of residential and day care institutions wield a power similar to that of head teachers and can rarely be challenged, let alone defied. Few homes are in any sense democratically run, routine smooths over differences and tension is projected on to the outside world, thus contributing to each home's further isolation.

Rites of passage

External control is the counter-theme to individualisation; both run through the whole of social work. The introduction to power-dynamics comes early in professional inculcation. Training courses, instead of providing a setting where students can, by experiment, enlarge their experience and judgement, still constrict responses into what is professionally acceptable. The liberal attitudes of some tutors are not always matched by those of placement supervisors. Students are subject to individual tutorials for reasons of 'confidentiality' and every sign of anxiety is subject to personal interpretation. Not all of it is as crass as one tutor's attempt to link a mature student's unease about the length of a nine-month placement to the period of gestation, but it can be extremely threatening. The personal criticism is nearly all one way; a difficult tutor or recalcitrant supervisor are nearly unassailable. Few supervisors subject their own work or reports to a student's detailed assessment. Disagreement over practice can result in failing the course. It is not even as if supervisors are in any way licensed; they are often appointed at random and post-certificate experience is the only qualification. Many regard having a student as a chore and the message is clear: create no difficulty and you will get by.

I would not want my general argument to suggest that there is no place at all for individual supervision and encounter. Groups are not always appropriate for certain types of discussion; nor are they necessarily economical of time and effort. Furthermore, groups can be used to suppress and control their less articulate or confident members, unless the structure and leadership emphasize sharing. What I do assert is that the intrinsic worth attached to one-to-one interaction in the social work setting, whether under the guise of supervision or of casework, far from making people feel valued, tends to limit rather than to enhance the individual's capacity as a social being; not only that – it usually acts to reinforce the pre-existing distribution of power within the relationship.

Leading by the nose

Because social workers, like all liberals, are reluctant to admit the realities of control, most of its exercise is underhand. There is of course an explicitly bureaucratic element deriving from the local government tradition of departmental rather than individual responsibility but social workers confuse the issue by attempting to introduce a professional structure. I shall suggest later that these are not as contradictory as they appear but their clash does create a profound anomaly between the enactment of casework, in which individual assessment is supreme, and a denial of responsibility to workers within the agency, so comprehensive that in many departments there is a control of correspondence reminiscent of boarding school or prison. In a few places social workers have not even been able to sign their own letters. A professional justification is offered, that the team leader must be aware of everything that is happening both to advise and to cover during absence, but the real purpose is simply work-supervision to ensure that the agency's priorities and responsibilities are carried out.

This dishonesty is parallelled in the personalisation of issues, especially by social workers who are climbing up the rickety rungs of the management hierarchy. Individual supervision is frequently used as a means of maintaining the supervisor's authority. Disagreement is often treated as personal disloyalty to the managers; but when under pressure the managers have little hesitation in picking on their junior's weak spots, even in team meetings. Unworkable decisions are defended for fear of losing face; public opposition is countered by private manipulation and accusation of subversion. The caring services, as well as being ineffective, are often extremely unpleasant to work in.[14]

Blowing the gaff

I have argued that individualist ideology, emotional stress and occupational control weigh so heavily on social workers that they can escape only by developing routine responses, gaining promotion or leaving the job. Some people break down. There are offices where nearly all the social workers survive on tranquillisers. A survey reported from Bradford suggested that at least one-third of sick-leave is due to depression or mental stress. At basic grade we have only twenty days' paid holiday. Whatever altruism we possess is quickly submerged in the struggle to survive.

Many people argue that this pressure is largely the fault of reorganisation, but I shall suggest in the next chapter that there are more fundamental processes at work which also affect our clients' lives. The problem is that it is easy to be overwhelmed by global difficulties; we are trapped in a conspiracy of compliance because to challenge one aspect of the social work edifice eventually leads to challenging it all. When faced with the reality which makes social work necessary, radicalism is the hardest option. The alternatives are to maintain both private and public illusions by keeping one's perceptions firmly at the individual level and pretending the work is worthwhile, or to develop a cynical and martyred perseverance. Giving, says Pearson, is a deviant activity in a profit-oriented consumer society.[15] Social work attempts to convert that potentially subversive and widely felt desire into an activity whose self-deception is a suitable tribute to our society and which legitimates its rapacity.

5
The lament for caring

Social work has always been considered an essentially humane and compassionate occupation, but as stress envelops its practitioners we have become increasingly incapable of relating even to each other. Personal expression is limited or distorted by statute and hierarchy; the writing of reports is more important and time-consuming than the encounters which supply their content. The feelings which Richard Titmuss once described as creative altruism, and which many thought were the mainspring of social work, have become subjected to an incessant process of covering oneself against mishap. An area officer in my department was recently heard to remark that if the paperwork is all right, everything is all right. I have already surveyed many of the factors which have created such turmoil but it is worth reiterating the dimension for which social workers have themselves been largely responsible, the consistent splitting of individuals from the groups of which they are constituents. On one hand we divorce ourselves from routine administration and continually castigate allegedly unfeeling bureaucrats, whether in local government or in the D. H. S. S. On the other hand we insist on being controlled by former social workers who have little or no experience of management and are probably both reluctant to undertake the task and inherently unsuited to it. Faced with the consequent disorganisation, an increasingly popular response has been not to confront such splitting but to institutionalise it still further by calling for an organisational structure which will reintroduce the personal element and allow social workers to get on with their proper business of 'caring'.

It is unfortunate, but no coincidence, that this approach should have been widely espoused by social workers of different persuasions, including two highly committed critics, Zofia Butrym and Bill

Jordan, who write from opposite ends of the social-democratic spectrum.[1] Such agreement does illustrate how wide is the common liberal ground which practising social workers have to share, but is based on a misunderstanding and underestimation of the strength of the processes at work, as well as a false nostalgia for previous specialisation; neither Butrym nor Jordan has, so far as I know, worked within social services area offices, one having been a medical social worker and the other a probation officer. After briefly reviewing their positions, I shall argue that radicals have to reject the assumptions about caring on which they are based as being both divisive and conservative. I shall give further thought to their organisational proposals in Part III.

Retreat into casework

Butrym's argument is founded on faith, on her own explicit Catholicism, on her belief that our present society has the needs of its members at heart, and on her conviction that it will be able to meet them. She does not, however, discount the value of scientific knowledge and is a firm advocate of a properly diagnostic approach founded in a professional relationship which treats the client with the respect deserving to a 'unique moral agent'. She advances a trenchant restatement of traditional casework orthodoxy which contains much that is worthwhile, but, in my view, ultimately founders in its values, in its failure to understand society in any historical context and finally in its practical recommendations. Butrym, reasonably enough, selects three value assumptions, which though of an abstract and general nature underlie social work: respect for the individual; the social nature of humanity; and human capacity for growth and change. Butrym recognises some of the intrinsic difficulties involved but distorts them by insisting on individual uniqueness as the epicentre of judgement and action. I shall explain and jusify this a little later. Also, although she uneasily dismisses the idea of society as a homogeneous consensus, she is not able to relate the ensuing conflicts between competing groups to the relationship between social worker and client; she appears to assume, for instance, that the control exercised by the social worker is by and large for the client's benefit and that conflicts of interest will subside if the client is dealt with firmly but lovingly. She resurrects the old adage of loving the sinner and hating the sin, but while recognising that ambivalence may ensue she nowhere admits that the nature of sin may be subject to secular definition according to interest. She is also hopelessly passive in her interpretation of our social role; she agrees that we should not be simple agents of adaptation, but advocacy does not really appeal to her and she would like to limit us to feeding information 'to those who have the power to change structures and reallocate resources'.[2]

This lameness results from Butrym's attribution of our present ills to lack of definition and politicisation. About the latter she is vitriolic: 'The avoidance of a personal close involvement with those who threaten one's own precarious sense of wholeness can be compensated for by generous gifts of money or the conduct of public campaigns for improved conditions.'[3] Or, one might add, by professional social work. Butrym cannot allow that it is our social and economic organisation which dismembers us. Lack of definition is sounder ground, but Butrym herself exacerbates the traditional confusion. She stresses the importance of a focus on social functioning, the reintroduction of relationships and, leaning slightly overboard, the promotion of the caring content in all manifestations of living. But she also asserts that the primary function of social work is the relief of suffering. It is precisely on the implications of such relief and the conflict it poses with her other objectives that the major recent controversies in social work have arisen.

Butrym strongly criticises those who have prescribed a concentration on the supply of material benefits and sensitively observes that what counts is not just success in securing them, but 'whether the acquisition of what was needed and desired has been a positive personal experience, enhancing his [the client's] sense of self-respect and worth, and giving added confidence for future living, or whether it has the opposite effect of undermining him further, making him feel barely tolerated or pitied, a social liability carried grudgingly but inevitably by a "responsible" society'.[4] Jordan, on the other hand, bases his position on the argument that our benefit system has been structured precisely to create the latter effect and that social work has been used both to disguise and reinforce it. Yet Jordan himself, though rejecting the old casework ethic, has consistently attacked the involvement of social workers in service delivery and what is now glorified as the 'unitary' model. Since he has himself been actively involved in the Claimants' Unions, the most radical and effective movement of its kind, and is, moreover, the author of two unpretentious but highly valuable books on practical social work, to which I shall return, radicals must take his views seriously.

Jordan's work has to be seen in the context of the Conservative government of 1970–4, whose Secretary of State for Social Services, Sir Keith Joseph, sought to identify poverty with those caught in a small but hereditary cycle of deprivation, on whom the principal attention of the social services should be focused. Jordan devastates both the policy and the assumptions behind it. Poverty is not coterminous with deprivation and both tend to be perpetuated by the services provided to meet them. In practice welfare provision has always been residual and selective; the extent of relief has been dictated by the requirements of capitalism at different stages, but has always been defined by the principles that financial support is 'conditional upon the willingness of the family to take responsibility for its own members', that it should go mainly to those unable to work and should not interfere with the work ethic, and that it should maintain law and order. The denial of relief may lead to riot, over-generosity to idleness. Relief has therefore been inseparable from financial and moral supervision and a collective judgement of unworthiness on those who accept it. The stigma of failure has been the essential concomitant to all benefit systems; a decent standard of living for everybody has never been a right, despite Labour's juggling with the terminology of National Assistance in 1966. Reformers have found their attempted distinction between the upstanding but badly-off independent labourer and the helpless pauper obliterated by the vagaries of capitalism as it mercilessly discards those for whom it has no use, the old and the structurally unemployed. Even the insurance system has failed to ensure minimum universal standards: the more privileged have contracted out; the rest find their contributions are no longer self-financing, so that their standard of living becomes subject to political decision and they face reliance on the more degrading system of supplementary relief.

The Conservative emphasis on selectivity was, Jordan argues, indirectly influenced by pressure groups like the Child Poverty Action Group, which presented poverty as a social not an economic problem and therefore more easily ameliorated. Social workers, pressed by radicals who stressed the obtaining of material benefits as their prime task, became sucked in to the administration and supervision of relief. Poverty was once again treated as maladjustment; control became more intrusive. Yet selectivity consistently fails to work; it divides and demeans, it reinforces dependence and creates its own culture of poverty. Jordan's answer is to separate social work completely from any sort of financial relief; there should be a universal guaranteed minimum income and we should abandon our pervasive intrusion into the lives of others, which instead of preventing calamities makes them the more likely to occur.

Jordan's history of public welfare and his diagnosis of its constraints are both compelling; but his prescriptions are ideals, not solutions. In *Freedom and the Welfare State* he goes further towards explicitly accepting that true welfare can exist only in a different kind of society where, for instance, work in the sense of earning one's living is dethroned as the prime requirement of a worthwhile life; and he acknowledges that his prescription of a universal minimum income means a drastic revision of economic priorities which the present dynamics of society cannot tolerate. However, he offers very little hint of how such a society is to be achieved and seems to draw back from the consequences of his analysis, writing as if the ideological reversal which he argues for can be divorced from sweeping economic change. He is reluctant to identify the source of change in the working class as a whole, which he sees as irrevocably divided, nor does he confront the issue of power. Instead he sees claimants as a collective pressure group which he sometimes refers to as a new class, increasingly resembling the 'mob' of which nineteenth-century philanthropists were so terrified. But the only factor which gives claimants any homogeneity is their total or partial dependence on the state for benefits, and even that experience is individualised. They have no weapon other than disruption or moral blackmail, and cannot on their own change the nature of claiming, any more than students can in isolation change the structure of education. Benefits can be withdrawn more easily than colleges can be closed. By treating claimants' problems as being of a special nature Jordan makes their actions into an administrative struggle with possible political consequences rather than a political struggle with administrative change as one of its major demands. He thus perpetuates the very syndrome he is trying to escape from, the hiving off of claimants into a separate ghetto. The struggle of the poor and unemployed will only be successful when it is no longer their fight alone.

Perhaps the best illustration of the flaw in Jordan's position is the move which is being made by David Donnison, now Chairman of the Supplementary Benefits Commission, to introduce flat rates of benefit supposedly high enough to obviate the need for discretionary grants. The only benefit so far introduced is the Non-Contributory Invalidity Pension, which has the neat effect of being just high enough to disqualify the drawer from claiming supplementary benefit, but is too low to allow saving for exceptional needs, especially at a time of inflation. The combination of such measures with the cuts in social service expenditure has meant that social workers have had to dust off their *Charities' Digests* and transfer begging back to the private sphere.

One of the reasons why Jordan fails to offer any practicable strategy is that he overstates his basic premise that the stigma attached to the current use of social services is caused by social work control over certain benefits. He is of course right to attack the discretionary control attached to their allocation, but wrong to suggest that the tainting of social work lies in this sphere alone. Jordan fiercely castigates radicals who saw casework as the root of oppression in social work and urged its replacement by material aid. But, although radicals may have overstressed the efficacy of material aid, the essence of the critique was surely correct in reversing the traditional priorities of casework with its focus on and judgements of the fundamental personal difficulties which lay behind the 'presenting' problem; the tendency to ascribe this to failures of individual adjustment was reinforced by the fact that social workers were not usually in a position to help solve the presenting problem anyway. A small study of clients of a Family Advice Centre conducted in 1971 led me to conclude 'that clients who came in for help with problems which they couched in personal or emotional terms were more likely to receive a sympathetic response than those who presented their needs as material, or, particularly, financial'.[5] Mayer and Timms found a similar phenomenon.[6] Radicals have argued that the elimination of want in society will not cause an end to all social and emotional problems, but that these problems may be both expressed and dealt with in a quite different way from any current conception of social work; and that, in the meantime, concentrating on a client's material needs is a more honest approach than the traditional one. In so far as dependence has been maintained or reinforced, this has been a function of the nature of social work in our society rather than a result of the increase in discretionary benefits. The mistake which many less political radicals made was to see social work itself as an effective medium for any major change. Those who saw the need for a greater injection of politics were in turn forced by the values then prevailing, to overemphasise the universal efficacy of material aid.

Finally, Jordan shares with some radicals a failure to distinguish casework as an ideology from casework as a method. The former should be repudiated, the latter recognised as one way of helping others, which sometimes is the only avenue open to us and which we then have to make something of. Bob Deacon, reviewing *Poor Parents*, expresses the dilemma slightly differently.[7] He argues that Jordan correctly defends the *idea* of casework 'as a helping relationship based on compassion for people in trouble, sorrow, need and sickness', but does not dissociate himself at all from the totally fake theories of human relationships and behaviour that have formed the basis of casework *practice* under capitalism. In his concern to argue that casework is justified quite separately from a poor-relief function of social work, he fails to acknowledge that the ideal of casework he depicts can never be, and has never been, achieved in a society that so distorts human relationships. Deacon's terminology is a little loose, but the underlying critique is correct. Jordan does in fact reject the traditional psychodynamic format of casework, and, as we shall see, the transactional approach of his earlier work contains the seeds of a radical casework. But two examples reveal his somewhat ingenuous idealism. In his earlier books, most of the cases he cites are examples of his being manoeuvred into providing practical assistance, but to no avail; a more realistic personal approach did bring results. Money, he concludes, is no substitute for love and attention. The goal is to free people into making something meaningful of their lives, not to pay them off. Yet that is exactly what capitalism does. Jordan describes the case of James, a muddled and somewhat disturbed teenager, on probation for possessing cannabis, whom he successfully rehabilitates. But in the process of being forced to act as a replacement father, Jordan appears completely to remove James's hostile feelings about society, which, he argues, are based on projection. This may be slightly unfair criticism, since the whole story is not told, but it does seem clear that Jordan's purpose is to stand for the potential good of capitalist society of which James should learn to take advantage. In the end James may have become a good citizen, but it is doubtful whether, in the social sense, he became a freer person. Also, in *Freedom and the Welfare State*, Jordan, now much more explicitly radical, offers the hypothesis that only Victorian social work provided any justification for intervention within freedom, because he considers that the structure of Victorian society was such that client and social worker were responsible to each other in a network of reciprocal obligations; only when society is an organic whole will the dilemmas of intervention be resolved. To some extent this is true. But not only may his conclusions about Victorian social work be open to challenge. He does not seem to see that only an organic society not based on class or exploitation will create the freedom he desires. Organic relationships may create a sense of wholeness, but the freedom to be exploited is perhaps one we can do without.

Both Jordan and Butrym argue that the personal element has disappeared from social work and place some of the blame on radicals. Before examining their own recommendations, I want to suggest first that in so far as social work feels less personal, this is part of a much wider process quite extraneous to social work, and, secondly, that the radical input has not been a removal of the personal element but its transformation, that the caring which they lament was based not on universal values but on those current at a particular era, which can now be seen not as a source of individual fulfilment but of individual constriction and, at times, oppression.

Deskilling and the division of labour

The reorganisation of social work brought about an increased involvement in administrative tasks and put social workers under considerable pressure. I considered some of the causes of this in Chapter 1, and clearly such alterations did introduce a greater element of impersonality, particularly in leaving even less time to be spent with each client. (A Home Office research report in 1969 found that child care officers spent about 40 per cent of their time with clients.[8]) Alternatively, written work and administrative duties were neglected. But when the development of social service departments is looked at as a whole and in context, many of their present-day features can be seen as part of a more general process affecting the whole world of work. Although social work is usually thought of as a rather special occupation, it is essential to realise how much experience we have in common with other workers if we are to resist the temptation to escape into some professional limbo.

First of all we have to realise that, in Benington's words, 'Local Government has become Big Business',[9] and although our connections with private industry are rarely direct, social services budgets, normally the largest after education, are increasingly subject to corporate management techniques and many of the problems we meet are the direct result of the entrepreneurial activity of other branches of the authority, either alone or in conjunction with the business world. We cannot therefore reasonably expect to remain immune from the business process.

When I wrote in Chapter 3 that social workers could more and more appropriately be seen as members of a new proletariat, people unfamiliar with recent Marxist analysis may well have detected an element of wish-fulfilment. To some extent that is true; in so far as we have a choice, I have no doubt about what alliance we should choose. But what this development implies is not the embourgeoisement of the working class but the increasing proletarianisation of the middle and professional classes as ever tighter control is exerted over their work processes. As Corrigan and Leonard point out, the Registrar General's 'bizarre' classifications have been used to suggest that more and more workers have been moving into skilled or white-collar occupations. In fact, 'in every major manufacturing industry the basic labour process has become less skilled in the sense of a craft skill and more skilled in the sense of being able to put up with a repetitious task for nine or ten hours a day'.[10] Braverman, who has written an extremely readable Marxist classic on the subject (itself a rare feat), goes so far as wanting to abolish the term 'white-collar' altogether.[11]

What is happening is the rationalisation of labour in order to reduce its cost, a process which Marx described but whose inspiration Braverman traces to Charles Babbage, writing in 1832. Babbage's all-important principle was that the employment of craftsmen capable of performing a whole task more than doubled manufacturing cost as compared with a process which broke a task into an optimal number of subdivisions each needing the use of minimal skill, since less skilled workers would command much lower wages. The later introduction of managerial and technical control associated with Frederick Taylor refined these divisions by beginning to separate entirely the conception of a task from its execution. The division of mental and manual work and the consequent hierarchy of knowledge were used to reinforce control over each step of the process. Braverman carefully documents the spread of such methods into every form of occupation.

Not only does such an analysis help us comprehend the way in which we are subject to routine control apart from the official requirements of our job, which have already been discussed; it also allows us to begin to understand how the structure of social work has developed since 1970. The Seebohm Committee did not fully conceive the generic social worker, but the fusing of specialisms turned out to be a necessary initial by-product of reorganisation. B. A. S. W., by virtue of its constitution, was forced to extol generalism as the essential basis of a new and superior profession, but illusions were soon shattered as such occupational skills as social workers believed they possessed became diffused and lost in the constraints of having to cope with being organisation people. There were nowhere near enough of us, and our agitation threatened to make us expensive (though it was middle management who reaped the greatest benefit because social workers became trapped in a special salary scale which put our earnings well behind those of comparable local government workers). At first, large numbers of unqualified people were taken on simply to meet demand; later it was realised how useful such cheap workers were and their position became institutionalised – the use of untrained assistants has expanded in both field and residential social work as well as in the health service. They have little status and are easily controlled because they are presumed to lack knowledge and their clients, mainly the elderly, have low priority. Gradually, as management attempts to define our jobs more closely, a subordinate hierarchy is being created by a division of labour based on Babbage's principle. It is likely that the vogue for 'patch' work will increase this trend. Teams based in outlying offices are likely to have a heavy bias towards providing basic social services through home helps and social work assistants. Specialist workers (having escaped from the attempts in some areas to treat them as being in dead-end jobs) may well now develop into a professional elite, though it is not yet clear how much autonomy they will be permitted within their fields. Alternatively there may be more specialisation by skill or task. In either case specialists will be much more vulnerable to the increase in centralised control we have seen since 1978, because they are likely to be more isolated with less access to the formulation of general policy. While some departments restructure to achieve bureaucratic control, others, which appear to be devolving power, may simply be diluting it.

The 'impersonalisation' of social work thus turns out to be a general result of economic organisation from which we cannot escape except by challenging that system of organisation itself. Professionalism, as we shall see in the next chapter, offers no escape except for an elite few. But first we have to question the nature of that personal caring which was thought to be the heart of social work and consider whether its return, in whatever form it was supposed to exist, is really going to be as liberating as its proponents suggest.

Immanuel Kant, unsung patriarch of social work values

Alasdair Macintyre concludes his survey of the history of ethics with the observation that we live with the inheritance of a number of well-integrated moralities, and he suggests how the same action may be subject to quite different interpretations according to the ends, rules and virtues of the particular morality adopted, since there is no longer any generally accepted standard of arbitration between them.[12] Social work itself reflects these moral contradictions: our theory, now largely shorn of explicit religious justification, derives unambiguously from a Kantian respect for persons; our practice is based on crude utilitarianism, the pursuit of the greatest good for the greatest number; and both are challenged by a developing morality in which Marxism has been a major influence. I want to digress briefly about Kant, not in the pretence of any expertise, but in order to place what social work considers to be universal values firmly within one philosophical approach to morality.

Kant's *Groundwork of the Metaphysic of Morals*[13] was written towards the end of the eighteenth century, when the rapid changes which were enveloping Europe had still not reached his eastern Baltic town of Königsberg. He was nevertheless fully aware of what Macintyre calls the growing divorce between moral rules and the goals of life, and sought by an intense application of pure and practical reason to establish the existence of universal truths independent of anthropological interpretations of society, thus making an absolute morality possible. Kant attempted to link the stern notion of duty with the fact that humans do welcome some sort of reward for their actions, even if it is only the satisfaction of feeling that they were justified. He was also concerned to establish principles of human conduct which reconciled the supreme freedom of the individual with the constraints and gratifications of living in the society of others who also possess such freedom. If the following summary of his principal relevant line of thought seems garbled, my own interpretation will be partly responsible, but it should be remembered that Kant was less able to divorce himself from religious thinking than he would have liked, and that unlike most modern thinkers he assumed a teleological approach; that is, he took for granted that everything which exists has some ultimate purpose. In addition, some of his arguments are both inconsistent and difficult to understand.

Kant begins by assuming that the only thing in the world which can be taken as good without qualification is a good will. Reason exists to inform the will about its duty and thus create a good will. Kant argues that if the purpose of reason and will is simply to create happiness, neither is a very effective instrument; instinct would have been much better. There must then be some other end, whose existence is in itself an absolute value and from whose existence spring certain laws: every rational being should be regarded as such an end, and there is an absolute duty to obey the laws which can be derived from that assumption. Kant divides rules of conduct into those which offer some definite satisfaction and those to be followed simply because of duty; but no moral worth arises from actions pursued for reasons other than obedience to duty. In fact, the harder an action is to perform, the greater is its moral worth, and effort is more important than success. Actions are to be judged on their intentions rather than their actual results.

Since the existence of each rational being should be conceived as an end, an absolute value, duty enjoins us to act taking other people into consideration as well, and Kant derives from this the principle of universalisability – namely, that in any given situation, each of us should act as we would wish anybody else to act in similar circumstances, a rather more sophisticated version of 'Do as you would be done by'. We should therefore never treat humanity *simply* as a means, but always at the same time as an end. Kant also argues that existence of reason and the possibility of good will presuppose the existence of freedom, though he admits that perfect freedom would not exist outside a perfect society, or what he called a 'kingdom of ends'. Thus the essence of Kant's groundwork is to start from individual existence and perception and work towards a social system which fully recognises individual value.

The power and attraction of Kantian doctrine lies in its apparent success in removing morality entirely from any subjective social order. It endows each individual with the privilege of being a supreme moral agent, yet by rooting morality in an impersonal principle valid for others as well as oneself, it posits common humanity and interests. Of great importance is Kant's construction of a supposedly secular morality entirely consistent with religious belief. Such characteristics are familiar components in discussion of social work values, and while I want to suggest neither that these values stem directly from Kant, nor that they stand or fall entirely with his structure of reasoning, their weaknesses and limitations are open to similar criticisms. Alternative philosophies may well provide social work with more applicable and realistic principles. I shall criticise four planks of Kant's position: the possibility of rational action; respect for individuals; the glorification of the will; and the independence of morality from social structure. My remarks must be taken as observations rather than conclusive arguments.

Social work presupposes with Kant that rational action is both possible and desirable, assumptions which have come under attack from the anti-psychiatry movement whose existentialist base stresses the necessity of unfettered and often irrational choice. But we do not have to go quite so far; it is sufficient to recognise that we live in a society whose pretence of logic only serves to disguise its economic and political irrationality, and whose power is so permeating that the only defence may be one of apparent unreason. The respect which Kant enjoins for persons is based on the combination of making each individual the supreme arbiter of morality and then guiding and controlling conduct by making each one take account of the equivalent position of all other individuals. It is an attractive schema which succeeds in contrasting pure and absolute morality with prudence or interest; unfortunately its positive contribution to good conduct is considerably less than its initial promise. The principle of universalisability is a laudable ideal but in itself is devoid of practical content. It tells us nothing definite about the way we ought to behave or about the relative weight we should attach to means and ends in particular circumstances. In fact, as Macintyre points out, almost any rule can be universalised, given sufficient ingenuity and qualification. Even if the principle could be refined, it still lacks power; Kant assumes that if people act correctly, others will imitate the example which has been set and change will follow, a belief founded in wild optimism. And finally it seems empirically untrue to suggest we make our own moral decisions, when so much of morality is dependent on economic priorities and received custom and practice. In sum this particular version of respect for persons offers no positive criterion for action, is open to widespread abuse and ultimately does little more than provide a spurious moral refutation for attacks on individualism.

Kant's association of goodness with acts of will is frequently echoed in social work theory. One book about social work, written in 1960, proclaimed that 'not depending for its justification on results, no failure can therefore discredit it',[14] a recurrence of Kant's dictum that the moral worth of an action does not depend on the expected result. From Kant's emphasis on will is derived a secular ideal of pure dedication as the supreme motivation, and its corollary that if we cannot be happy we should at least be deserving of happiness, a principle of whose worth many social workers have tried to persuade their clients, though without much success. The nobility of such sentiments disguises their unreality and social danger. If specific results are unimportant, and if the notion of duty based on respect for persons is as empty as I have suggested, then anyone who seeks to base their actions on such principles will find that duty has been assimilated to the socially dominant structure of society as a clarion call to conformity. Furthermore, since belief in the existence of universal principles implies that conflict cannot arise between principles but only from the baser passions, and since those principles are bound already to be enshrined in the dominant morality, whatever it is, radicals will find themselves further discredited by the attribution of base motives like self-interest.

The purpose of this digression has not been to do philosophical justice to Kant, still less to arrive at a definition of morality, but to suggest some of the pitfalls of a moral philosophy based on the kind of individualism prevalent in social work and to prepare the ground for a similar discussion of caring. It is true that freedom of some kind is a prerequisite of rational and responsible choice. Yet the society which calls itself 'the free world' depends for its prosperity on the use of people as a means of creating wealth. In so far as the experience and purpose of the proletariat differ from those of the dominant class, so their moralities are distinct, despite continuous propaganda on the behalf of the latter. Any location of moral standards outside social structure ignores the implications of such divisions in society. Even our expectations of individual potential are accorded by rank, and to pretend otherwise is to do those who are worse off a grave disservice. 'Respect' is only too often a cover for pity and even contempt.

Because social workers are concerned with social difficulties and individual pain, a concern which extends naturally to the protection of minorities and of the downtrodden, they often seek to justify their compassion by appeal to the value of individual uniqueness. The Kantian morality, highly appropriate for a market society, also acts as a protection against tyranny. Yet individual uniqueness is a product not of our *moral* capacity but of our genetic, spatio-temporal and social identity. In fact we share the ability to confer identity on each other, and it is from what we share, rather than our individual uniqueness, that radicals argue we should derive our standards of action. I have argued that ultimately Kant has little concrete to contribute to the argument over how priorities should be distributed between the protection of the individual and the development of social forces, let alone to how such decisions might be taken; historically the needs of the ruling class have been predominant. However, important concepts like human rights do not have to be derived from Kantian principles; socialism offers the first opportunity for centuries to resolve the false antithesis between society and the individual.

Moral argument can be endless and, when in doubt, social workers are quick to rely simply upon their feelings of care and compassion. We have now to consider how even these basic human qualities are enlisted to preserve the ideological legitimation of our society.

The false credibility of the caring ideology

Perhaps the most profound human activities are centred around our attempts to come to terms with or escape the separateness which is a condition of human existence. Eastern thought is built round feeling at one with all living things; Western tradition emphasises human unity in love. A prosaic definition of such activity might locate its essence in the attempt to convey to other people that their existence has been noticed and that it matters. Many would say, 'matters for its own sake'; I have already cast doubt on the usefulness of such a coda in morality; when talking of love it is even more obscure.

The idea of loving people for their own sake is supposed to convey both their uniqueness and their commonalty, but in fact conveys neither. Sometimes its implications are reprehensible: Butrym explains 'acceptance' as the extension of unconditional love to people regardless of how attractive or unattractive they may seem; C. S. Lewis simply describes Gift-love as loving the unlovable.[15] Butrym is rightly concerned with rational and emotional investment in our common humanity, which she calls 'agapé', a Greek work originally meaning fellow-feeling but more recently used in Christian thought to express communion.[16] But although we have to explain and value fellow-feeling, Butrym's use of 'love' ignores the fact that we do not all recognise the same fellows. The Greeks, for instance, distinguished sharply between themselves and the barbarians whom they enslaved. Christianity, on the other hand, seeks to extend agapé to everybody on the grounds of their basic shared attributes, thus enabling the capitalist, however large the camel and small the needle, to bask in the same irradiation of God's love as the most menial of his workers. The use of agapé both presupposes and recreates the idea of an integrated and ordered society, with the additional advantage of appearing to minimise rank and class; as I have argued above, such caring is used to reinforce the social order. Caring itself, which originally meant little more than diligence, has become corrupted and confused by the overtones which it has acquired. I would like to see the word 'love' at least temporarily expunged from the social work vocabulary, not with the intent of eliminating human relationships but of clarifying them.

In talking about personal motives, I suggested that a major problem with giving was the superiority it endows upon the donor. At the personal level, giving fosters obligation and loyalty. But any organised giving, whether based on private philanthropy or public welfare, is immediately impersonal and the obligation is obscured by an inherent stigma, which, as Jordan argues in *Poor Parents*, is exploited for economic purposes. This impersonality is the more severe when welfare is explicitly associated with control. The most fundamental contradiction of social work is that impersonal control is expected to be maintained by the expression of personal caring. The obverse is that those who are denied the most basic source of identity in our society – namely, an active part in the production process – are supposed to feel that they matter by being provided with a personal service from hirelings or volunteers in order to compensate for their lack of worth or for the love which their kin lack the opportunity to give. As Pinker points out, individualising welfare is supposed to tailor services to need but 'the most personal forms of social service are likely to be the most humiliating for the beneficiary'.[17]

Caring brings its own rewards, not least by showing clearly that it is we who are competent enough to care; it is a hallmark of adequacy. If clients master their problems, we can always find ways of sharing their success, even when we contributed little or nothing. When clients fail, we may feel guilt for the reasons discussed in the last chapter, but it is clients themselves who bear the brunt; they failed even though we tried our hardest. I have also discussed the moral advantage and self-justification which caring confers, independently of results. The benevolence behind which the profession masquerades can drive clients to palsied impotence as it absorbs the impact which they try to make; alternatively it provokes the apparently negative act of the perpetually rejecting and rejected child 'picking out the caring adult's weak spot and clobbering him or her with it in the most painful manner possible'.[18] It is the only way we can be forced to remember our own unlovability. One further advantage is that choice in the relationship tends to be the prerogative of the carer, who in most situations has the freedom and security of being able to withdraw, not perhaps at will, but by, for instance, changing jobs, seeking training or gaining promotion. Clients rarely enjoy such privilege, and if they exercise it they may well be judged for the apparent incapacity to accept help.

The most damning indictment of the caring ideology is its innate insincerity, which often disguises what genuine caring does take place. We are expected to make up for the physical and emotional deprivations our clients have suffered by offering them an illusory personal interest. We have to exert our personalities to stimulate, stifle or channel the clients' own emotions, without becoming involved ourselves – a cardinal offence. We have to appear honest and intimate with people we would never otherwise meet and probably do not trust, whose interests and amusements we may not share, and with whose temperaments, cultures, language and life-styles we may be at odds. We are paid to use our persons to manipulate clients into being honest and intimate with us. Halmos offers the dubious defence that '"behaving as if" is not an act of dissembling but a genuine movement towards an ideal'.[19] Of course, trying to understand can well be genuine and dissembling sometimes necessary. But we are not talking in a context of universal love but of a callous society which will palm people off as cheaply as it can or, as Jordan puts it in a slightly different argument, with 'the wholesale giving of second-hand goods and second-rate sympathy'.[20] What we are engaged in is nothing less than licensed emotional prostitution, from which our gains are moral rather than financial, but from which we reap the same handicaps; just as prostitutes often lose the capacity for real sexual response because their professional persona intrudes into their private lives, so social workers can lose a capacity for spontaneous emotional response. And as often as not we compensate by despising our clients, just as prostitutes do. I do not want necessarily to be seen as condemning prostitutes, but I think we should not dress our own activity up in language it does not deserve. An ideal society would need neither prostitutes nor social workers.

Of course mutual relationships are important and possible, but they mean really making oneself vulnerable; the stress and insecurity of social work militate heavily against exposing oneself to further pain, and stepping beyond the role can make one liable to accusations of unprofessional behaviour, which is often little more than confusing what one does feel with what other people think one ought to feel; it is like letting down the side. The problem for radicals is that by trying continually to open up the possibilities of relationships we not only challenge professionalism but confuse ourselves as well because we are still inevitably caught up in it. Titmuss used to talk of the social services filling a moral void in our society, and to some extent we cannot avoid such compartmentalisation of human feelings. Yet if social workers are really to live up to their pretensions of moral concern, they have not only to recognise how far their own capacity for relationships has been corrupted but also to resist that process.

The rule of expediency

Libertarian radicals have disputed the caring nature of social work because of its connection with control. But the issue is not so much the existence of control itself, for care and control are in practice inextricably connected, even at a personal level. The idea of *social* control is essential to any form of society, though societies may be ranged according to the extent and overtness of the control which they need. In our society we have to ask by whom is control exerted and in whose favour, and radicals reject the social control which we have lovingly to enforce, because it is based on a defence of capitalist interests for which benevolence is only a mask.

In practice, the caring ideology is limited to a stuttering expression of concern, and although we are sometimes able to offer real friendship it does not inform our major decisions, which are based on expediency. It is quite clear that social workers often take or enforce decisions which are manifestly against the interests of their client. At the most limited level are decisions arising from family disputes, where interests conflict; social work debate has been forced to tackle such problems by asking who the real client is, but, unsurprisingly, has been short on answers; even outside such a limited framework, there are no absolute solutions. We do attempt to 'value' the people against whom decisions go, but if they persist in challenging our rationale, they are more often than not relegated to the status of nuisances.

In fact, the notion of caring is so worryingly inclusive that it often deeply affects decision-making. Objective difficulty, personal insecurity and woolly ideology afflict our liberal judgement with such paralysis that necessary decisions are delayed, half-heartedly enforced or lapse. Alternatively, decisions may be taken with quite inappropriate ruthlessness. The best general example is of social workers who insist on doing emergency night-duty for fear of being thought uncaring and then find themselves committing people to mental hospital in haste at dead of night because they are too tired to think straight. Another example is the rash of children removed from their parents because of suspected non-accidental injury, a proper source of concern where action is sometimes necessary but needs always to be well thought out.

I was involved as an outsider in one such case where Rosita, the six-year-old daughter of a Chilean refugee, attended school on two successive days with heavy bruising on her buttocks but perfectly ambulant. The school informed the N. S. P. C. C., who unilaterally removed Rosita to the local children's hospital without any proper investigation. Rosita still spoke little English; she had lost her father on the day of Pinochet's coup and had seen her mother brutally beaten up by police in Argentina. The strain had already caused some wild behaviour, which the beating was her mother's last desperate attempt to control. Now she was subjected to a further separation which she found hard either to understand or to tolerate. There was no doubt that her mother was overemotional and in need of special understanding and support. Nevertheless, the paediatricans, on both medical and social evidence, argued for Rosita's immediate return home. The N. S. P. C. C. and police insisted on prosecution and the local authority was pressurised into receiving Rosita into a children's home, where nobody spoke Spanish and which was even further away from her own home. She received excellent care there, but her anxiety increased. The social workers were in a difficult situation but justified the decision by saying that if they did not bring care proceedings the mother would be prosecuted; privately they considered the N. S. P. C. C. decision was mistaken, but felt it necessary to preserve good relations. In the end they applied for a supervision order only but even then the case was dismissed and, after nearly a month, Rosita returned home, while her mother was offered the voluntary supervision she had always said she would accept. The point here is that mother and daughter seemed to have become pawns in inter-agency relationships. It is also worth noting that if an order had been made, there was no guarantee given by the police that they would not prosecute the mother anyway.

Caring as moral and political control

I have already written of the general bias of caring ideology towards the *status quo*. One might, though, expect it to have enabled clients to enjoy a greater degree of individual choice. However, far from liberating anybody except in the crudest sense of rescue, the general run of official caring tends to demand far stricter standards, of which most of its recipients inevitably fall short. There are, of course, exceptions, and the number has been growing with the influx of liberals and radicals. Nevertheless, few homes or hostels free their residents, whether child or adult, from the tyranny of repetition and imitation to which they are subject in most families. Tom Hart's *A Walk with Alan* tells of Alan's assertion that 'for the majority of people caring for children . . . care meant turning out carbon copies of themselves, socially acceptable, hard-working automatons – they were to be remoulded, reshaped, retreaded, pressed into the mould of respectability with the morality of those who had care of them, based upon their upbringing, their religious inclinations'.[21] Alan spoke from bitter experience but we all know what he says is true. Even now, as Tom Hart comments, a small home for children in the middle of suburbia is not a home in the natural or family sense, it is an institution and institutions have rules based on socially acceptable, not family, norms. Respectability is more strictly enforced since residents tend already to be considered deviant and any erring simply confirms their status. To take one example, not in homes, nor hostels nor hospitals can we tolerate sexual activity, let alone homosexuality, even though it is known to occur. Both field and residential workers are openly discouraged from showing sympathy to gays, let alone tolerating homophilia among themselves. Promiscuity is frowned upon, families are sanctified, and marriages are to be kept intact if at all possible. Those who seek different forms of expression are still, whatever impression professional journals may give, labelled as sick. As Halmos commented years ago, 'the ubiquitous admonitory clauses have given traditional morals a kind of clinical and scientific respectability'.[22]

Individuals and families: production and reproduction

'Liberty as a right of man', wrote Marx, 'is not founded upon the relations between man and man, but rather upon the separation of man from man.'[23] If our age is more than any other scarred by individual angst, it is because the ethos of individual freedom and responsibility which we respect is a buttress of free enterprise and competition. Similarly it is the dominant middle-class virtues of saving and long-term planning which social workers seek to implant in clients who seek immediate gratification. Thrift is, of course, a traditional expression of an insecure existence, but our present practice derives from the bourgeois need to accumulate capital for reinvestment and growth, and from an assumption of increasing prosperity. Individualism is the dynamic of production; it distracts attention from social forces, makes it more difficult to pool experience and burdens us all with an exaggerated guilt.

The only natural social unit recognised in capitalist society is the family, which in whittled-down form is a cell performing a number of vital functions. Because it occupies such a central position it is hard to criticise, and crude attacks on family life, while attractive to those who are aware of having been unhappy in it, tend only to stiffen the resistance of those for whom the satisfactions of the family, however limited, are all they dare look forward to. Yet our present emphasis on the health of the small unit we call the family is only a reflection of the way we live, as is our concept of childhood. Philippe Ariès, himself no Marxist, wrote in his classic study of the subject that before the seventeenth century 'the density of society left no room for the family. Not that the family did not exist as a reality: it would be paradoxical to deny that it did. But it did not exist as a concept'.[24] In our society the family's main function is to reproduce suitable labour power. It introduces us to the world, defines our place in it and teaches us the meaning of authority and acceptable forms of personal and sexual satisfaction. But society does not hesitate to interfere when its interests are suited. The accepted role of women within the family fluctuates according to employment opportunity.

The size of the family has been reduced, conveniently forming small, easily-transferable units which confer sufficient mobility to follow the labour and housing markets. Even more important is the usefulness of small units as the most convenient and profitable targets for consumer marketing. A plethora of goods, many unneeded and even unwanted, are advertised (with an appeal mainly to women) and foisted upon families. Industry achieves wide sales but consumers suffer duplication, waste and the expense of having to buy things in small quantities. And, of course, as purchases increase, so does property, binding its possessors ever closer to the capitalist ethic.

Most damaging of all, as work becomes less and less satisfying, and as women, rightly, demand greater male participation in domestic tasks, the family has become a refuge from the harsh economic tussle, a 'tent pitch'd in a world not right',[25] and the hoped-for source of emotional sufficiency it cannot possibly provide. Individual wills and expectations clash sharply in a setting incapable of bestowing such satisfaction. The myth of passionate romance is one on which many relationships founder. Alternatively couples develop the teamwork which Fromm describes as a 'well-oiled relationship between two persons who remain strangers all their lives . . . an alliance of two against the world, and this egoism à deux is mistaken for love and intimacy'.[26] Thus private has been exalted over public, the legitimate expression of love funnelled into an ever-shrinking container, while the family's priorities and modes of expression have been increasingly determined by broader market forces which it is too small to resist. The ultimate irony of mass capitalist society is that the variety it promotes is quite illusory, the individuality it worships no more than bedecked conformity.

Social work embellishes and preserves these forms of relationship which are neither ideal nor natural but moulded by a particular form of production in which the worker is alienated from his product and in which all members of society are alienated from each other. To quote Marx again, alienation is transcended only if 'the individuals reproduce themselves as social individuals'. Mészáros, in his well-known study of alienation, comments on this thought as follows:

> Thus, the individual in a socialist society does not dissolve his individuality within the general social determinations, on the contrary he must find an outlet for the full realization of his own personality (Gesamtpersönlichkeit). In a capitalist society the individuals can only reproduce themselves as *isolated* individuals. In a bureaucratically collectivised society, on the other hand, they cannot reproduce themselves as individuals, let alone as *social individuals*. In both of them the *public* sphere is divorced from the *private* one and opposed to it.[27]

On education Mészáros remarks that 'the crucial issue for any established society is the reproduction of individuals whose "own ends" do not negate the potentialities of the prevailing system of production'. He goes on to argue that:

> the capitalistically reified social relations of production do not perpetuate themselves *automatically*. They succeed in this only because the particular individuals 'interiorise' the outside press-ures: they adopt the overall perspectives of commodity-society as the unquestionable limits of their own aspirations. It is by doing so that the particular individuals 'contribute towards maintaining a conception of the world' and towards maintaining a specific form of social intercourse which corresponds to that conception.[28]

The traditional function of social work is to interiorise, lubricate and perpetuate such ideology and to press its adoption on those who suffer most under it.

The unequal relationship

We have seen how any helping relationship is by definition uneven, because one party to it has to put itself wholly or partly in the other's hands. This dependence may foster resentment, loyalty or both, but it also attracts an inevitable stigma whose extent, suggests Pinker, can be determined by three functions – the depth of need, the time over which it is likely to stretch, and the social distance between helper and helped.[29] Butrym rather cavalierly asserts that when people need help, they are not concerned about equality in the relationship.[30] Of course people in need do not wish to be further burdened by the concerns of others. But the fact that desperation can cause abasement does not mean that the humiliation is felt any the less keenly. It is, moreover, significant that whereas middle-class people are expected to assert their rights, most of our clients tend to be looked at askance if they attempt the same, and whereas a sacrifice of status on one occasion may be acceptable, its permanent loss ought to be intolerable.

Radicals do not deny that unevenness cannot be entirely eliminated from the helping process. The challenge is instead to the extent, distribution and significance of the resulting stigma. We have first to realise how extraordinary it is that dependence should be so stigmatised at all, an attitude rooted largely in the capitalist emphasis on individual achievement, which makes failure the more reprehensible. Yet about one–third of everybody's life is spent in some kind of dependence, though those rich enough to employ servants can pretend it is not so. If our mutual interdependence were more readily recognised, and if the value of a life were not to be judged mainly by one's ability to make money, dependence in one area of existence would not so colour all the others.

Apart from its deterrent value, stigma has the effect of increasing the distance between helper and helped and thus also increasing the former's power over the latter. The effect of this bias on individual relationships has been a subject of recent social work concern, and will be discussed later, but that imbalance is subject to and in part determined by the wider balance of class forces. The long-standing cultural gap between social workers and their clients is a reflection of our social alliance with the bourgeoisie. To the limited extent that such superiority inspired confidence, it was therapeutically functional as well as politically rewarding. How this worked can be illustrated by the operation of dynamic psychiatry, an early ancestor of modern social work, which was critically described as follows by a French physician in 1818.

> It is always landlords who operate upon their subalterns, never the latter on their superiors; it would seem that magnetism always works downward, never upward. The officers who so easily magnetised in their garrisons no doubt accomplished marvels upon poor soldiers who felt much honoured that marqueses, counts, knights, would be willing to gesticulate over them.[31]

But the peasants were under few illusions as to the ultimate uselessness of therapeutic movements like magnetism. Ellenberger sanguinely records the fate of Mesmerism, interrupted by the French Revolution.

> The peasants, instead of sitting at the foot of magnetised trees, gathered around 'liberty trees' to listen to revolutionary speeches. Many of Mesmer's aristocratic disciples emigrated: others perished on the scaffold.[32]

The fate of most social workers in modern times is likely to be less dramatic, not least because our function is more disguised. Mass consumerism, the rudiments of further education and a wider social intake into the occupation have narrowed the cultural gap and our self-perceptions have radically altered. Yet despite the transition from tweeds to T-shirts, our social task in the broadest analysis remains just as repressive, and the bureaucratic direction of our activities conspires to create a further divide of which we are now as much the victims as the perpetrators.

Escape routes

Many of the criticisms I have made of the current organisation and practice of social work are also made by people who adopt a viewpoint quite different from that advanced here. But although organisation and personalities play their part, the radical position goes deeper in maintaining that the fundamental causes of our difficulties lie in the functions we are expected to perform. The advent of radicalism and Seebohm reforms have certainly sharpened the contradictions and given them a different form but they have always been present. The fashionable nostalgia for the old specialised departments will solve nothing. It is true that *we* feel the personal element has been lost; it is true that standards in *some* areas have fallen. But it is necessary both to distinguish how much has simply been a result of upheaval, and to realise that the old departments were not the embodiments of continuity and caring which some people imagine and remember. Then we were foolish enough to work even longer hours, although we probably felt slightly less out of control. Many welfare departments, which had low budgetary priority, worked to extremely inhibiting and unfeeling standards, particularly to the 'undeserving'. Mental welfare officers were more knowledgeable and reliable in filling out applications for the compulsory admission of patients, but their cosy relationships with psychiatrists, which the latter were so sad to lose, often did not operate to patients' advantage. The much vaunted children's departments, though based on the idea of personalising official involvement with children, which was, to be fair, a turning point for the improvement of social work, were in their time bitterly criticised for the stigma they conferred on difficult families, the abuses they condoned towards the homeless and the failure of much of their residential care. Reorganisation and changing standards have made us all much more self-conscious, and being more aware of our weaknesses is a considerable factor in the stress we feel.

In the next part of the book I shall discuss the major strategies which have been offered to social workers. I have argued here that social workers can have little impact on the major social factors causing individual distress, that social workers are themselves at the mercy of those same forces, and that we need both to admit how much we ourselves are potential consumers of the services we provide and to gain an adequate sense of ourselves as social agents.

In order to show any real caring, we shall have to step out of the roles in which an uncaring society has cast us.

Part III

Practical Strategies

6
Striving for technical solutions

Now that our functions appear to be defined within our agency, rather than the social work of agencies being determined by a limited official function, it has become more urgent and also more difficult first to decide what it is that social workers actually do, and secondly to justify it in face of mounting criticism. Our seeming inability to live up to the claims which have been made for us has prompted some cynics to shudder when they hear of attempts at evaluation, lest the newly-crowned emperor of public welfare is revealed in mortifying nudity.

Nonetheless, those who believe in the actual or potential efficacy of social work are constantly engaged in trying to define the 'inalienable' essence of social work and its constituent skills, and to break down the tasks of social work into manageable form, using social scientific techniques. There is, however, a split in both the orthodox and radical wings as to how much weight should be placed on organisation and how much on the individual social worker, thus giving rise to four identifiably different strategies which I shall call managerial, professional, revolutionary and libertarian. Each strategy approaches the problems, tensions and conflicts faced by social workers in a different way, although none of them is complete in itself. I shall discuss the two radical strategies in Chapter 7.

None of these strategies operates at the level of social policy; only the revolutionary strategy is overtly political. In general, they are concerned less with debates about legislation, selectivity or similar issues than with how social workers and their supporting/controlling departments can best confront the tasks they are set. The official strategies do, however, presuppose a general liberal consensus that social work of some sort is a good and essential element in society, and are initially more concerned with organising social work than justifying it; the assumption is that the better organised we are, the easier justification will become. Indeed, the fact that it is possible to talk of organisation independently of policy demonstrates the burgeoning independence of the social services and the ability of social workers to wear political blinkers.

For this reason it is not possible to identify either official strategy with any political persuasion. One cannot, for example, suggest that conservatives advocate the managerial approach, while liberals support professionalism. If anything, the roles are reversed, with conservatives and radical liberals espousing the personal independence of professionalism which offers some freedom from organisational restraints and a little bit of space for mavericks, while more orthodox liberals go for social engineering. Nevertheless, all hold in common that social problems can be removed by properly-thought-out policy and implementation within the present economic dynamic of society. It is this premise which radicals reject; however, more detailed criticisms can also be made.

Managerialism

I have deliberately avoided *titling* this strategy bureaucratic because the bureaucratic theme runs through all official manifestations of social work, even if its acceptance is at times uneasy or resentful. In particular, I want to avoid the mistake of regarding bureaucracy and professionalism in social work as if they stand in moral and logical opposition at the present time.

I shall justify this further when discussing professionalism; meanwhile I propose to offer a summary of what I define as managerialism, necessarily brief because I am not a manager, although the ideology is beginning to seep insidiously into social services control and planning, largely through the efforts of the Brunel Institute of Organisation. Managerialism derives not from social work but from organisation theory, much of which has been developed in the United States with reference to business corporations. It is prescribed by academics, management consultants and planners and is of increasing importance in a public sector grappling with apparently enormous budgets without any of the guidelines to efficiency and success familiar in the unfettered market. It is of considerable attraction to former social workers who now find themselves in administrative positions with no clear definition, although its practicability rarely lives up to its promise. Effective management consists in the optimal use of scarce resources and managerialism in social work is the belief that the major problems confronting social services can be overcome by developing organisational structure and operational techniques suitable to the task in hand – namely, 'the prevention or relief of social distress in individuals, families and communities, in liaison with other statutory and voluntary agencies'.[1] Managerialists would admit that such a definition begs many questions but believe that it is a sufficient basis on which to organise. In its simplest version a department is seen as a unified hierarchy functionally geared for adequate service; however, this hierarchy should not be a 'cast-iron frame' but a 'membrane-like structure which allows each worker some particular cell or space in which he may freely operate'. (In other words, put a lion in a safari park and he'll think he's free.) Such a structure allows for some goal difference, but, conclude the Brunel researchers, 'unless there can be some consensus, however broad, on common aims and the main divisions of work, then the word "organisation" can hardly be employed to describe the situation'.[2] Thus, given a major conflict, organisation theory goes out of the window. Hierarchy is seen as the only viable structure, though it may be broken by co-ordinating functions. The relationships between the different levels are managerial not supervisory except for 'experienced' social workers, who, in the Brunel typology, are seen as floating independents, in a co-ordinative or developmental relationship to the rest of the department. The managerial role has been described as 'deciding what should be done, and getting other people to do it,'[3] though Brunel states it more cautiously.

Managerialism offers two different approaches to policy implementation. One is 'the rational or quasi-rational model of decision-making in which co-ordination is achieved by formal co-ordinating machinery, with centralised powers to direct subordinate decision centres within a single corporate structure'.[4] This option is exemplified by Planning, Programming and Budgeting (P.P.B.S.), famous in other spheres for the production of such white elephants as the F.111 aircraft. Its application in welfare (mostly in the United States) has been either inefficient or disastrous because, like cost–benefit analysis, it suffers from 'inherent inflexibility and methodological weaknesses', or, more bluntly, the fact that planners' values are rarely the same as those of the people they plan for. The second approach is now more generally favoured, a liberal pluralism and reliance on 'spontaneous adjustment between partisan groups'. The

Brunel hierarchy is an attempt to contain this pluralism within an organisation. However, it completely evades the fact that centralised planning, forecasting and controi are becoming more and more abstruse. On the one hand, managerialism favours technical answers to problems; on the other, it is forced to have them evaluated by competing interest groups which may reject those answers entirely. The claimed solution is, of course, a consensual corporate unity, gained by an acceptable task definition and maintained by an effective representation and communication system which ensures that the directorate keep closely in touch with the rank and file. Maximum delegation downwards and minimum accountability upwards are the watchwords. To sum up, managerialism is based on a loose but functional hierarchy, technical planning and organisational unity.

As applied to social work, managerialism is an ideology in search of a constituency. An increasing number of senior social services officers are attending managerial courses, many of which seem to preach that hierarchy is embedded in nature but teach little about management in practice; subordinates continue to be caseworked rather than managed, and although there are some instances where administrative problem-solving techniques are useful, much of the need for them would evaporate if social workers were given the opportunity to control their own roles in the organisation. Brunel proudly quotes how its distinction between transfer and referral helped intake and long-term teams to clarify their relationships in Wandsworth, but if the teams had not been artifically split from each other and the different social workers had been able to understand each other's problems, I doubt whether a research team would have been needed. Larger-scale problems reveal the fundamental incoherence of managerialism, a set of techniques elevated to a philosophy which operates among its own pure flow charts and founders on encountering the complexities of reality.

A department versed in managerial theory can present a façade of competence; Brown arrives at the theory's logical conclusion by asserting that a department's external relations are as important as the quality of its internal management,[5] an assertion which social workers around the country who suffer almost daily from managerial incompetence can greet only with hollow laughter. Radicals need, however, to be clear that there are other reasons for opposing managerialism, especially its belief in functional organisation in an area of conflicting interests compounded by intense competition for resources. Sometimes the effects are trivial – for instance, the tendency to appoint people to organise the relief of separately identified needs, like child-abuse or the single homeless, and then considering the problem will be solved. More serious is the pressure, however delicate, towards implying the possibility of consensus. Radicals argue that the social services are fundamentally *dys*functional organisations caught in an irreconcilable conflict between those who lay down the conditions for their existence and those they are intended to serve. While the former wish to assign the minimum possible resources, recipients, once their expectations are aroused, demand as much as they need. Moreover official policies – for instance, that delinquency be controlled – are always undermined by fiscal meanness. The result is that social workers, who are supposedly paid, among other things, to safeguard their clients' interests, bring the conflict *into* the agency, often linking it with their own demands as well.

Thus the agency is *not* a whole; it contains an interiorised division between those working directly with clients and those responsible for management and rationing which no form of representation and mutual discussion can solve. There is no more unenviable post than that of area officer, who is supposed to embody both functions at once; it is not surprising that most opt for the easier life of supporting management. We are not all engaged in the same task, as the managerial myth would have it, and our relationships must proceed in recognition of that fact. I do not advocate destructive hostility; we do need a *modus vivendi*; but those who enter management with liberalising intentions have to realise that, while they may be able to perform some sort of enabling or even protective function, they now represent a different interest and are isolated from the main body of workers. If they step out of line, they risk far more unpleasant sanctions than do those still in the field.

There is, however, one bright spot for radicals in this approach. If our managers do try to manage, instead of trying to please everyone and satisfying nobody, and I have no doubt that they should, the issues of interest and control will be very much clearer, as will be the consciousness of social workers as workers. It will then fall to social workers to ensure that we too organise appropriately.

Professionalism

'Professionalism' is one of those words, like 'self-determination' or 'democracy', whose vague descriptive content may be less important than the effect which the user of the word wishes to have on the audience. According to context it carries either a positive or a negative value-charge and is often used to persuade people of the worth or otherwise of a particular practice without conveying any very definite information about it.[6] One example of negative connotation is the slightly derogatory ring of 'welfare professional', an echo of the old attitude to professional cricketers, the trace of a sneer at those who demand payment for engaging in activities better performed for the enjoyment, merit or effect alone. Self-styled professionals, on the other hand, stress their altruism; the acceptance of fees becomes almost part of the service. Community service, high standards, expertise and independence are part of the positive connotation, and professionals sometimes appear to be claiming a monopoly over these obviously desirable attributes, a claim which often confuses their critics. Status is another connotation, valued but underemphasised by aspiring professionals: the radical case is that status is such an overriding consideration that 'professional' becomes virtually synonymous with 'elitist'.

After briefly commenting on the weaknesses inherent in the professional ideal, I shall argue that not only is the social work claim to professional status shaky on its own terms, but it also has dangerous implications for all those involved in the personal social services. I shall further suggest that the conventional contrast between professionalism and bureaucracy in social work and the escape to a 'purer' practice is based on a fundamental misunderstanding of the necessary functions and attributes demanded of social work in present society. I shall not consider the notion of 'semi-professional' since it is parasitic on the major professions.

Paths to professional status

The essence of professionalism is not a commitment to service and the maintenance of standards but the belief that these and other goals can be achieved only by organisational independence and peer control, that values can be maintained only if professionals themselves have the sole responsibility of monitoring their own activities. Only in this way, it is argued, can the client have confidence in the individual professional whom he approaches for help. I shall comment later on this assumed basis of authoritativeness. Here there are two points to make. First, that the standards which are enforced do not derive from clients; they are in practice merely measures which provide a minimal protection from physical or financial exploitation which would damage not just the client but the image of the profession itself; more positive goals are based on optimism. A senior consultant told the inquiry into St. Augustine's Hospital that consultants were responsible to themselves and the profession; the gruelling training and examination procedure was, he asserted, sufficient to ensure that successful candidates would invariably seek to maintain the highest standards without reference to anyone else.[7] Secondly, the inevitable conclusion to be drawn from this belief in professional independence is that professionalism is not the expression of the inherent nature of particular occupations but a type of occupational control: 'a profession is not an occupation but a means of controlling an occupation'.[8]

If we regard professionalism in this light, its attraction to social workers becomes clear. The thrust towards expertise, itself attractive in that it offers hope that some problems at least will become soluble, is strongly larded with a bid for self-determination; an escape from the tyranny of local authority supervision and routine, and from the disdain of more established professions. There is justification for the dissatisfaction felt by social workers, and merit in the promotion of our particular perspective of helping people, which is the only one to consider people in the context from which they derive their identities, rather than, say, as a collection of symptoms and responses. It is therefore sad that these should be distorted by an attempt to seek parity of status with, for example, medicine, which is reflected in the disproportionate bias towards medical social work in the membership of both the American and British Associations of Social Workers.[9] The two other strongest constituencies of professionalism outside academia appear to be among managers who seek to retain a social work identity and a minority of younger trained workers who either believe in the advancement of social work technique or else seek justification for the rule-breaking into which they are forced by the demands of the job in traditional professional values.

The attempted identification of social work as a profession proceeds by comparing attributes and by emphasising social workers' unique knowledge and skill. The first argument is of a syllogistic form: professions are activities identifiable by particular traits or functions; social work exhibits most of these traits, therefore social work is a profession. From this conclusion further syllogisms arise asserting social work's right to the recognition of other professional attributes and its need to be organised as other professions are. Whatever may be thought of the logic of this argument, the principal flaw lies in the major premise which is based on a naïve acceptance of 'trait' theory. In fact, no agreed list of professional attributes exists; most are just ragbags tailored to suit the needs of whatever group is using them to aspire to professional status. The most amazing feature of the argument is its readiness to accept the professions' own definitions of themselves without any consideration of what led Shaw to castigate them as 'a conspiracy against the laity'. It is absurd that social workers should seek to ape the very characteristics that many of us have found so objectionable in doctors, merely so that these very doctors should treat us as equals.

The second path is more subtle and proceeds as follows. It is generally recognised that social work is a skilful task. Although some individuals are more suited than others, the relevant skills are acquired rather than innate. If they are acquired, they must be teachable; therefore there is a body of knowledge which is unique at least in relation to the exercise of those skills. The possession of knowledge implies expertise, which itself confers status. However, this status is conditional on public confidence that the expertise is being used in the public's interests; if knowledge is abused, the profession will decline. Thus the simple identification of a skill leads to the exaltation of the membership, not so much, it is alleged, in their own interest but in that of the people they claim to serve.

There are a number of variations on this argument, and many do not follow it through the whole way. The most controversial step is that which proceeds from the possession of knowledge to the granting of status in recognition of special expertise. The radical priority is, of course, the sharing of knowledge, however derived, and not allowing it to be corralled into a privileged reservation.

The mistaken search for exclusive knowledge

Social work knowledge is both diffuse and overvalued; attempts to make it exclusive are farcical and damaging. But I do not thereby suggest that knowledge is irrelevant, only that it should not become a fetish, pursued for its own sake. Little opportunity for constructive thought is allowed to social workers. Post-training courses are rare and usually deal only in 'advanced casework'. In-service training rarely rises above the elementary. The recognised professions are permitted study time. Many social workers are not even allowed to experiment with, say, groupwork, let alone read a book during work-time. This pressure has the double role of keeping our perceptions firmly at the level of individual cases, and of concealing how inadequate and even puerile is a good deal of so-called social work knowledge.

What is unique in social work is not our knowledge but our praxis, the way knowledge is applied; what we know is important only in so far as it aids our understanding. We draw on an immensely wide variety of sources; there is hardly a human science which is not in some way relevant. Even when social work is defined simply as intervention to improve social functioning, much of psychology and psychiatry is not excluded. Nor can we properly study our own work because so many variables are involved; controlled experiments present ethical and practical difficulties. Some research is possible but usually only work which provides background information proves useful. Studies of efficacy are always questionable, Goldberg's *Helping the Aged* being a case in point.[10] Some work shows social workers in a favourable light, but other studies have produced such worrying findings as a higher mortality rate among the supervised elderly, more frequent child-battering among clients receiving social work attention and deterioration among delinquents. Scott Briar concludes his review of casework by observing that social workers always think that they have done better than they actually have.[11] Such findings get little prominence for obvious reasons; they are also probably as unreliable as studies which purport to show the opposite. We do well to treat them all with suspicion and not to claim them either as justifications or invalidations. The real questions are quite different.

Once again the underlying assumption of all such research is that if only intervention could be properly quantified and we could develop new and effective techniques, social work could really begin to justify itself. In some smaller-scale and more clearly-defined instances this may be true. But the fundamental argument of this book is that the nature of the problems we deal with is far beyond being affected by technical tinkering. One example might be the enthusiastic adoption of the time-limited task-centred approach to social work, founded on an initial contract with the client. Initial research suggested that work on this basis could be more effective. But in 1977 social work journals were full of criticism for the depersonalised and indeed unequal relationship which is imposed. I shall discuss contracts and bargaining in Chapter 8 but meanwhile cite this changing attitude as a symptom of the fact that no new technique will ever of itself meet with consistent success.

There is, however, a broader and more political point to be made. If the real social function of social work is the maintenance of social consensus, and if our job is a form of second-tier socialisation, then the improvement of our techniques is in part a contribution to the technology of repression. Once again, contract theory is a good example; the idea is that the social worker will perform certain tasks which have been requested by the client, if the client will reciprocate in certain ways. The contract has the superficial appearance of an equal bargain, but in practice, unless the client is abnormally strong-willed and disruptive, the power to determine the nature and scope of the contract lies almost wholly with the social worker, and this bias is institutionalised when a supervision or probation order is in force. Furthermore, techniques will be developed not according to client need but according to government and other external priorities. In this regard the state of social work is closely analogous to that of psychiatry, which has far more powerful weapons of intervention available but operates in a sphere where accurate knowledge is heavily lacking. As Jordan forcefully argues, medical knowledge is now often out of the hands of the profession and many practitioners are little more than technicians.[12] Doctors receive their information and instruction from the pharmaceutical industry, which also determines where research resources should be directed. One result is the ever increasing development of capital-intensive equipment, the use of which has low priority for the population as a whole but yields higher profits to the manufacturers and higher status to the users. Another is the plethora of identical and relatively useless drugs and medicines on the market, all with extravagant claims but whose major contribution is to increase consumption and sow confusion among both prescribers and users.

Belief in the value of knowledge induces a belief in training, though this is often more a process of professional socialisation. Social work training is a messy business and poses far more questions than can be discussed here. However, dissatisfaction is rife and perhaps the only group to be consistently conscious of possible benefits is mature students, at last able to discover and assess the rationale (or lack of it) behind what they and others have been forced to do during their previous work experience. I remember feeling that much of the time on my two-year course was wasted, though I did emerge with a feeling of confidence which it took as much as six months to convert to depression. Observation suggests such experience is not uncommon, though some persist in attempting to convert the promises of social work into practice, while others repudiate those promises from the beginning. At any rate all the evidence I know of suggests that training has very little effect on agency practice. In the children's departments both Packman and Davies found that the number of trained officers in a department had little effect on the services provided; variations depended on quite different factors.[13] George's research into fostering found that practice was guided by conventional wisdom as inculcated into departmental culture, not by the detailed knowledge available; there was little difference between the work of trained and untrained officers.[14] American research in the 1960s found that even in private agencies, trained workers were as likely as not to adopt agency policy as a prime determinant of their work, whatever the needs of clients (the bureaucratic orientation), and confirmed the conservatising effect of rank.[15] To be fair, professional standards can also be invoked to support radicalism, but this does not appear to be an effect of professionalisation itself. I would suspect that reorganisation in the United Kingdom has probably increased the influence of bureaucracy on trained workers despite their increased numbers, a suspicion reinforced by the observation that departments boasting a high number of recognised 'professionals' are often both more conservative and less responsive to client need than many others. Within departments a strict hierarchy operates, the opinions of 'professional' workers being given far more weight than those of the less experienced but more enthusiastic workers, who perform as stressful work for less money and who are often accorded no recognition by management at all.

The emphasis on knowledge has another disturbing effect on potential recruitment. As courses increase their academic content, entry into the professional ranks will depend more and more on prior academic competence, without any evidence that this will be of benefit to clients. It is becoming much harder for people without degrees, let alone 'A' levels or 'O' levels, to gain places on courses. Even the number of mature students has been cut back. Social work is becoming a profession of graduates, thus effectively increasing their distance from the majority of those who seek help, and closing the ranks against outside challenge. The desperate attempt to make social work a repository of detailed scientific knowledge is desensitising us in the unworthy cause of professional legitimation.

Finally, the attempt at exclusivity is causing needless professional rivalry, exemplified by the often bitter feelings in the mental health field between social workers and community nurses. The latter represent the nursing profession's attempt to break out of the institutional straitjacket and usually base their actions on a desire to extend the ward into the community. They are directly responsible to psychiatrists, who obviously prefer them to social workers who are beyond their control and often appear ineffectual. Social workers, on the other hand, tend to be opposed to the traditional medical model of illness and many view this development with alarm. We would rather abolish the ward than extend it. At one level the argument appears simply to be about the aims and effects of particular types of intervention, but the outcome is determined in a struggle for occupational territory, and instead of pooling knowledge and skills, victory finally goes to the group most successful in exerting influence and winning what new resources are going.

Authority and status

Advocates of professionalism maintain that professional status is not an end in itself but a means to assuring clients of a high standard of service. I find this claim disingenuous, misguided, divisive, and inaccurate, especially in the case of social work, where standards are determined by government and agency priority. I shall return to this last point in the next section.

The benefits of professional status to its holders are well known; they are marked out as people deserving of public respect and gain financial rewards which, if less than those of directors of industry, nevertheless put them into an upper income bracket, where they can keep up a lifestyle proper to their position in society. One source of high status is the fact that little if any manual work is involved; more important, however, is public confidence that these people can be entrusted with information and decisions which they will not use to further their own interest. As Johnson points out, the root of the claim to professionalism is the practitioner's need to have his or her abilities taken for granted in the diagnostic and treatment relationship; if this were not so, the argument goes, the practitioner would be divested of the authority and freedom needed to make quick decisions.[16] The first point to make is that it is but a short step from justifying status because of the need for authoritativeness to justifying authority because of status. A large number of professionals are carried through their working life not by individual confidence in them but by the prestige and self-protective measures of their professional body. Secondly, if professional status depends upon a diagnostic relationship, professionals will obviously do all they can to maintain that relationship. In social work that means a continued stress on casework as the essential activity of the profession. B. A. S. W.'s evidence to the Butterworth Inquiry bears this suspicion out:

> The social worker's primary area of responsibility to his client is his responsibility to use his skill in the therapeutic use of relationships in the one-to-one setting, the family group, the small group and the community group to the maximum benefit of his clients. . . . During this relationship the client usually enters a phase of dependency. . . . It is known that many clients will never achieve independence.[17]

Despite the lip-service paid to other settings, there are few more explicit statements of social casework as the general task of the profession. The disingenuity of the claim to status through authoritativeness is that it increases the likelihood of continuing dependence, it enhances the life of the practitioner, and in its justification of increased social distance it is profoundly conservative.

At least in so far as social work is concerned the claim to authoritativeness is itself misleading since we have no grounds for making it except in a few tightly-defined situations. We have no professional answers to most of the problems our clients bring, and I have argued that it is self-deception to imagine that we could have. We can often help sort out what has gone wrong but we have no prescription for progress, and clients are often much more realistic about our role and potential than professional optimism allows us to be.

Finally, professional status is divisive because it distances us not only from our clients but from workers in similar occupations. Social workers seem far less interested in understanding important activities like nursing or occupational therapy, which are by statute ruled to be ancillary to the medical profession. It is with doctors that our professional lobby seeks parity. The claim to privilege also antagonises workers in, for example, housing and education, not to mention in our own offices, for it is, above all, class-based. Middle-class people do not like having authority exercised over them, so, aided by financial or educational advantage, they carve out occupational structures which permit them at least some freedom of judgement. As I argued above, more and more white-collar jobs even in social work are becoming filled with routine content; professionalism is an attempt to escape from the boredom and control which this trend has brought, but depends for its success on limiting the escape from complete alienation to a few select categories of people. Radicals have to recognise that this is a struggle in which all workers are legitimately engaged, and repudiate such a narrow reinforcement of occupational privilege.

Professionals or bureaucrats?

This question is usually posed as if one answer is exclusive of the other. Since few people admit to being bureaucrats, professionalism is presented as the only viable alternative, offering an escape from routine, a sense of personal responsibility and the possibility of real individual service. But such prospects are pure sales technique and bear as much relation to reality as does a travel brochure artist's impression of an unfinished hotel. Whatever the position may be in the traditionally recognised professions (and in general it is not dissimilar), social workers are not independently contracting practitioners but are subject to administrative stringencies, managerial control and ideological direction. The framework within which we have to act is enshrined in statute, the practical standards and guidelines we follow are delineated in agency policy and our objectives are set by political decision. Our clientele is, as Johnson observes, guaranteed by the state in what purports to be a collective and uniform responsibility for welfare.[18] However we interpret this intervention, its organisational consequences are with us to stay.

Bureaucracy is not simply a pejorative term associated with paperwork and inflexibility of regulation; it is in part 'the organising activity of the state', and as such represents a particular form of political mediation and control, which has become an increasing feature of all modern societies. Bureaucracy is the logical result of attempts to rationalise the workings of the capitalist economy; officials derive their apparently neutral status from their intended role as mediators between class antagonisms or between the individual and society, and attract hostility both because they cannot escape allegiance with the dominant source of power and because their own organisation does possess a creeping momentum of its own. In public administration this momentum is not sufficient to lead bureaucrats solely into following their own interests and ruling society; although they are delegated some power to regulate the workings of an economic system incapable of self-regulation, and are thus often involved in contradictory actions, they both disguise and catch the flak for the needs and workings of capital. One central contradiction which has been a theme of the present economic crisis is the extent to which capitalism can any longer afford the regulative machinery it has found necessary and the threat to the consensual society it has attempted to create if it shakes off these bonds. Of course, not all social workers are employed by the state, but private organisations too are licensed by the dominant ideology, which their existence normally helps to reinforce, and display the same organisational tendency towards pursuing self-interest.

Few, if any social workers can escape bureaucratic functions, but this does not mean the demise of the professional. Instead, social-democracy offers professionalism as an antidote to the bureaucratic machinery whose expansion has been engendered by social reform. The role of the professions in a bureaucracy is to counter the collective effect of strategic intervention by building in more flexible and individually oriented functions, which demand individual competence and increase external accountability. By infusing professionalism social-democrats hope to argue that the success of reform depends on the competence of those carrying it out, and can more easily ignore the viability of the reforming activity itself. They are also able to make government more flexible and palatable by making its fringes elastic enough to adjust to individual need. Finally they believe that the commitment to individual welfare which is characteristic of professionalism will maintain democratic values within officialdom.

Social work ideology fits these roles perfectly. A professionalism based on the ideal of individual liberty but with a profoundly normative content can appear to be tailoring the system to the needs of citizens while it legitimates an often coercive element in the otherwise private domain of families and individuals who have caused or appear likely to cause upset and offence. This interference is sugar-coated with respect and love, a doorstep sales bargain offer of freedom. The privileged position which professionals enjoy hides the fact that they are victims of their own illusions, supposedly representing the interests of the ruled but doing so without mandate and often without conviction. The purpose of the professional in a bureaucratic structure is a combination of maintenance fitter and trouble-shooter, whose job it is to keep the system working.

This professionalism is not independence but fits in neatly with the hierarchical and cellular organisation advocated at Brunel. I have already referred to some of the evidence for bureaucratic orientation among professionals. Neither social workers nor even probation officers are free agents; we are firmly under the control of our departments and case committees. There may be possibilities of more delegated authority, but this would always be open to revocation, especially when unorthodoxy is suspected or proclaimed. If our job even in part is to control our clients, then we ourselves must be subject to control, and should the threat to order in society increase, so will radicals be watched much more carefully. The suspension and reprimanding of the London probation officer, Geoffrey Parkinson, in 1977 for allegedly suggesting to clients that some crimes were less reprehensible than others and bargaining with them over the payment of fines is one case in point. Another is that of Martin Cumella, sacked by Birmingham Corporation for allegedly putting a boy in moral danger by allowing him to spend the weekend with the only couple to have taken an interest in him for years, the wife having previously been convicted of prostitution. It was generally agreed that Cumella's militant reputation as a union shop-steward was the underlying motive, a point confirmed by his reinstatement after an all-out strike had forced a special committee to consider the case. It is difficult to act too harshly against radicals in such situations, since unwelcome precedents may be set for more respectable social workers faced with equally unwelcome alternatives. It is, however, possible to monitor and harass them. The most general threat is that any open criticism of departmental policy even by permitted means endangers chances of promotion and risks secret blacklisting. Radicals can find their hours more carefully monitored, their files rigorously checked, and extra work assigned. The personal resentment felt by management can result in rumours being spread with the intention of isolating radicals by depicting them as oddities. Increasingly management go for appointing 'safe' people in senior posts; job interviews have been known to centre around such important social work issues as the control of militants.

Of course, radicals are not the only ones subject to control. The individual supervisory system, which I have already discussed, and the local government tradition of departmental responsibility mean that everyone has to account upwards for what they do, write and say. But the limits of accountability remain undefined; more often than not, it is the fieldworker who carries the brunt of responsibility, however limited his or her actual delegated power may be and whatever the deficiencies of the department. Supervisors are becoming equally vulnerable if things go wrong, though there are encouraging signs that the scapegoating of individual fieldworkers or supervisors (as opposed to a proper allocation of responsibility) is now being more strongly resisted. One result has been a tendency for some social workers to cover themselves by paying more attention to the faithful enumeration of statutory visits and inspections in their files than to the real content of either visits or records, or to other priorities which discretion may indicate or necessity demand.

To conclude, it seems that professionalism is not an alternative to bureaucracy but an essential part of the bureaucratic strategy. In so far as workers are freed from petty organisational restrictions, professionalism can be a liberating influence.

However, there are two profoundly conservative implications. By attempting to escape routine work, professionals put themselves apart from other workers to whom they do not permit such freedom. By their stress on individual cases and their attempts to juggle the rules in order to prevent clients losing out too much or too often, they disguise the general purpose and workings of the welfare system in such a way as to destroy its major gain: when welfare is mediated by the state it should become a collective and impersonal right. Welfare is transformed from a personal to a social issue. Professionalism reverses this step. The irony of the attempt to maintain democratic values in public administration by injecting professionalism is that it should result in a partial loss of rights for those who become its clients.

The impossibility of a pure professional social work

Every profession carries its own image of its essential activities, and relegates other tasks to routine status. The essence of police work is catching criminals. 'When a policeman can engage in real police work – act out the symbolic rites of search, chase and capture – his self image will be affirmed and his morale enhanced.'[19]

The essence of social work would be more difficult to define; some would speak in terms of planned interventions geared to improve the social functioning of an individual or group. Behind both the charitable and technical approach lies an expectation of personal relationships and expression.

The tragedy of social work is that its place in society permits neither an escape from routine nor much possibility of personal contact, and no reform or reorganisation can escape that fact. Both Butrym and Jordan, whose positions I discussed in Chapter 5, advocate the removal of administrative functions from social workers and, of course, they are right to assert that many of these are unnecessary. But in attempting to limit and define a role for social workers, they fail to see that we are lumbered with a whole variety of disparate functions because that is the only way our welfare state can be made to work. Generic social workers did not exist so they had to be invented. Moreover, both authors, especially Butrym, appear to assume that the fate and functions of social work are somehow in the control of its practitioners. I hope I have already said enough to counter this assumption. Butrym soars into a realm of pure professionalism in which social workers, no longer tied to any particular agency function (a concept she regards as only of historical relevance at the present time), would be stationed at 'crossroads' like medical practices, D. H. S. S. offices and even major workplaces, or would work on a small local 'patch' where they would become 'familiar and trusted within the community.[20] What services they would be delivering or what statutes they would be enforcing she does not say, nor does she comment on how this trust is to be maintained. Jordan, on the other hand, correctly advocates a far more limited and residual role: social workers are only to be called in when the major social services, including those of income maintenance, prove insufficient; in his ideal welfare state we should serve only those who have a proven need for consistent long-term support. Yet he offers no strategy at all, except perhaps unilateral withdrawal, by which we can escape the present confusion, and by which people can gain the services they really need. Moreover his proposal to 'free' social work from the burden of providing financial assistance is utterly unrealistic. Without a source at least of petty cash, the job would be made immeasurably more difficult even in the best of circumstances. It is unjust to link his thesis too closely with Butrym's, for he certainly does not advocate an elitist professionalism. Nonetheless, without an adequate strategy for present use, his arguments can more easily be used to favour the development of professionalism than to procure the change in society which he considers necessary.

What neither Butrym nor Jordan fully considers is that social work is not of itself a coherent enterprise but a philosophy to whose adherents society has assigned various different and even contrary tasks. If some social workers wish to become psychotherapists or sociotherapists and can persuade the authorities to pay them, let them do so, call themselves by an appropriate name and recognise both their skills and limitations. If others wish to concentrate on service delivery in whatever form, let that be recognised and given its true weight. Even the simplest aids have to be humanely administered and their use can require persuasion, reassurance and education. Such skills are also a recognized part of social work and are abused only when used to ration and to stigmatise. We should spend less time trying to persuade each other of our relative superiority and more in discovering how we can work together on an equal basis. If we cannot do this with our co-workers, we will never manage it with our clients. Above all, let us forget the promise that social work offers any basis for proper and honest relationships. Our job requires that we treat people as 'welfare cases', an attitude which professionalism hardens. Only a radicalism which spurns both professional seduction and bureaucratic indifference by allowing encounters between real people in real situations and facing the personal vulnerability involved can dare to attempt to be really personal.

I have argued that the case for professionalism has to be regarded with the utmost suspicion, both because of its dangerous implications and because it is internally incoherent. The seducing qualities it offers – altruism, high standards, individual responsibility, an escape from bureaucracy – are either illusory or covered up in practice by the rat-race of occupational prestige. In pursuit of these unexceptionable aims, social workers have become lured into a decaying nineteenth-century and class-based occupational tradition which has little relevance either to our job or to present-day requirements. Kay McDougall, discussing the obligations of a profession in the early days of B.A.S.W., stated that a profession is not an occupation but a way of life; 'We are judged', she went on to say, 'by how we are seen to behave towards clients and towards each other.'[21] In the very attempt to arrogate all these qualities to our way of life, and by that action excluding others from it and separating ourselves from our clients, social work professionalism stands condemned by its own criteria.

7 The radical challenge

Radicalism in social work is an accumulation of social and political critiques from a variety of sources. The uneasy coexistence of these critiques results from the contradictory position in which radicals find themselves. The springboard of radicalism is a rejection of social work in any of its present forms as anything but an institutionalised substitute for the caring relationships which people in any predicament could expect and enjoy in a less exploitative society. On the other hand many radicals believe that those who are exploited or rejected by society should pursue their rights as forcefully as possible, and social work offers one method of helping them towards a position to do so. Radicals are also faced with having to earn a living themselves and resisting their own exploitation. The resulting contradictions make it difficult if not impossible to act consistently. Facing up to them, and simultaneously attempting to maintain open and honest relationships with clients in conditions which favour deceit, make radicalism a vulnerable and painful undertaking. Add the fact that the involvement in union and political activity which radicals consider indispensable can itself either be boring or attract intense hostility from established interests, and our commitment becomes yet more unenviable; the courage, caring and capacity for work which are required make real radicalism a daunting task. Those who criticise radicals for taking an easy way out merely betray their own naïvety with such misplaced insult.

I now want to flesh out the differences between libertarian and revolutionary radicalism but, although I shall make more criticisms of the former, as far as social work is concerned I believe the two strategies to be complementary. However, major change can, in my view, come about only through an underlying commitment to revolutionary organisation. Without an active participation in this type of struggle libertarians risk irrelevance or a drift into liberalism. On the other hand, revolutionaries who concentrate solely on organisation can become blinkered to the purposes of change and develop a puritan and harshly moralistic disposition.[1]

Labelling, deviancy theory and anti-psychiatry

These critiques have been of considerable importance to the radical platform, and it is necessary to offer some preliminary comment on them before discussing strategy in more detail. The impact of labelling theory is illustrated by the fact that its basic premise has become platitudinous. Most liberals now accept that moral and behavioural categorisation are not objective accounts of behaviour but self-perpetuating judgements which serve the interests of those who make them, and more often than not reinforce the behaviour which is being condemned by making its perpetrators appear as a separate class of person. Words like hooligan, criminal, client, psychopath all work in this sort of way. The application of this theory to social work reveals both its value and its weaknesses.

Labels have an important function in social work, despite our attempts to resist them. Just as people with at least one conviction are more likely to be brought to court than first offenders, however trivial the offence, so the existence of a label aids social workers in diagnosis under pressure; for instance, people behaving oddly are far more likely to be compulsorily committed to mental hospital if they have been patients before. Labelling may sometimes be represented as being to the client's benefit. Shortage of resources forces us to tailor our descriptions of clients to meet the provider's requirements. Applications to residential establishments will emphasise the qualities in which the staff are most interested and clients will be expected to live up to their previous symptoms. Working in an area where resources for the mentally handicapped far outstrip those for the mentally ill, I find myself much more likely to classify borderline clients as handicapped. Alternatively a client's plight may be exaggerated to get them a place, no doubt at the expense of somebody else. Moreover, because we have become more aware of the deleterious effects of initial labelling and are therefore more reluctant to make a firm commitment to diagnosis, a label once applied sticks much harder. Sometimes the existence of a label is more important that what it actually says, a condition astutely and wittily depicted in Spike Milligan's television series *Q6*, in which every participant and object bore a blank or illegible luggage ticket. However, understanding the effects of labelling does not mean that we should or even can avoid categorisation altogether. Furthermore, a theory of behaviour based on social reaction not only implies that people, once labelled as different, actually become so; it also represents them as passive creatures of the labeller. Deviancy theorists have attempted to go further by emphasising deviants' own contributions to the value and logic of their actions. But simply accepting deviants' descriptions of themselves will not do either, except when seen as part of a dialectical conflict between different descriptions. Radicals need to be able to validate deviants' self-perceptions without necessarily agreeing with them.[2]

Perhaps even more important to social work than deviancy theory has been the anti-psychiatry movement, because the emphasis which Laing and others placed on *social* diagnosis enabled social workers to enlist them as allies in the crusade against medicine because they seemed to root the development of mental disorder in the family sphere, which social workers often claimed for their own. It was ironic that this co-option of Laing should have occurred at a time when most local authority social workers were authorised to apply for the compulsory admission of patients to hospital, and it took a little time to sink in that the critique could also be directed at our own traditional practices. Although we were able to take advantage of the added technical understanding deriving from Laing's approach to disorder, the development of anti-psychiatry's political implications and of alternative therapies became the province of libertarian groups functioning on the fringes of the official health and social services.

Because so much of the theory and self-justification of social work depends upon a theory of the personality and interaction which is rooted within a currently conventional approach to disorder, and because social workers as a group have (often wrongly) become associated in official circles with the Laingian perspective, it will be useful briefly to discuss mental disorder before considering radical social work more generally.

Politics and madness

Anti-psychiatry is at present in disarray; it is, wrote Peter Sedgwick, a discredited party in which nobody will admit having carried a card.[3] Its insights have been eclipsed by the failure of the exaggerated claims made by some supporters, and, more fundamentally, by certain practical weaknesses inherent in the libertarian position.

The kernel of anti-psychiatry was and is the restoration of intelligence, motivation and respect to the person whom medically-based theory classes solely as ill. Madness was a strategy devised to survive unlivable situations whose root was in the oppressive and distorting form of family life under late capitalism. Some even argued as if schizophrenia was the only sane reaction to the intolerable normalcy of the real world. Thus while medicine, as Pearson succinctly puts it, is dedicated to the extinction of madness, anti-psychiatry is concerned with its elucidation.[4] Clearly Laing's stand against authority in both diagnosis and treatment was of great significance for radicals.

The attraction of the Laingian position is obvious and its value is indubitable. It is not, however, self-sufficient. Of the many different criticisms which can be made, two will suffice for our purposes. Firstly, no criterion is offered for distinguishing which particular disorders are caused primarily by illness (for instance, by toxaemia or tumours, to take two non-controversial examples) and which are genuinely 'behavioural expressions of an experiential drama'.[5] Of course, diagnosing an organic condition should not mean a denial of its experiential aspects; their context and significance must, however, be affected. On the other hand, feelings and fears based solely on social apperception can be unbearably agonising in unadulterated form; some balance has to be struck between gaining awareness and the disabling pain which can result, especially if the experience is involuntary. Furthermore, some people's strategies lead to situations which cannot be regarded with indifference. Laingian anti-psychiatry appears to offer no guidance on such practical decisions and in essence seems limited to the provision of a compassionate and tolerant environment for individual 'trips'.

Secondly, while Laing and others have given us a poetic description of what it is like to live 'in the often fibrillating heartland of a senescent capitalism',[6] they have little or nothing to say about what causes the ugliness of social reality or how it is to be changed. The libertarian diagnosis can, with minor variations, be blamed on capital, technology, over-population, or even the decay of old-fashioned values. Laing indicts the world but offers no strategy for change; indeed, in reply to Ssasz's attack on Laing's Philadelphia Association as a hotbed of communism, he has been reported as denying any connection with socialism at all. Yet the constriction of the anti-psychiatric operation can be partly attributed to the operation of capital. Priority in medical research is given to the invention, duplication and marketing of pharmaceuticals and high-technology equipment which generate a high reward on investment. A few small-scale, long-term, labour-intensive projects may be licensed by the N. H. S. to buy off persistent critics, but they have little economic logic.

Although the weaknesses of libertarian anti-psychiatry have been evident for some time, British Marxists have not in general given much attention to constructing any different framework.[7] The most helpful perspective for social workers so far suggested is to use Marxist analysis and group support to break out of the mystification with which capitalist ideology surrounds those with mental 'symptoms'. Though deficient in this field, there is no doubt that Marxism helps people to re-externalise guilt and pain imposed by the individualisation of problems and reverses the anaesthetised passivity which our society inflicts. Groups organised around specific areas of oppression like the Women's Movement offer the hope of genuinely collective support and response. However, not only do we find that some Marxists have personal problems which cannot be resolved in this way, we have also to deal with clients for whom socialism does not at first sight seem relevant to their private ills. Yet even these have political content. What, for example, are we to make of the lonely old lady who believes that hordes of Ugandans are parachuting down on to her house from gliders? Surely, among other things, she is expressing an unconscious reflection of society's hysteria, internalised to her own plight.

There have been a number of Marxist experiments with therapeutic communities, but the most significant has probably been the short-lived Socialist Patients' Collective (S. P. K.) in Heidelberg during 1970–1.[8] Reacting against some particularly restrictive regulations, including the barring from psychotherapy of patients over 35 or without a school-leaving certificate, a psychiatrist and fifty patients forced the University Clinic to grant them self-governing facilities by an occupation and hunger-strike. After a year of harassment the collective was finally broken up by armed police following an alleged link with the Baader–Meinhof urban guerrilla groups. Within that period they had evolved an entirely new therapeutic praxis which challenged the traditions of medicine and the mental hospital. Each new patient received a full physical examination to eliminate organic causes. The next step was a form of counselling with a more experienced patient of his choice in order to promote a relationship of equality and remove inhibitions about finally participating in the full self-governing group whose purpose was the socialisation of each person's knowledge and experience in order to achieve a political analysis of illness. By this process the mystique of psychiatry was removed and individual patients gradually gained the sense that recovery from symptoms lies within the power of ordinary people if they have the attention, company and solidarity of a larger group to begin finding themselves again.

Above all, the therapy was political. Combining anti-psychiatry with a Marcusean belief in the power of deviance, the S. P. K. adopted the philosophy of *Krankengut*, the worth of illness. As opposed to the Laingians, who appeared to say that no-one is ill, the S. P. K. argued that all of us are ill if only we would realise it. Illness is collectively produced by the workings of capitalism but is manifested in different individual symptoms. Health is an out-and-out bourgeois concept because it is nothing more than availability for exploitation. But instead of the unitary concept of illness which has so bedevilled radicals, the S. P. K. substituted a dialectic: illness contains a progressive element, a protest against the capitalist way of life, and a negative element, a restraint or paralysis of functioning, reinforced by individual treatment.

These conceptions of disorder and of therapy are, I think, of great value to radicals. However, the S. P. K. ended up in isolation, not least because they attempted to make illness explain too much. Although their ideas presented a considerable threat to the establishment, they failed, as far as I know, to gain organised support, partly because of the general atmosphere of modern German politics, but mainly, I suspect, because exaggerated claims by an apparently deviant group of identification with the working class as a whole easily leads to the alienation of outside help. The survival of any radical group, particularly one as threatening as the S. P. K., depends on careful work in building organisational links with the stronger organisations of the working class; if they neglect these links, disintegration will follow. The Philadelphia Association has ended up by catering largely to the affluent middle class; the S. P. K. was simply crushed.

Community work

Community action was an even more potent rallying point for

radicals, but here too hopes have been disappointed. 'Community' was to be the magic carpet of libertarian radicalism but turned out to be as limited as other forms of social work, not, as caseworkers had predicted, because it was unable to resolve individual problems, but because even at their own level communities proved to have too little power to make more than minor gains or undertake more than symbolic actions. The radical potential of such work is often undermined by localism and competition; where cohesion is created, it is, much more often than not, for the purposes of social control. Military writers are quite clear on this subject; they call community work 'counter-organisation' to win people over to the government and 'frustrate the enemy'.[9] From a radical point of view, community organisation and action can be an effective defence for people; it can also break down some barriers of isolation. It is not, however, powerful enough to be a medium for significant change.

Libertarian social work

The weaknesses of anti-psychiatry and community work are those of libertarian social work in general: it is less a strategy than a patchwork of initiatives. The best exponents of the libertarian case I know of are the Americans Clark and Jaffe.[10] They argue that 'only after an extensive process of personal change is an individual competent to dictate what programs are feasible for larger numbers'. Such change is to be accomplished and spread by the establishment of 'transitional communities' based either around practice and experiment in a residential setting or around task-centred advice and activism. In these communities people are to be enabled to discard their enforced roles, including those of helper and helped, and to work together to create a sharing of experience and a collective security. The task of their members is to raise awareness, and promote the possibility not only of opposing the prevailing order but of feeling better for it, and that difference is more rewarding than conformity. Some libertarian groups, communes or co-operatives are introverted and cannot really be considered as transitional. However, libertarians who are working for change do not just see the alternative society quietly springing up within the framework of the old one, but stress the role of wider community activism and participation in the belief that if institutional barriers and prejudices are broken down, the road to individual freedom will be wide open.

Though often sharing a Marxist critique of capitalism, libertarians attempt to achieve revolutionary change without abandoning the simple and essential freedoms of primitive rebellion. But because of the consequent distrust of organisations and institutions, libertarian groups work on a small scale and continually face isolation or absorption into the welfare network.

The problem of money

Every venture has to function in a capitalist world and has to accept some degree of compromise in order to survive. It is no use abolishing money if rates and fares have to be paid. The term 'transitional community' can cover groups ranging from therapeutic communes to simple advice centres, but all of them need continuous financing. Fund-raisers are faced with the need to choose between community appeals, which in one sense make the people they work with poorer than they are already, and approaching public bodies, charities or private business for donations, in which case they risk inspection or even management of their activities. Politics risk dilution by having to be expressed in semi-professional terms.

The alternative to sponsorship is a shoe-string existence which may set an example but can also result in an undermining of the project's worth. This has been particularly true of groups based on a critique of psychiatry because, whatever their ambitions, they have generally been limited to helping people who share their initial assumptions, and rarely have the resources in space, time or people to cope with those who display apparently unreachable aggression, delusions, desperation or disruptiveness. Eventually they too have to fall back on hospital treatment, often after far too long a delay, and professionals point to such failures as proof of the over-ambitious nature of the critique. Against this, it must of course be pointed out that the balance of resources is one-sided. Economics, the emphasis on nuclear relationships and the battery-chicken design of much modern housing all militate against the organic growth of communal groups capable of responding consistently to stress. In such a context one success is worth many failures.

Stealing libertarian clothes

Some alternative ideas appear to have sufficient potential for innovating professionals to take them over or steal their methods with the intent of reinforcing society rather than recreating it. The success of informal advice centres has forced central and local government to legitimate such activity, and where possible found their own. Advocacy has been institutionalised into the structure of social services with the recognition of welfare rights as a specialism and no longer sports much pretension to radicalism, though it is surprising how many social workers still do not actively take up their clients' cases.[11] Tenants' associations are frequently encouraged by housing managers eager to have a buffer to help them cool out grievances. Similarly, many public authorities have eventually realised how the funding of their own advice centres can not only squeeze out the radicals but add a protective function. One example at national level is the government-sponsored advisory service for immigrants (U. K. I. A. S.), which sorts out procedural complaints but is prevented from confronting the oppression of the immigration process itself. It is possible that a similar fate will befall the women's refuges which are opening throughout the country. Authorities ignored the problems of battered women until Erin Pizzey's squat in Chiswick. Now there is an attempt to set up local council-controlled refuges which are conventionally run and exclude the possibility of building up women's consciousness.

Sometimes co-option is more effective than replacing a facility. This was what happened to the squatting movement of the 1960s, which suffered defections by liberals anxious over militant tactics and by revolutionaries. Many squatters saw the housing problem as one of matching homeless people with empty houses, and were willing to accommodate with councils which were prepared to grant suitable concessions. The left argued that no amount of squatting would of itself solve the housing problem; a concerted movement was needed and the squatters should not allow themselves to be bought off. The arguments, which were mainly over short- and long-term perspectives, became muddled and ended with both sides accusing each other of betrayal.[12] As a few councils realised that it was possible to make better use of short-life property, they began negotiations which culminated in detailed agreements permitting squatting associations to manage such property on the council's behalf. Overnight the squatters' leaders became cheap-rate bureaucrats and, although their administration was flexible and humane, their impetus was lost. The number of homeless has remained as large and the squatters' organisations were limited to providing advice rather than practical help. Though some working people did, as Ron Bailey says, gain the experience of successful struggle against the state, by 1977 rents were soaring, construction was stuttering to a halt and squatting had become for the first time a criminal offence.

The fate of the squatters illustrates the dangers of participation, another empty vogue which has come to nothing, partly because without a radical restructuring of the agency the interests of clients and of social services are often opposed, and partly because it is mere tokenism, the presence of a reliable client on a policy-making body who wields little power but legitimates decisions. Such representatives often become part of the new establishment. Libertarians within the social services often perform a similar function, acting as tame radicals to prove the department's breadth of vision. Outside the institutional system those who reject formal organisation can at least feel that they are acting with some sort of revolutionary purpose. Within the social services there is little to distinguish such radicals from professionals who believe simply in 'outreach', or making social work more accessible to clients. Decentralisation, patch systems, welfare-rights work and intermediate treatment are some of the attempts to make services relevant; they are hardly the stuff of radicalism and have the advantage, from an official point of view, of containing discontent and increasing neighbourhood control. Such proposals do not have to be opposed; they can bring improvements, but cannot in themselves change the purpose or character of social work. Similarly an informal style and new methods of personal communication are gaining popularity; used correctly they can break down certain inhibitions, but they are only techniques, not a philosophy. Encounter groups have become the Tupperware parties of the progressive middle class, and these cosmetics of the new social work cannot disguise the aging of the profession.

Overcoming isolation

There can be no doubt about the absolute necessity of a wide-ranging network of alternative facilities which operate on principles opposed to conventional ideology. Nor must revolutionary socialists underestimate the need for personal change. My purpose in criticising this approach has not been to denigrate, but to illustrate its limitations. Working at the grass roots confers authenticity without much corresponding power. On the other hand, joining a governmental body cannot but institutionalise to some degree; need is no longer felt but becomes something to be dealt with as conveniently as possible. This dilemma can be further illustrated by two examples. The first is an advice bureau in a decaying urban area which bombarded the housing department with complaints so that the workers there were on the receiving end of criticism and abuse for policies and organisation over which in most instances they had no control. As a result of their exasperation, they won union-branch approval for industrial action; they would no longer accept any calls from voluntary organisations. The council were delighted and the bureau stymied. Those social workers who opposed such action were generally felt to be just as bad.

On the other hand, as social workers we can only form a partial liaison with grass-roots groups and have to be careful not to try taking them over. Richard Bryant has described how social workers tried their utmost to assist one mining community during the long strike of 1972 but found they could not escape suspicion. He concludes that

> in times of crisis and national conflict, the public identity of professional workers cannot be divorced from how local groups view the total institutional structures of which the professional worker is a part.[13]

If radical social work is to be of any practical effect, it must find a way of breaking down institutional barriers. The revolutionary socialist thesis on which this book has been based is that just as we can begin to understand the demands and organisation of our job only if we analyse it as workers within a capitalist economy, so we can break through both the artificial and the more substantial barriers which divide us only by linking up as workers with the labour movement and the organisations of other exploited groups. The rest of the chapter will discuss this strategy in more detail, and it can be usefully applied to the two examples just quoted. The harassment of obdurate officials, whether trade-unionists or not, is clearly justified if persuasion fails. Nevertheless it is dangerous simply to regard institutions as monolithic. In order to persuade officials of one's worth, it may be important to consider what can be done for them. In one social security office with which, as a social worker, I was continually in dispute, the atmosphere changed considerably after I offered to raise support for their wage-claim in my own union and to co-operate with whatever industrial action they decided on. A similarly sympathetic approach by the advice centre to the housing department might well have produced a better response.

About Bryant's comments, one must suggest that reaction may depend not on the individuals involved but on the public identity which they choose. Obviously there were also cultural factors at work in his example. But offering help as a trade unionist is a very different matter from doing so as a social worker. One's union may come in for ribald comment, but the relationship becomes not one of compassion but of shared struggle, and whatever knowledge or resources one may possess by being a social worker are of only secondary significance.

At another level, an active proletarian consciousness seems vital for the development of alternative therapy. We do not need less therapeutic skill but its very different expression. As an Italian writer has commented, we need to be able to 'relate the problems of those needing help to the social, political and other issues in his or her community which generate those problems'.[14] The Marxist mental health team in Gorizia, which she discusses, stresses the importance of common class understanding and consciousness in order to remove the traditional therapeutic roles and categories, and discover new ones 'grounded in needs expressed by the working class'. Only an active participation in the labour movement can create and maintain such consciousness as well as spreading a different understanding of illness among workers' organisations themselves.

It is for this reason that revolutionaries generally prefer to work in the local authority setting. Voluntary organisations appear to offer more freedom but are often even more petty and conservative in internal policy. Both their projects and their staff tend to be isolated from mainstream development; while their experiments may be valuable, much of their importance is lost unless they are applied throughout the principal system by which our work is organised.

Foundations of a Marxist strategy

In order to be effective, radicalism has to be underpinned by trade-union and, indeed, political organisation, not just for our own protection but to ensure our continued relevance. Liberal critics have picked up a long-standing uncertainty in the radical camp by claiming that Marxism has little to contribute to actual practice; conservatives have been riled enough to suggest that if we see such little use in social work, we would be better employed elsewhere. I hope that this book and the perhaps more temperate account of Corrigan and Leonard will at least demonstrate the relevance of Marxist explanation; furthermore it could, I think, be shown that

Case Con, despite what many thought was strident rhetoric, has had a very considerable and beneficial effect on the way the job is done. In the next chapter I shall look at practice in general terms. We must, however, admit that the potential for change in or by social work is very small; radical prescriptions often disappoint on paper because they seem either impracticable or simply tame, depending on the extent to which liberalism is capable of absorbing them. Once again it must be stressed that the major change must be in attitude rather than technique; radicalism must aim at changing the way we regard ourselves and our clients. We do not offer principles and techniques which masquerade as being fundamental to morality or value-free but are in fact a disguised form of politics. Instead, we declare overtly political principles some of which can be legitimately expressed in social work and others in more directly political organisation.

Joining the union

Union membership is hardly the most glamorous of attributes; the unions, we know, tend to be clumsy, bureaucratic, inept and limited in function. NALGO, to which most social workers belong, still calls itself an association; there can be few less inspiring rallying points for action even though radicals have gingered it up considerably in the last few years.

Nearly all social workers now accept the need for some collective association to protect their interests and secure more favourable pay and conditions, but there is disagreement over what type of association it should be, and a general reluctance to participate actively. Radicals argue that the major criterion for choice should be the capability of our organisation to form links with other workers on an equal basis. This means supporting other workers' actions as we hope they would understand and support our own.

In addition, we have a particular contribution to make by attempting to ensure that the labour movement protects and promotes the interests of workers not directly represented within it, like pensioners, housewives and the unemployed. It is of vital importance that organised labour finds some way of allowing these groups to participate. Trade unions are the most powerful existing bodies for the protection of workers' interests and in matters concerning clients we should be in no doubt about the extent of their influence. Local links are maintained through trades councils, which, though often bureaucratic, are sometimes prepared to take significant action. A minor example will suffice. All of us face an increasing burden of fuel debt, which is often beyond the means of claimants and the lower paid. During 1976 instances abounded of young families and elderly people having their fuel supplies cut off. Trades councils not only contain delegates from unions whose members are required to perform this task; they also nominate representatives to the gas and electricity consumer councils. In my own trades council a long-standing industrial militant who was on the electricity council spoke on behalf of the executive against a motion originating from the Right to Fuel Campaign by asserting that there were no cut-offs in our area which caused hardship. A social worker delegate from NALGO was immediately able to counter this statement with examples, the motion was held over, an investigation begun, and sufficient pressure was then brought on the Board to change its policy. Similar actions in other areas eventually produced a national change. This is a good example of how community and union organisations can complement each other.

But essentially we join the union to pursue our own interests, and social workers are at last abandoning earnest self-sacrifice in pursuit of better pay and holidays as well as working conditions which can improve the response to clients' needs. I do not mean paraphernalia like air-conditioning or pot plants, but space, telephones, administrative back-up and adequate staffing. In some areas the union has gained the right to be consulted about any innovations which may affect staff. Some grumble that unions have done little for social workers. From a sectional point of view that is true, but what have social workers as a body ever done for the union? Our precious self-regard has not made us a popular group in other departments.

More realistic complaint can be made about the nature of unions in general. Radicalism in social work is the harder because it means radicalising the union as well. Unions appear not just to outsiders but also to their members as monolithic structures with incomprehensible and niggling rule-books, in which participation without detailed knowledge is all but impossible and whose officials seem not only to be more intent on a 'constructive' relationship with management than on cultivating their own membership, but to be doing very nicely out of it. This is not necessarily the fault of the officials but of the whole Topsy-like structure of unions. Prolonged vilification will achieve as little as organisational tinkering. What is needed is a rank-and-file policy which will develop members' interest in and knowledge of the union so that they can use it better. The accusation of niggling is understandable but usually arises out of a misunderstanding of union function and ignorance of the issues involved. A scheme which management represents as the path to a better future may look very different from ground level. Also, unions exist to protect all their members both present and future. If, for instance, a new job is allowed to go through on an inappropriate grading, the post-holder may be irrevocably disadvantaged and a precedent will have been set. Restrictive practices do make some sense from the workers' point of view and will continue to do so as long as workers' interests are considered last by employers.

For many social workers the greatest fear of becoming involved in a union is the possibility of strike action, although even professional associations are being forced to endorse the withdrawal of labour on occasions. I would refer here to my arguments about 'caring' in Chapter 5, and ask at what point social workers actually care enough to make a stand over an issue. While militant tactics are not to be embarked on lightly and many problems can be resolved short of direct confrontation, a readiness to back up one's demands is sometimes the only way to achieve them. Although any strike must include provision for genuine emergency and apparent militants have on occasion visited clients about whom they were extremely concerned during a strike, one suspects that reluctance to withdraw results at least as much from an unconscious fear of proving inessential as from genuine concern or political opposition. Nor is going on strike any easy option; it can mean working harder and longer than on a normal day because of the need to gather and solidify support.

Imagination will supply a host of tactics which stop short of total withdrawal. In Sheffield the upgrading of welfare assistants was secured by all sections of the social services refusing to use telephones except in emergencies. On the other hand, the formation of night-duty teams has been won only by a refusal to perform those duties. Other successful withdrawals have been to prevent victimisation and to obtain adequate working accommodation. Many of these have received the sympathy or active support of clients who are affected; it is vital to involve clients as much as possible. Sometimes militant action has been taken directly on behalf of clients, usually against cuts in spending or in cases of homelessness. These have involved occupying offices or other buildings, or, as in the famous case of the Islington squatters, literally taking to the barricades in their support.[15] Clients should, of course, make the ultimate choices about such action.

Apart from gaining the immediate goals, there is an additional purpose to militant action which affects both clients and social workers. The point of organising together is to assert some choice and control over one's own life and work. Those who take part may develop a sense of importance and self-respect which they never before possessed. New skills can be learnt and clients in particular may for the first time gather confidence and pride as well as gaining a sense of belonging if the action is on a reasonably large scale. If we believe that we are imprisoned by the structure and expectations of society, we have to make ourselves strong enough to break out.

Any union action needs a democratic decision in order to be fully effective. The best union organisation so far suggested for social services workers is based upon the recognition of worksites as the basic unit, each with its own shop steward elected from among the membership. Depending on the size of departments these stewards should form a committee or committees with direct negotiating rights with management. Stewards need to have official time off from work in order to carry out their duties, which include maintaining a continual flow of relevant information between members and their representatives. NALGO is at present moving towards a universal shop-steward system but some of those in existence are hardly worthy of the name. Union members, particularly those who complain about lack of democracy, should stir themselves to be clear about the available alternatives and to make what seems the most effective choice. Many people fear getting sucked into overwhelming involvement but apathy is one of the greatest time-wasters. It only takes a slight general increase in interest and participation to make union business far less onerous.

Some social workers accept all these arguments but hesitate to support NALGO, not least because of its inefficiency. But a union is what its members make it. Historically it is the most appropriate and, despite a clumsy structure which mirrors that of local government, it has been changing character over the last few years. Though known as the gaffers' union, over half its members earn below the national average wage and have been stirring. In some areas frustration with NALGO's bureaucracy and the local domination of the union by senior officers have persuaded social workers to transfer to NUPE. This move can offer some local advantages but is not always welcome to other NUPE members, and in wider negotiations, where NUPE is bound into exactly the same cumbersome Whitley Council procedure, it offers considerably less representation.[16] NALGO also has a well-known action group of several years' standing which has exerted considerable influence, not least in pressing for a shop-steward system. Others advocate a separate union, either based around B. A. S. W. or a separate social workers' grouping. But B. A. S. W.'s exclusivity and irrelevance hardly makes it the nucleus of a new union, while the small group in the north-east who have started a British Union of Social Workers (B. U. S. W.), which they hoped would also gather in residential workers, home-helps and other social services, has failed to gain much support. Such groups have little to gain from being associated with us, and the move to smaller unions only encourages fragmentation. It is probably significant that B. U. S. W. was founded by a social-work tutor. The most important aspect for radicals of being members of NALGO or, at a pinch, NUPE, is the direct connection they have with other local authority workers. Cross-departmental contact at worksite level is urgently needed to improve our understanding of each other's problems and hence our performance.

The social work strike of 1978–9

The discussion of unionisation above was written before the events of 1978–9, which saw social workers on strike in sixteen local authorities over the right to negotiate locally for regrading. The average length of the strikes was about three months; but social workers in Tower Hamlets were on strike for nearly nine months, and whereas Islington social workers achieved a locally negotiated settlement after only a few weeks, social workers in Newcastle were, in early 1982, still disputing what they regarded as the punitive terms on which they had been forced back to work. Some aspects of the strike have been covered in Bolger *et al.*'s *Towards Socialist Welfare Work*; my own comments are intended to be complementary, but an adequate account is still needed, not least because a process of selective professional amnesia has consigned both the achievements and the experiences (good and bad) of the strike into an obscure corner of social work history.

The action originally caught many social workers by surprise, for even those who were local union activists had not always followed the progress of the claim through NALGO's procedural machinery. It was not until social workers in Southwark, Newcastle and Tower Hamlets withdrew their labour during August 1978 that most of their colleagues elsewhere realised that there was even an issue, and that it had been official NALGO policy since the 1977 conference to seek local negotiations for regrading. It was then up to each NALGO branch to formulate a claim based on the increase in duties and responsibilities since 1971 (a widely accepted negotiating process), to present it to its local council, and, depending on the response, to determine what action to take. The pace at which this was carried out normally depended on the degree of unionisation already achieved. When negotiations proved impossible to sustain, each branch then had to decide whether to strike, and this accounted for the piecemeal progress of the action. Some branches, like Bradford, voted narrowly to remain at work; those which did strike were mostly in metropolitan areas (Cheshire was a notable exception) and from councils controlled by the Labour Party. In general there was widespread support for the claim for regrading, both within the social work profession, and among NALGO members as a whole. However, many people found the arguments for local negotiations more difficult to accept (they are discussed in *Towards Socialist Welfare Work*) and used these reservations as a reason for opposing strike action.

It soon became clear that the employers had decided to retain a national prescription, and were more interested in using the regrading claim to apply more control over what they saw as undesirable social work militancy in the professional sphere. A first offer was firmly rejected; as solidarity began to spread, both the employers and NALGO's national negotiators seemed taken aback by the organisation and commitment shown by the local strike committees supported by an *ad hoc* body, the All London Social Workers Action Group, and the NALGO Action Group. A wide variety of tactics were used to make the strikes more effective by hitting the employing authorities in areas where closure or inconvenience would have more impact than in Social Services Departments. The strikers reasoned that many authorities might not be too displeased at having their social services halted. There were pickets of town halls and civic centres in attempts to halt post (successful) and fuel (less so). This was an entirely new experience for most social workers and one which forced them to reassess their relationship with the labour movement; many were astounded by the co-operation shown by members of other unions like the post workers, and even security men. But even where councils were put to massive inconvenience, as in Tower Hamlets and Liverpool, they did not budge. Meanwhile some basic social services were maintained depending on who had been called out in the different areas and on the number of non-strikers. Some strike committees, including Sheffield, where there was an agency shop agreement with only a handful of social workers belonging to unions other than NALGO, maintained a strictly controlled emergency service, with the branch issuing instructions to other NALGO members in the department, and the councillors stressing the need to avoid needless provocation of the strikers. However, most NALGO branches (representing all local NALGO members) moderated their support by proving reluctant to escalate the action; this was encouraged by the national negotiators, who, despite the policy of recognising local claims, seemed to be approaching a national settlement. Additional restrictions were imposed by NALGO's own archaic rules which, for example, allowed NALGO members to break their own union's picket-lines, while requesting members of other unions not to do so. However, striking social workers did benefit from the rules over strike pay (soon to be changed after the strike) which maintained income at 55 per cent of gross wages, a generous level of support from other members of NALGO without which the strikes might not have occurred at all, but which sometimes caused embarrassment when approaching other workers for support.

At the end of November the employers made a national offer dividing social workers and social work assistants into five grades. To the negotiators' reported surprise, it was rejected by eleven out of the twelve NALGO District Committees. But despite this near unity, a very similar package, with a small margin of local flexibility couched in terms advantageous to the employers, was presented very shortly afterwards. Despite a further rejection from the strikers, the National Executive Committee decided to resolve the impasse by putting the offer up for debate at a national meeting of all local government branches, many with no social work members but with a financial interest in ending the strike. This reliance upon an uninformed decision posed interesting questions about union democracy which have never been fully discussed. But with the date set for 26 January 1979, several weeks ahead, all hopes for further progress were frozen, an apt metaphor as pickets struggled through a bitter winter period, and the focus of the strike changed from pressurising councils to persuading the rest of the union to reject the Executive recommendation. Only Islington social workers managed to achieve a local settlement. Finally, the national conference accepted the report after an acrimonious debate which reflected credit on neither side; local committees were left to negotiate their own interpretations of an unwanted 'agreement' which the employers were intent on applying as literally as possible, knowing that the strikers were now under strong national pressure to settle. One by one the striking branches returned to work, until in April only Tower Hamlets was left with a solitary struggle lasting until the summer as social workers there fought proposals for major cutbacks.

There are many problems in assessing the results and effects of the strikes. The emotive issue of whether it was morally right to strike became more clouded because of the complex and different claims, the different experiences in each strike area, especially in dealing with rifts both with non-strikers and among the strikers themselves, and finally because of the long drawn-out process in which it became increasingly unclear whether our main opponents were the employers or the union. I shall offer some brief comments first on the trade union, and second on the social work aspects of the strikes, in the knowledge that mine is at best a subjective and limited account.

The strikes did not achieve their main purpose of demolishing the national prescription for grading, nor did they result in any immediate and substantial improvement in pay for a significant number of the strikers. These disappointments and a resentment both against the union leadership and the employers left a bitter taste in many strikers' mouths. In some areas management sought to exploit the new framework to penalise those who had been on strike by placing them initially on the lowest level and introducing quotas and assessments as barriers to progression. But those responsible for devising the gradings had, by all accounts, little direct experience of fieldwork, and at local level both sides tended to agree that the different tiers of responsibility made little sense in practical terms, the more so after the Standing Conference of Strike Committees recommended that the union negotiators should begin by interpreting the levels so severely that, if they were rigidly adhered to, most offices would grind to a halt. As the stronger areas achieved more advantageous settlements, a process of evening up occurred, though the national system remains as unworkable and potentially divisive as ever, is quite unsuited to decentralised work, and is still used to penalise newly trained and unqualified workers.

But if the strikes were certainly no outright victory, they were far from being a defeat, even in financial terms. It is highly unlikely that the improvements that were won could have been gained without action. Other workers in social services have, in general, done less well, and contracting public expenditure would have rendered any more substantial improvement in grading out of the question; it is likely that prolonged negotiation would have achieved far less, except perhaps for an elite few. Instead, a combination of local settlements and wage drift have brought more and more social workers on to the higher scales except where strict quotas exist; although there is still no adequate match up between job responsibility and salary, we are at least closer to comparable occupations.

Strictly from a trade-union viewpoint, the strikes, although costly, were, I think, successful at many different levels, not least because awareness of the union was vastly increased, and with that went a degree of commitment rarely seen before in NALGO. Individual social workers gained a quite different view of the social power structure in which they and other workers are involved and developed not only a new assertiveness but quite unexpected forms of collective experience and solidarity, some of which are described in *Towards Socialist Welfare Work*; one spin-off was a significant improvement in our physical health. A great deal was learnt about the relationships between different local authority and health service workers, especially since social workers were forced to go out and sell their action. However, the intensity of such experience was not shared by those who refused or were reluctant to participate actively, and was seemingly quite incomprehensible to social workers not on strike. The lessons of self-organisation, both within and between authorities, and the strength discovered, have stood us in good stead when fighting the depredations of Thatcherism. A decisive break in tradition had been taken; now that the exhaustion and resentment have worn off, social workers are not only more prepared than before to take industrial action when it seems necessary, but also, before they commit themselves, are in a much better position to ask searching questions about its aims and effect. Finally, I think that the union as a whole learnt valuable lessons, some of which were put into practice the following year in the highly successful national dispute over comparability payments for all local government workers. It must also be said that the leadership, despite what was in my view a mistaken assessment of the action and of the employers' offer, have remained publicly firm in face of criticisms of social workers from other members resentful at the use of the strike fund, and have, quite correctly, emphasised the role of Annual Conference as the major decision-making body.

The link between these considerations and more professional issues is that the strikes were not simply about money, but were an expression of the rising tide of disillusion and resentment at the demands made on social workers and the structures in which they were expected to operate. Here again, despite severe problems, the actions were, at a local level, positive experiences for many, perhaps most of the participants. As I suggested above, being on strike was for many people a real opportunity to exert some democratic control over the structure of their daily lives. This feeling was obviously stronger for the most committed, but, once the decision to strike was taken, many of the opponents rallied round to help make the action successful. Unexpected talents came to the fore; the strike committees were open, reporting to regular mass meetings, producing bulletins, and involving workers who had not necessarily played leading or active roles before. As in most industrial struggles, individuals learnt skills, from public speaking to duplicating, which could later have a wider application. While for some this was making the best of an unwanted situation, for others it was the flowering of new opportunity for self-expression. Most of all an assertive and pervasive solidarity arose, entirely replacing the fragmentation and competition of ordinary working life. This aspect was so marked that one Director of Social Services, having called a mass meeting of staff after the return to work, actually invited those who had found they had a talent for organisation to consider whether social work was really the appropriate occupation for them; she seemed unaware of the double meaning which could be attached to her words.

Of course, the longer the strike wore on, the more jaded everybody became. But going back to work was an emotional upheaval, for a few almost akin to bereavement, though it felt different in every authority and probably on every work-site. Most fieldworkers were determined to remain grouped together in order to maintain our collective spirit and resist possible victimisation. In Leeds the Social Workers Action Group was formed; in Sheffield, fieldworkers' groups were set up on the work-sites and part of the strike fund used to launch a social workers' magazine as a continuation of *Strike News*. The national grouping of strike committees attempted to transform itself into an informal organisation of all social services shop stewards including residential and administrative workers. This helped build some bridges but soon became unwieldy and collapsed. In some places there was hostility from management and also from colleagues who had objected to the strike and picketing; there were definite attempts to reassert control, though managers were nervous. But, in general, as we sought to reassess and renew working relationships which had been broken for many weeks, there was a growing feeling, encouraged by liberal managers and the professional lobby, of 'Let's forget it ever happened'. Except where there was a need to remain grouped together to fight cuts, the overt solidarity of fieldworkers gradually disintegrated and staff turnover eroded group memory. The individualistic processes of social work reasserted themselves, though less comprehensively than before.

From a social work point of view, the strike was, in the end, probably rather less significant than anybody thought at the time, except in so far as public interest was kindled, although in the media much of the debate was still poorly informed and caught up with the usual hostility to striking workers. Those of us who had hoped to use the strike to discuss and initiate radically new forms of relationships with client groups were disappointed, though many healthy discussions occurred with individual clients, especially on returning to work. In the initial stages we were not only very busy, but also needing to rethink our own positions: adopting the exclusively trade-union consciousness which was needed both to prosecute the strikes and to resist our professionally induced 'guilt' meant that we became somewhat closed off, a phenomenon which affects most industrial strikers as well. Decisions had to be made whether to run emergency services; some areas refused to do so on the grounds that they would simply be allowing the employers to diminish the effects of the strikes. Others, like Sheffield, where the agency shop arrangement gave the union more control and where fieldwork services had halted almost entirely, ran limited services which provoked much discussion. Also, because clients were, as usual, isolated from one another, it was impossible to contact them directly, if this had not been done before the strikes. Finally, the hostility of the employers, the press, B.A.S.W. and social work journals forced us into a false insularity, though it taught us a good deal about those bodies. Many residential and other staff still at work did their best to mollify clients in need, especially children in care who were unable to achieve planned moves; others, however, took the opportunity to vent the inbuilt hostility to social workers I have mentioned earlier in the book. In the end the fulminations of those representing official social work thought proved to be largely ill-founded. In Sheffield, when we somewhat belatedly took to the streets with a petition, we were amazed at the general level of support and the amount of contact which passers-by seemed, directly or indirectly, to have had with social workers; similar experiences were reported elsewhere. Subsequent surveys have suggested that the public standing of social work was not much affected and that clients were generally, but not always, tolerant and supportive (see, for example, *New Society*, 7 May 1981, pp. 216–18). Undoubtedly there were some who were hurt (as indeed we were, for being driven, as we saw it, to withdraw our labour). But without wanting to minimise those feelings, we considered the long-term interests of the service to be at stake; if nothing else, the problems of paid caring on behalf of a tight-fisted state were starkly highlighted. The impact on unmet need is still harder to judge. We were caught in a trap not entirely of our making and were often judged by double standards. Either we maintained we were essential, which left us open to accusations of callousness; or, if we argued that we were not in most instances a life-and-limb service, we were said to be undermining our case. The D.H.S.S. published an inconclusive survey of the effect in Tower Hamlets; in Sheffield co-operation was refused by NALGO and subsequently by the Department for fear of official bias. The incoming Tory government eventually set up an enquiry which reported in May 1982 (Barclay Report).

The strikes also taught us something both about other agencies' ability and willingness to intervene and help clients if there were extra moral kudos in doing so when we were unavailable; and our emergency service gave us valuable insights into management priorities under pressure. Residential placements or payments of cash seemed much easier to obtain as unnecessary procedures were circumvented now that management was pressing social workers for help, rather than the other way round.

All in all, the strikes were a prolonged and confused episode in social work history which did have important repercussions for social workers in reassessing their place in the power structure. Despite the difficulties and recriminations I do not believe the effect to have been negative; certainly those social work departments which took no part but were subsequently able to wring benefits out of the new gradings made considerable gains. From time to time I hear or read about residues of bitterness in some places. It was inevitable that such feelings should have been generated and should linger because the very fact of the action undermined so many assumptions on which the social work hierarchy is based; not the least of these was the well-known social work game, 'I'm on your side really you know?', played by social workers with their clients and managers with their staff. In my view this was an egg worth breaking. But the greatest difficulties seem to have occurred where there was acute management intransigence; the lesson of that should be obvious.

My own reaction after restarting work was one of disorientation; the experiences were so disparate that it was hard to relate to them, and while others kept up their new militant consciousness I found my interest drifting, for a while at any rate, more to the specifics of the job and to the task of trying to find some way of recreating both for clients and for ourselves the enhanced and exhilarating freedom from orthodox modes of expression which we, as strikers, had from time to time been lucky enough to enjoy. However, such exploration has been possible only in the context of struggle against the restraints imposed by government cutbacks affecting services, living standards and workers' organisations; part of that resistance has been based upon the foundation of our experience of industrial action.

Limitations of union work within the agency

Workers in all trade unions are becoming readier to take up a much broader range of issues, despite attempts by government and courts to stand in their way. But in our sphere of work there is still a great deal of uncertainty as to how far trade unions should become involved in 'professional' issues like the scope of residential care or mental welfare duties. There have been instances of managements refusing to listen to social workers' views on such topics when they are speaking as union members. This is absurd. At an institutional level, unions and affiliated bodies are asked to make nominations or give evidence to many different public bodies, including school governing committees, the magistracy and health authorities. While unions are naturally reluctant to step out of their recognised sphere of competence, they attempt (or should attempt) to represent the broad views of the labour movement on whatever matters are up for debate or decision. Many social workers have no other way of advancing even mildly socialist or class arguments about the content, priorities or funding of their work; even when they have tried to do so, as in Leeds, they have been forced back into the union machinery because of hostility from management or employers.

But such a broadening of scope brings its own problems of legitimacy. Although it is the responsibility of shop stewards to lead as well as represent their members, they have, in such matters, to be even more aware than usual that they may be advancing too far down a different path from many of their members. If there is a consensus, the union position will be unusually strong. But class-based arguments, especially when applied to specific or small-scale topics, may well not carry the majority, even of shop stewards. Additionally there are many situations where different interests among members are affected or where (as in the restructuring of social services towards greater democracy and accountability) socialist principles which might lead trade unionists to support such moves may conflict with the bureaucratic protections offered to members under their existing service conditions. To abrogate such protections without obtaining alternative safeguards would be the height of liberal folly; the council would get the prestige, while social workers take the bombardment. If the union runs too far ahead of itself in advocating change, it may leave its members defenceless. Alternatively its credibility may be undermined, especially if a shop stewards committee has been allowed or seduced by a weak or cunning management into acting as a surrogate or second-tier control over its members. It can also happen that arguments about change degenerate into procedural wrangles, the importance of which is lost to the general membership, who are then manoeuvred by management into seeing the union as a blocking mechanism, remote from the interests of the membership. To sum up, a move from the traditional shop stewards' tasks needs a great deal of preparation. One helpful step can be for shop stewards to sponsor working parties or forums for discussion of policy issues; these can often be more successful than similar management-sponsored ventures. But such discussions or consequent interventions should not be separated from the union machinery, which is still the only effective way both to organise and to protect members advocating radical or socialist change.

Unions and politics

Joining a union should not be a purely self-interested act but a recognition of a direct link, a shared fate, with all those who are exploited by the owners or controllers of capital. Union membership can provide a sense of solidarity extended far beyond one's own workplace. It is sometimes hard to feel this when engaged in routine minutiae or the inevitable bickering which characterises much inter-union activity, but at times of crisis the fundamental spirit rises again. Right-wingers argue that unions should be concerned only with their own pay and conditions; this is a travesty of what unionism means. It also ignores the fact that pay is now an overtly political matter. However, unions do suffer one major structural defect which inhibits their potential as instruments for change. Although they are at present the most powerful force directly available to workers, they are irremediably tied to the economy which engendered them. Unions were not formed to overthrow capitalism, however crucial a part they may play in doing so, but to defend workers from the onslaughts of employers so that they could gain as many as possible of the fruits of capitalism for themselves. The consequent artificial division between economics and politics is responsible for much of the blinkered fumbling of union business. It has also led to governments seeking and achieving union support to shore up a failing economy. Anarchy and poverty are posed as the only available alternatives to exploitation, and unions, by their traditional logic and structure, are led to conform as far as their members will allow. This is why union commitment to social change depends on rank-and-file pressure.

Political consciousness, though basically determined by economics, is of an essentially different order involving, above all, imagination to see how things might be otherwise and an attempt to create appropriate change. Political organisations are more limited in membership since they demand commitment to a set of ideals and exclude those with contrary beliefs, but broader in scope since they admit anyone to membership, no matter what their occupational status. They are more flexible both in thought and in action than unions can ever be and should be capable of synthesising differing experiences in order to provide inspiring and practical leadership. Socialist parties differ in the emphasis they place on leadership and organisation; some radicals distrust them altogether. Yet there can be no denying the need for activity and thought on this level. Radicals, it seems to me, have no option but to adopt allegiance, if not to a definite organisation, at least to a general political trend. The essence of radicalism is that it never stops questioning but drives on through all the different spheres, refusing to accept divisions and compartments until it reaches a genuine synthesis of thought and action. Limiting radicalism to social work practice would be of little more objective value than being, say, a radical cyclist.

Now that the welfare state is once again a political battleground, the division between politics and union affairs is even more arbitrary. Unions come under fire from their enemies however they react. Restricting themselves to economic matters brings accusations of narrow-minded greed. Broader intervention is called political interference. But the present assault upon public expenditure is not just about our wages and livelihoods, nor even about the services we provide, but about the sort of society we wish to live in, the distribution of whatever economic surplus exists, the extent and nature of employment, the selection of economic priorities, and the interests they reflect. Trade-union policy will be crucial in deciding the outcome.

Politics and social workers

The attempt, refusal or undertaking of help for others is not a neutral activity since it assumes a certain limit of possibilities. Social work orthodoxy attempts to preserve the fiction of neutrality by suggesting that the social worker is informed by certain professional values of a universal character. Radicals argue that such values are either so universal as to be empty of significance or else part of a particular liberal ideology whose peculiar conceit is a denial of its own existence as an ideology. Social workers' advice and practice in particular situations are bound to be affected by their stance on, for instance, unemployment, women's liberation, homosexuality, emigration to South Africa or joining the Army. It is only fair to inform clients of our premises where appropriate. More than that, if respect for clients means anything, it includes their right to agree or disagree and to be supported or contradicted as the occasion demands. Occasionally political discussion forms the major part of an encounter; more usually it is preliminary to the task in hand.

Those who accuse radicals of using social work as a political platform appear deliberately to underrate the sensitivity of most radicals, the impatience of clients and the extent to which the accusers themselves are political performers. It does not take much observation to see how often clients' opinions and values falling within a conventional range gain acceptance and approval, while more unusual attitudes meet with silence, surprise or reproval. It is blithely assumed by writers like Butrym that a Christian motivation necessarily enhances the quality of social work and therefore operates to the client's advantage while politics can only manipulate.[17] Most radicals lean over backwards to avoid pushing their views on to clients, because we value freedom; our radicalism makes us conscious of how much our position can be abused. Yet while the merest whiff of politics evokes official censure, Christian social workers who campaign against abortion, discourage their clients from using contraceptive pills, show hostility or spread rumours about social workers who cohabit or are gay, gain respect and promotion. The religious approach, because it is more acceptable, is perhaps more open to abuse than the political. It would be ostrich tactics to ban either religion or politics from the social work arena; what matters is their application. Crude evangelising or propaganda that exploits clients' lack of power are clearly unacceptable, as, of course, is racism.

Dealing with racism and sexism in social work

I have, I hope, already emphasised the way in which our existing social expectations and institutions are biased against minorities and against women for the placing of this section not to be seen as mere tokenism. The explicit and detailed attention which these issues need has begun to be provided elsewhere. I think, however, that it is worth making the point that the social services, both in their structure and the manner of their implementation, cannot help reflecting such bias. Radicals will naturally challenge such institutionalised discrimination, but need also to examine their own behaviour for traits which reinforce socio-cultural patterns of domination. An understanding of the structural relationships between immigrant or black communities and the economy or state is not sufficient if it leads merely to a brittle white liberalism which takes no account of real conflicts or personal challenge. I think it is hard to work directly with black people without becoming more and more involved in the struggle against racism; certainly I have found the roots of a greater trust between myself and black clients when I have been able to meet them or their relations at demonstrations or other events. This consciousness should also make it much harder to pass over racist remarks by colleagues or white clients. It is important never to be seen to collude in such sentiments even at the risk of time-consuming and possibly fruitless arguments; silence only confers respectability and prolongs prejudice. It is also necessary to be aware of differences within the black communities. As a result, I would find it impossible to work with clients who are racialist enough to be active members of a fascist party unless they were open to argument. I would not be prepared to allow my help to be used indirectly to oppress others. If I find a person repugnant by temperament or belief, I would refer them on. I do not believe either that there is any place for racists in health or social services employment.

Sexism is of course much more prevalent, and sometimes even the norm; it pervades all the major areas of social work concern including the employment and income opportunities denied to women during recession, unequal treatment at the hand of legal and fiscal systems, oppressive expectation within the family and sexual harassment at work or outside. Although sometimes I think that strict segregationism by feminists defeats their own ends, it is clear that only women's self-organisation can hope to overcome the assumptions about women's inferiority, domestication or objectification that permeate our society. Given the success of organisations like Women's Aid and the Women's Therapy Centre, it would seem that there could be real opportunities for much more explicitly feminist social work; this need not initially be in the form of 'consciousness-raising' groups, though these would play an important part. For example, counselling offered by women for women, both in individual and group settings, is something that Social Services Departments could and should quite legitimately offer, especially in authorities with socialist aspirations; and there is also a Women in NALGO group.

One final note: sexual discrimination at work, whether against women or gays, is still prevalent and many departments operate, if unconsciously, on double or inconsistent standards of sexual morality. If these issues are raised directly as they affect us, we should understand rather more about our expectations of clients and our attitudes or behaviour towards them.

8

Opening out: limits and contradictions

It will be apparent from the discussion in the last chapter that what divides social workers who adhere to some kind of revolutionary philosophy from the rest of our colleagues is an unwillingness to commit ourselves wholly to those activities which can officially be construed as 'helping'. Because we are sceptical of their ultimate efficacy, we choose instead to devote a considerable amount of our time and energy to work which we argue is the only road to a longer-term solution to the problems which people in our society have to face. Whereas professionals, as Kay McDougall puts it,[1] turn their occupation into a way of life, revolutionaries seek to extend their way of life into their occupation, steering the difficult course between their own beliefs and values, those they are expected to purvey and enforce, and those of their clients. Sometimes, as in the case of the squatters, radical perspectives conflict, but if revolutionaries must understand that people's need is sometimes so urgent that they cannot afford to wage a long-term struggle, so groups which win their demands from the authorities need to realise both that their gain is likely to be ancther's loss, and that there are probably large numbers of others, so far unable to organise, who have similar needs. A victory loses much of its worth unless its lessons are extended; pressure-group and revolutionary politics may overlap but in essence they are quite distinct.

Given the inherent constrictions on social work which I have described, radicals, and especially revolutionary radicals who stress long-term strategies, have to confront two questions. Can there in fact be any form of social work which is genuinely radical? If not, can remaining in social work be justified? I have already suggested some kinds of answer to the second question and will return to it at the end of the chapter. I shall now attempt to pursue some of the dilemmas and possibilities of social work practice in a more positive way than hitherto.

Radicalism and socialist social work

Radicalism in social work, despite all the inherent difficulties, is not only viable but essential if we are to point the way to a new non-authoritarian caring. But the search for radical approaches has been constricted by the very concept of radicalism itself, which demands too much and offers too little. The quest for a form of radical social work which can not only be practised, but can also take its place on course curricula, has succeeded only in providing a broad umbrella for criticism, dissent and sporadic counter-organisation. The concept is too demanding because it cannot allow the incorporation of radical initiatives or the institutionalisation of radicals into tame dissenters without losing its essence; yet, as many critics have argued, the only other answer is to move outside the welfare establishment. Further, radicalism is no longer the property of the Left, if indeed it ever was. Our criticisms of the bureaucratisation of welfare and the self-deceptions of liberalism have been taken up by the New Right, riding on a tide of crude anti-statism. Some of the attacks on social welfare and professionalism by writers such as Morgan, Brewer and Lait coincide, if somewhat obliquely, with our own.[2] But their reassertion of authority, order and efficiency sits uneasily with their emphasis on freedom of choice, which of course is simply the freedom of the market. Brewer and Lait catch social work off balance by exposing the wooliness of its objectives and its lack of quantifiable effectiveness; they quite rightly demand some better justifications than self-professed good intentions. But the way in which they link their positivist approach with the introduction of the military concept of *triage* (after relief of suffering, help only those to whom prompt and thorough attention will probably make a difference in outcome) is either crude, cruel and almost certainly ineffective social engineering, or much less helpful than they suppose because of the ambiguous situations we have to deal with, and the very broad range of the phrase 'relief of social suffering'. The introduction of supposedly valueless quantification is in fact an aid to much closer control of both workers and clients, often for dubious ends. But at least such writers, despite failing to understand how social forces shape society, recognise that welfare is a political activity; others like Halmos or Davies use otherwise interesting ideas like 'equilibration' or 'maintenance' to deny the practical politics (as opposed to policy) of welfare work altogether, thus surrendering to the reality of state control.[3] Finally, when arguments similar to those of Morgan or Lait are used by Thatcherites to justify reductions in the living standards of working people, their intent is clearly unmasked. Nevertheless, as the authors of *Towards Socialist Welfare Work* point out, both the Right and the social democrats have a strategy: the Left must also devise one to counterpose and not rely on mere assertions of radicalism. These authors, among several others, now talk explicitly of socialist welfare work.

Of course, this rather grey phrase begs many questions, not least the meaning of 'socialist'. But recognition of the ideological content of welfare has legitimated both discussion and some possibility for practice in a broadly socialist framework. Paradoxically, although the explicit introduction of socialism may appear as evidence of sinister conspiracy to both Right and Centre, it will enable social and other welfare workers to frame much more explicit values, aims and objectives. Although equivocation renders socialism as full of pitfalls as purity does radicalism, the socialist ideal is both clearer and more realistic about achievable ends. The organised voices of socialist doctors or lawyers may often have been weak and ineffective, but they have certainly been accepted as legitimate and have had influence on both policy and practice. However, workers in important but more limited spheres like midwifery may find that their objectives (in the case of midwifery, the demystification and demedicalisation of birth and motherhood) may be more relevantly grouped under a banner of radicalism that will attract more widespread support from people who do not regard themselves as 'political'. But attempts to place tight boundaries around the recognised sphere of social work comment must be strongly resisted.

The explicit introduction of socialist ideals into social work organisation and practice does not mean that radicalism is outmoded. While it is pleasing that social work may become, at any rate in part, more closely linked to socialist ideals rather than being an isolated moral crusade, the dangers of reformism and incorporation remain as enticing as they have been for the Labour Party throughout its history. The radical tone must remain if the dangers I have discussed in the Preface and in Chapter 2 are to be avoided.

Working for Labour councils

Some of these possibilities obviously relate closely to the politics of local councils. In Tory areas socialist social work may have to be limited to defending services and individual clients or groups, interspersed with radical campaigns. But with all the major parties taking increasingly ideological stands on welfare, councillors are likely to take an increasingly detailed interest in achieving their own ends, thus opening up many old debates about the independence of professions or officials. Working for a Labour council may present more opportunities for innovations in structure; however, differences, not only on the lines of traditional socialist disagreements, but also between socialists who hold different positions in the state structure, will become much more apparent. To start with, many of Labour's old guard, especially at a local level, may well be far more interested in corporatism and the prestigious running of the local state than in simple welfare issues. Such paternalism tends to discourage even basic attempts towards democratisation. Councillors will also have politically expedient pet projects of their own which will, at best, only reflect some welfare interests. More radical councils (a very small minority) are more likely to place welfare among their main priorities and to have the courage both to defend their budgets and attempt some organisational change. But they, too, are likely to find themselves quickly on the defensive against economic difficulties not of their own making and the bias of state machinery; they then have to call on their workers (and/or ratepayers) to make sacrifices for ends that seem beyond the councillors' power to deliver. A vigorous campaign in Lothian during 1981 waged to save jobs against the direct intervention of the Secretary of State for Scotland lost any chance of success because neither the Labour Group nor the work-force as a whole were prepared to take the very risky step of united all-out action. The Tory insistence on greater central control of budgeting for local government and the use of the cash limit and penalty system have threatened to outflank Labour councils by forcing punitive rate increases. Understandably, councillors and workers are, unless pressed to extremes, reluctant to stand and fight; Labour groups may then resort to mystificatory and self-justifying tactics like the bungled referendum about cuts in Coventry during 1981; rather than trying to save services, the council was really trying to get itself off the hook by getting public sanction for the cutbacks. In an exercise boycotted by the Left, 22 per cent of the electorate turned out, most of whom preferred lower rates to retaining services. Although the cuts in the education budget which followed were resisted by a solid NUPE strike which eventually won reinstatement for the dinner ladies who were being made redundant, it was only at the cost of forgoing wage increases, which eventually gave the councillors the savings they were looking for. And there of course is the rub; whatever their intentions, the councillors remain social workers' employers and few seek to win any sort of trust from their employees; instead, like so many trade-union conveners turned personnel managers, their sympathy cannot be relied on because they are often much more rigid and dangerous enemies than those who have always been part of management. In a dispute (like the social work strikes) the best that can usually be expected from Labour employers is restraint from provocation, but that is small comfort. It must also be remembered that individual councillors stand in particular personal risk if they go out on a limb; the experience of the Clay Cross councillors who took Labour policy literally and defied the 1971 Housing Act, only to be bankrupted, stripped of their political status and forgotten by the Labour establishment, is still cited as a reason for having to accept oppressive legislation.

These are notes of warning aimed at structural problems in trying to achieve 'socialism in one local authority'; they should not prevent us from welcoming the advent of reforming councils and pushing them as far as they will go. A really informed and committed group of councillors may not only be able to permit and fund a much wider range of activities, to achieve changes in organisation which permit at least a small transfer of power, but also to break down some of the barriers between politicians and professionals in welfare matters. But such changes can only occur where all concerned recognise that major conflicting interests are at work, and do not exact a forced and false unity as the price of experiment.

Alliances between different groups in the Labour movement are fundamental to socialist change, which cannot simply emerge from individual practice without the development of socialist institutions. The Left will continue to differ on how far these can be created, short of revolutionary change, but there is plenty of scope for experiments in practice and in relationships provided the claims made for them are not too great. We must find every way we can to challenge oppressive or bureaucratic government; conservative and undemocratic trade unions, hierarchical schools and the present form of the family must all be questioned and defied where possible. One example of the chances and limits for experiment in the health sector comes from those GPs who have sought to organise their practices collectively, taking unexpected advantage of their positions as independent contractors to the NHS. The quality and range of patient care have frequently improved and there has been much emphasis on the use of non-medical personnel in preventative health and primary care, even extending so far as campaigns on issues ranging from nutrition to the perils of nuclear warfare. But within the collectives, even when pay has been evenly distributed, the authority of the doctors has inevitably remained paramount, because of their training, their structural status and the inability, in isolation, to find more socialist forms of accountability. These collectives are radical institutions guided by socialist principles, and perhaps that is the best we can hope for at present. It may of course seem perverse, even contradictory, to demand transformation while remaining sceptical of its practicality. But such scepticism is based on a real assessment of the shifting balance of social forces; we are working in a dynamic field with constantly changing perimeters. Recognising and noting these boundaries need not stop us from continuing to explore the space between in order to affect both the pace and the direction of change. To do so, I suggest we need at least three planks of understanding: the harnessing of dialectic, effective democratisation, and a spectrum of socialist practice including both defensive and oppositional work. All of these are living elements in current debates about practical socialism.

Harnessing dialectic

There has been some discussion in earlier parts of the book of how dialectic is not a simple posing of polarities, but an understanding of their intimate and dynamic relation to each other. The idea of welfare is central when discussing the contradictions of modern capitalist society; our health and social service institutions, produced from contradictory demands, have been and will become again a most important focus of class struggle. Some socialists argue that our most appropriate strategy is continually to press for welfare goals to be implemented whatever other priorities capitalist logic may pose. But even welfare ideology is subject to exactly the same process and to its own contradictions: for instance, such a strategy tells us nothing about how to regard the role of the family in welfare. To press for the implementation of policies to aid the family, when in fact we may want to see social reproduction taking a very different form, seems a curiously limited programme. It is of course generally conceded that the goal of socialism is a welfare society where production, as the slogan says, is for need rather than profit. But, as we have seen, our welfare structure has other roles as well: control, rationing, the reproduction of appropriate labour-power, or defensive concession to workers' demands, when it can be afforded. As a result, socialists do not only demand welfare, but justice also, and while welfare is often used as a means of achieving social justice, the two concepts can often be in opposition.

Of several possible examples, I shall cite only that of residential care for children. Justifications for residential care are a confused amalgam even in the liberal and therapeutic traditions, where the motives of rescue, compensation for deprivation and rehabilitation mix uneasily with the notions of control and punishment that are becoming increasingly explicit again. To a child, even (perhaps especially) when not at fault, any separation from his or her parents is likely to seem a punishment, the more so when it occurs through the exercise of bureaucratic and legal processes. Privately taken decisions about parental access or, still worse, abuse of the procedure by which local authorities have been able to assume parental rights over a child without necessarily involving a court only add to the process by which children's homes, despite very great improvements in local authority care, including experiments as radical as any elsewhere which are not always credited, remain tainted with the stigma of 'second best' even when they are not being characterised as punitive. The increase in care orders over the last decade has only reinforced such stigma – as does criticism of attempts (even if sometimes misguided) to improve the material standards of care as being the provision of palaces for delinquents. Conversely, the clumsy implementation of necessary safety regulations often creates a traditionally institutional atmosphere. The stigma seems to attach not only to children but also to residential workers, who in matters of pay, training and status still lag behind their fieldwork colleagues.

So it is hardly surprising that organisations such as Justice for Children that have the excellent objective of preventing children from being brought unnecessarily into care, and do extremely useful work in publicising the abuse of discretionary powers or over-hasty reactions to instances of child neglect, should propound principles some of which seem likely to strengthen still further the prejudice against facilities for those children, whom, they admit, cannot remain at home.[4] No socialist can do other than support those principles which apply to court hearings, namely to opt for the least restrictive alternatives, for the parties' right to legal representation, and that decision-making should be both visible and accountable. But two of their more general principles, for family autonomy and for the most limited interventions, cannot so easily be taken for granted. *Justice for Children* rightly quotes the *Finer Report on One Parent Families* (1974), which states that the object of achieving welfare must not be permitted to weaken or shortcut the normal safeguards of judicial procedure; they also stress the need to make satisfactory services available on a voluntary basis (voluntary, that is, for the children concerned). But simple and individualistic support for the family as prime social unit may make effective help much more difficult, well though it may succeed in protecting children and families in weak economic positions from arbitrary state intervention. A socialist approach to this dilemma would be to support the legal initiatives of this radical campaign, but to seek at the same time to extend the model of residential care towards a new mode of living communally with children, to make this and other support (in schools, for example) both more accessible and acceptable to children of all social conditions and ultimately for parents. True justice for children would involve allowing them a much greater role in all aspects of daily life: our society is notorious for adult attempts to pretend that children do not exist or, failing that, to segregate them. One step would be to promote much more flexible, non-stigmatising and short-term use of local residential provision, in the same way as help is provided in many areas for the elderly; one reported experiment was the Denaby Red House, opened as one of the original Educational Priority Area schemes.[5]

Thus socialists need to grasp both the legalistic arguments which reassert children's and indeed parental rights, and the apparently contradictory position of making 'care' more attractive. The importance of the issue is that it goes beyond the 100,000 or so children in care. As Cynthia Cockburn argued in *The Local State* (1977), family policy in all its aspects is at the root of social policy; Rustin has shown how the whole development of social work as a profession is linked with increasing emphasis on the family as a principal object of social policy.[6] At stake are the extent and nature of state provision both within and after a market economy. The lesson of this example, as of many situations described earlier in the book, is that we need continually to take account of contradictory pressures; in fact we must expect them to be present. The more we assert one alternative, the more the possibility of the other is raised. Sometimes we may want both; sometimes we shall seek to exclude one altogether; we must found our decisions on the way in which these conflicting interests match up with the contradictory forces within capitalist society as a whole. That partially involves recognising that our perspective is of little use in isolation: both our aims and our practice have to take full account of the second plank of understanding: the need for genuine democracy arising out of both individual and collective experience.

Democratisation

The call for greater democracy has traditionally been a plank of all radical platforms since the eighteenth century. Within social work some of the most important arguments were put crudely by *Case Con* (mainly in the context of industrial relations). By and large liberal social workers neglected the issue in practice, except for some token efforts, and the major impact came from groups such as claimants and the disabled organising their own protests. Within Social Services Departments foster parents have forced much greater formal account to be taken of their views. The National Children's Bureau has successfully given the impetus to the formation of 'Who Cares?, an organisation for children in care. Some social workers are also using documents such as *Clients are Fellow Citizens*, published by B.A.S.W. to explore the issues of participation.

But democratisation is something much more thorough, and the case for socialists taking a 'strategic stand' for direct democracy and accountability, given the lack of a suitably vibrant mass movement and the practical difficulties of formulating progressive welfare practice, has been most forcefully advanced by the authors of *Towards Socialist Welfare Work*.[7] They analyse many of the failings of existing welfare structures as the result of a social democratic ideology which has created institutions which pretend to be value-free and administered by experts, while patronising and alienating their clients. There can be no doubt of the value of such an approach, containing, as it does, demands which highlight the issues of the control and direction of welfare agencies and policies in the context of class conflict, and not only legitimate but emphasise the importance of collective action. Bolger *et al.* point out how, especially in child care, the welfare process excludes people from all sorts of decision about their own lives, and then blames them when things go wrong. They argue rightly that the demand for democratisation can be a touchstone of whether practice is progressive. As Ron Bailey has put it, we need to ask every day: 'Which way will I put the pressure, up or down?'[8] In individual instances we may often have less scope than this proposal implies, but radicals and socialists are here provided with a practical and positive principle to work from. Where we fail to put pressure upwards, we must find other ways of compensating.

And yet there are problems with this strategy of which socialists must at least be aware. Clearly democratisation must offer something more than the slogan of participation, which, I suggested in Chapter 7, is often little more than window-dressing for incorporation. The process must involve not just consultation but a real transfer of power, with unpredictable results. Democratisation is a surrender of power by at least some bodies, and comes hard to embattled liberals seeking support for progressive policies in the face of an orchestrated swing to the Right. Half-hearted ventures produce discrediting devices like the 1981 Coventry referendum mentioned above, which looked, from the outside, like an attempt to force the unions and the Left of the Labour Party into meekly accepting cuts. Also in 1981 Sheffield Education Committee decided to consult the public on the ending of corporal punishment in schools; parents and teachers voted fairly heavily in favour of retention. The council decided to abolish beatings anyway, only to be accused, ironically enough, of heavy-handed authoritarianism. Of course, the group most intimately concerned, the children, had no official vote; but by refusing from the start to make clear the purpose of the exercise, the councillors were, as far as consultation was concerned, hoist with their own petard. What they had missed was the need for a very active campaign in order to help create and coalesce the experience which would show why beatings were unnecessary, and to build a base for non-hierarchical discipline in schools.

The need for clarity of objectives is accentuated by the overlap between socialist demands for a fully democratic process and crude anti-statist feeling fuelled by right-wing populists. Workers in education have been grappling for some years with demands for accountability which carry disturbing implications. In the United States there is an Accountability Movement (part of the Moral Majority), whose aim is to wrest control of the schools from liberal professionals and to make them subject to popular and parental demand. Evangelical religious feeling has played a strong part in this and other movements; one demand has been the reinstatement of 'creationism' on the curriculum. More worrying still is the success which has been achieved in at least some states in imposing harsh productivity controls on both teachers and children, who are both assessed solely on examination results. In the worst cases children who do not do well are held back a year to repeat the lessons with younger pupils; teachers are simply sacked if their pupils' results are not up to scratch. There has already been some spill-over of such controls in British educational thinking.[9]

Such developments pose several dangers for socialists who do not take them seriously. My reservations about accountability are based neither on the desire to cover up sloppy work nor on what Bolger *et al.* rightly diagnose in some quarters as a typically social democratic fear of the unchecked power of the organised working class. The worst risk is that welfare, instead of being opened up to genuine popular control, is surrendered to hostile values, for instance evangelical judgmentalism; thus power passes from politicians or professionals to ministers and is mediated through their congregations. This is most likely to happen at times like the present, when the restructuring of capital undermines an ideology of welfare which has, even at the best of times, to function in a generally hostile environment conditioned by means of communication whose owners and managers have sectoral rather than mass interests at heart. Finally, both as socialists and as welfare workers, we still have to evolve satisfactory ways of democratising institutions which do genuinely attempt to arbitrate between conflicting interests, whether of groups or individuals, and within the working class. Bolger *et al.* do concede that without a socialist movement commanding wide support, attempts at change within the state will have to be limited. I think they underestimate the problem; we need to give much more attention to the building of such a movement; it may be that the opportunities for doing so within the work setting are, for most of us, too limited and that the attempt to democratise fundamentally oppressive structures may prove to be a luxury or a distraction. My warning here is not against the attempt or the demand, but against the illusion of success it may create unless we bear all the contradictory forces in mind.

To sum up. Welfare cannot lightly be rendered more vulnerable to other forms of ruling-class domination, especially when capital is reasserting the need for order and control. Welfare is not yet so corrupt, alienating or degrading that it can be so surrendered. We have therefore to distinguish liberal demands for participation, or right-wing pressure for a return to the exertion of individualistic power, from the very different experience of socialist democracy, that of a collective struggle for power within which we all share responsibility, which will create a logic of its own based on mutual respect, and which will enable us to transform at least some of the separate interests which divide us. I have already made it clear that I do not think this can be achieved directly through the state, though one of our most important tasks as state workers is to make the machinery responsive to the demands placed on it. All this may sound an ambitious, naive or rhetorical programme for the harsh 1980s. But if we can even assist in creating a broad base for social service users to pool their demands, our contribution will be worthwhile. To consider the practicality of such work, we must now move to what I have termed the third plank of a socialist-inspired social work, the distinction between defensive and oppositional work, first widely propagated in *In and Against the State*, and developed with more detailed application to the probation service by Walker and Beaumont.[10] In particular we must attend to the way in which these two styles can alternate or merge over time.

Defensive work

Walker and Beaumont rightly observe how defensive social work has been underrated by radicals. Setting our sights too high may be partly to blame; another factor has been the need to distinguish radical initiatives from those of mainstream social work whose intervention in institutions such as the courts has tended towards mitigation rather than defence. Once again an explicitly socialist framework not only gives more possibility of practical guidance, but also enables relevant analogies to be drawn with other bodies undertaking a similar role within the working class and subject to many of the same strengths and weaknesses.

The defensive mode of socialist social work is based first upon an understanding of the positions of differing individuals and groups within the class structure and in relation to the state; second, on a commitment to unmask the ways in which these positions affect those who form our constituency; and third, upon the development of tactics by which people can protect themselves and one another from the adversities arising from such positions. With clients this work means developing their knowledge and confidence so that they can fully exercise their rights; both one-to-one and group activities will be necessary. Within the agency it means laying the base for mutual and collective support so that we can take the risks and vulnerability both of individual caring and of social action. I shall discuss individual work first: although its effectiveness may be limited, one-to-one relationships may provide the best base for leading people through to group experience, the more so if the relationship is not 'professionalised'. Also it is possible to use the space allowed by the professional ideal and the privacy of casework to explore themes with clients which might not receive official sanction if publicly pursued. There seems little problem of legitimacy here, provided that the clients themselves see such exploration as helpful.

Socialist casework?

Work with individuals is almost always defensive (in political terms), though it may be an important prerequisite for future change. This is the more so for the majority of fieldworkers whose caseloads are dominated either by statutory obligations or the increasing economic burdens that weigh our clients down. The pressures of these latter problems force us especially to relate to our clients as individuals in the first instance; the same would be true of a claimants' union, though the important difference would be that individual attention to problems would not mean that claimants' difficulties were individualised; social workers who spend much of their time on financial problems should perhaps consider whether other solutions like specific advice and advocacy clinics or agencies would not be more useful. But, as I shall argue in a moment, this sort of advocacy is not the only stuff of radicalism; the dynamic and behavioural traditions within social work orthodoxy may also be harnessed to create the possibility of change, particularly in terms of the distinction I made earlier (p. 67) between resources and problems.

How then should we approach individual work? None of the old-fashioned orthodoxies will really serve: the analytic style is rarely appropriate and, if misapplied, is condescending, mystifying and often completely undermining. (The confusion perpetrated by some tutors and supervisors between the proper content of social work supervision and personal counselling has done as much damage as anything to the casework idea.) In recent years fashion has swung towards more active roles for caseworkers or therapists and to an interactional analysis which makes allowance for the separate identities and purposes of the protagonists. In this way the possibilities of conflict and of change have been built into the social work encounter. It is, however, typical of the developments in social work which I have described that the model in vogue, that of task-centred contracts, should be based on a commercial transaction ending in a finite exchange. Thus a social worker may promise a certain type of support to a client in exchange for the adoption or abandonment of certain behaviour. Social workers have welcomed the idea of such contracts since they not only purvey the illusion of equality, but suggest that we have something definite to give. But by concentrating on the contract, the model has become static and depersonalising, as well as disguising the inequality inherent in the relationship.

A more realistic and open-ended version of the model can be constructed, focusing not on the outcome but on the negotiation which precedes it – a process which should be directed at moving away from the institutionalisation of clients' difficulties towards a more genuine social and personal understanding. Much social work negotiation is determined by the social worker's tattered intent to maintain some sort of integrity and the client's desperate manoeuvres to preserve the vestiges of dignity. The ensuing conflict gnaws away all their energy. The only way to avoid this is to step outside the social worker and client roles entirely and to analyse the conflict for what it really is. The purpose of the negotiation is not to arrive at some artificial bargain, but to attain some degree of sharing. This sharing involves the attempt to transfer whatever knowledge, experience or power we possess; the power to explain, to resist, to be confident, to give; the power, at a mundane level, to disentangle bureaucracy and stand up for rights; in short, the power, however limited, of being a person. This cannot be achieved without a more fundamental sharing, not this time of power, but of weakness. In order to bridge the institutional gap which divides us from clients, we have to counter our apparent privilege by acknowledging (though not parading) not simply our individual weaknesses but our weakness as individuals. One aspect of the casework or groupwork encounter must, therefore, be a sense of individual struggle which, if shared, brings strength to both parties. Social workers must no longer be allowed to play at God.

Being a person involves the right to be known and to have our worth appreciated, to feel that we are not alone. This, I suspect, is part of what lies behind the qualities of homeliness and empathy which clients praise in social workers. It is not just a matter of finding somebody easy to talk with, but of feeling that one matters. John Berger characterises this event as 'recognition', an imaginative effort by the helper which not only bestows identity on the person who is being helped and on their problem, but links that person to the world by offering the helper as a comparable person as others too are comparable; in a word, the helper offers fraternity.[11] In the context of medicine which Berger describes, fraternity is compatible with some degree of paternalism. However, the social processes in which both we and our clients are both actors and victims have to be confronted as far as possible on a basis of equality. Jordan seeks to base such an equality on citizenship, thus reflecting his belief in the potential of a social-democratic society.[12] Revolutionaries regard that as midlead-ing; we offer an attempt at personal fraternity sustained by an understanding of our mutual exploitation by capital. In order to achieve any sort of recognition, we have to escape the structural deformities of our role.

Few clients will immediately understand or accept such a position; this is the disadvantage of applying Freire's dialogical model,[13] which requires some pre-existing awareness of oppression. But the point about both negotiation and dialogics is that, within the notion of sharing, they allow fully for the possibility of conflict. We do not have to agree with clients any more than they with us. In fact if we are to achieve some sense of each other as real people operating in a real world, some degree of conflict will be not only necessary but legitimate. The essence of working with 'difficult' clients is to convey the fact that the social worker too is a person who is ready to give but will not just allow himself to be messed about. Sometimes even in long-term work this will require quite harsh measures, including use of statutory powers. Provided that we can separate ourselves from the bureaucratised pseudo-caring which is thrust on us, such use of authority can be an occasion for growth even in radical terms. Within this context it becomes easier to understand the basis on which it is justifiable for radicals or socialists to engage in statutory work. We and our clients have to take realistic account of the demands made on us if we are to survive, but if we, as social workers, are able not to identify with our roles, both we and our clients can, perhaps after some initial confusion, attain a better understanding of events around us. This does not mean that we should take action we deem to be unnecessary, but that we should take every opportunity to offer non-stigmatising explanations of the social forces which determine the limits of action. Where clients' financial affairs are under discussion, and I seem to be the most appropriate person to offer help, I do so with the explicit suggestion that the client should regard me as an accountant, paid by the state to perform certain services at his or her request or to offer advice. I suggest that this is a perfectly normal arrangement for the large number of people who find tax and other matters hard to deal with, and I find that this provides a very adequate basis to discuss with clients how best they can manage their affairs, how they share certain problems with others, and steps of various different sorts which may be taken.

Another example is the composition of court reports, a game as elaborate as the solicitor's construction of a defence, the prosecution's arrangement of the evidence, or the deliberations of bench or jury. To attain any success in our aim of protecting the poor, the weak or the oppressed against the consequences of an arbitrary or bourgeois justice, we have not only to maintain our own credibility in the courts, as long as we are part of them, but also to remember that workers, too, demand to be protected against crime. There may be occasions when economic analyses may be acceptable as well as appropriate (structural and economic factors ought to be the only material provided in reports requested after conviction for offences like rioting), but normally they will be disregarded, as will an excess of sob stories. But we do need to ensure that our clients enter the courts as fully equipped as possible, that they know their rights, have some understanding of procedure and are adequately represented, especially when their views of outcome are different from the social worker's. We also need to recognise that, while some battles will be lost, we should monitor the style and bias of courts in order to influence patterns of sentencing. We can also refuse to collude with bad sentencing practice.

Where we are the direct executors of authority, the conflicts are still more difficult. Obviously the exercise of power is to be minimised. None the less there are occasions when an individual's social consciousness is so faulty that only a forceful outside intervention can hook them back into the real world. It is, however, essential to distinguish, both to oneself and to clients, the actions which are taken for genuinely therapeutic reasons, and those which are forced by a sheer lack of alternatives. Most instances of compulsory admissions under the 1959 Mental Health Act fall into the latter category, and should provide constant stimulus to try to organise such alternatives. Those who would like social workers to have no truck with any such action must consider whether clients would really be better served if these functions were the sphere of specialised workers who would inevitably resemble the police. But of course, however good we are at explaining things, especially after the event, we cannot expect to be any the more liked for it. As an old *Case Con* cover (no. 19, 1975) put it, showing a child faced with two social workers, one's pockets stuffed with Tavistock publications, the other carrying the works of Marx and Trotsky: 'I don't care which of you puts me away.'

To sum up, constructive involvement in statutory work can be justified both on the grounds of offering clients a different perspective from the official view in order to help them understand and choose realistic options which, so far as possible, safeguard their interests, and of preventing excesses or abuses in the administration of either justice or therapy. I shall have a little more to say about counselling and therapy in the section on skills. Individual work is important, especially where the social worker's scope is limited. But tactically it is often not far from being a last-ditch defence, and at best is unlikely to be much more than palliative.

Solidarity and alliances

The effective defence of workers and claimants demands the introduction of new elements of organisation and collective work, which can in turn form a basis for moving into direct opposition in order to achieve change. The simplest example I know comes from the work of a health collective which, in conjunction with local shop stewards' committees, began running a weekend health and safety clinic in a working men's club. From picking up individual queries, those involved were able to move on to active campaigning on safety issues. We need to learn through such practical experience how to work together in non-hierarchical (though not necessarily leaderless) groups, a much harder task than it sounds; and we need to do so with both colleagues and others, whether clients, volunteers or others; some groups will mix categories; others may organise around one category. Sometimes the short-term interest of these groups will merge; sometimes they will diverge.

The immediate focus, for most social workers, is the team to which they are attached. Teamwork has been the centre of an increasing amount of professional attention, much of it concerned with the efficient distribution of tasks, though the need for support is also recognised. It is this latter aspect which I want to emphasise, by stressing the experience and quality of sharing. If we are to understand and improve our work, let alone politicise it, we have to create a working atmosphere in which support and criticism can mingle. At present social work teams tend to group defensively against the demands of clients on the one hand and management on the other. They are divided within themselves by differential grading systems which reflect personal history rather than the job being done, a division likely to be reinforced if career grades are ever introduced. Most supervision is on an individual basis and team or area meetings become boring or routine events which members resent and often miss. Caseworkers' incapacity in groups is reinforced by the longing to bury themselves in individual problems and issues, without taking the responsibility of thinking through the implications. By reflecting in our reactions to each other the individual way we treat our clients and by shrinking from any public vulnerability, most social workers fail to gain any practical understanding of the value of shared experience and group support. Our defensiveness makes us afraid to venture; because we are so frequently faced with hostility, we fail to recognise that the best criticism derives from caring.

One major goal of radical social work has to be to foster teamwork, not just for its own sake or for the maintenance and improvement of standards which will result, but for its political consequences. A team which functions co-operatively is a break in the hierarchical command. The political conclusions which will be forced on any such team will lead it to extend its solidarity towards other workers and towards clients. Two consequences are likely to occur. Firstly, the working lives of team members will be enhanced if they are able to assert greater control over their jobs. (It must be emphasised that the control will not be complete; radicals are not seeking to *run* such a stunted enterprise as social work, but to protect themselves and their clients.) Secondly, the collective security engendered is likely to make social work a much more open affair, which will in turn allow clients a greater freedom in and choice over the help they get. It would then be possible to start groups in which both social workers and clients could participate on an equal basis in an examination of their respective positions; this would be the first step towards real participation. These groups might then be able to move to a discussion of their members' lives and problems at a more personal level. Such a development could be of considerable political significance if it became widespread.

Teams engaged in this kind of approach will need to form all kinds of alliances and will need to maintain strong union links, as their actions are likely to bring them into conflict with management. The hostility evoked by the reports produced by the Leeds Social Workers Action Group meant that it had to seek the official support of the local NALGO branch, which now acts as its publisher. Working with groups of social services users is no easier than ever it was. Despite professional assertions that groupwork is now accepted in itself, few departments seem actively to encourage it, especially as a tool for mainline social workers. Most often groupwork is seen as an extra: to be done either in caseworkers' spare time, with few if any resources, or as the province of special workers or projects, often with a 'community' or 'intermediate treatment' label. But the potential power of groups is illustrated by the advances made by foster parents in promoting their status and interests. Rarely, even in the mental health setting, is groupwork offered as a first-line approach. That groupwork in the orthodox sense should still in some places be seen as a novelty is quite extraordinary. But that neither radical nor socialist group-orientated approaches have had much impact, except in struggles against cuts which have provided the motivation and momentum to create change, is less surprising. Non-hierarchical groupwork with social services users requires abandoning a great deal of professional acculturation and to step as far as possible out of the paid social worker role. Myra Garrett puts the problem in its most extreme form when she says: 'Never trust a social worker.' Her account of the degree to which she had to step back and challenge people's expectations of her in order to get them to release their own potential serves as a most useful model.[14] Certainly within our own agencies there is no lack of need for those with similar problems, status or relationships to us to get together and begin to represent themselves. Following on from Myra Garrett's comment, I also have doubts about whether state social workers are any more the most appropriate people to represent their clients' group interests, because we still remain bound into the official system, and, as yet, lack any adequate direct accountability to such groups.

One of the most underprivileged groups are those people who, for reasons of long or short-term disabilities, whether physical or mental, do what passes for 'paid' work in day centres or rehabilitation units. Their wages are controlled in what often seems to be an arbitrary fashion, not always linked to work achievement or to the earnings limits attached to state benefits, which will not be the same for all users. Two principles seem fundamental and easy to implement: accounts should be open for users to inspect; and any profits, if they cannot be distributed through individual wages, should go into a common fund. It is not always possible for users to act for themselves without a great deal of support, but few social workers will be able to resist the pressures of 'therapeutic goals' for their clients or of the open conflict liable to be produced with day-centre staff as well as central management. And unless the centre staff are themselves united, it will be almost impossible to raise other issues like the question of contract labour for non-union firms. Individuals who do so are likely to become very isolated. There are already some workshops for the disabled which operate on co-operative lines. But elsewhere, outside bodies like the League for the Blind and Disabled (affiliated to the T.U.C.), the National Union of Students (already approached by some trainees in centres for the mentally handicapped),[15] the new Union for the Physically Impaired Against Segregation, or even charities like MIND, could perform useful representative and organisational roles. There are many issues which may prompt centre users to form a group which could approach some outside body – wages, benefits or struggles against cutbacks are the most obvious and widely shared. Socialist social workers involved with such centres should be pooling information and attempting, with centre staff, to allow meetings to be called. Staff initially sceptical of such a move may well find that, with the right support, users will be able to set up much more effective structures than some of the present well-intentioned but feeble attempts at democracy.

Oppositional work

The example above shows how initiatives, originally seen as opposing existing structures, can easily become incorporated. This should not, however, be seen as a discouragement to setting up channels through which users can press their demands, because, without organised networks, they will continue as passive recipients (or non-recipients) of services. As demands fluctuate, there is likely to be a fluid movement between defence and opposition to existing structures: a defensive strategy will include oppositional tactics, and vice versa. By *oppositional* I mean work which directly confronts the form, definitions and demands of the state. Such work may be negative, in the sense of refusing certain tasks, duties, impositions and categories; or positive, in the sense of creating new definitions and networks which seek to replace or significantly alter those of the state. Useful summaries of possible directions for opposition are offered in *In and Against the State* and in *Probation Work, Critical Theory and Socialist Practice*.

At their simplest, oppositional tactics are best described as 'client refusal', a phrase coined by Ian Taylor to denote a specific kind of political advocacy,[16] but which has a much wider application. At its most innocuous, client refusal consists simply in blocking the unjust suction of individuals into so-called 'therapeutic' situations where they lose control and responsibility. One of the earliest examples was the refusal by many groups of social workers in the early 1970s to receive children into care solely because of homelessness. Analogous is the refusal to accept clients for casework simply because in these times of monetarist economics they can no longer meet their bills. But this kind of response has to be backed by a readiness to offer alternative suggestions for people to organise; this needs to be done openly and publicly, because one of the major objects is not to let protest about hardship become defused by remaining individualised. The initial stages of confrontation within the courts also demand great solidarity. The National Association of Probation Officers has refused to prepare social enquiry reports on any defendant convicted of political offences, and it seems clear that this should be extended to defendants on riot charges, unless they request otherwise. Similarly a suggestion has been made that in courts where the bench, encouraged by the right-wing law-and-order lobby, seems blatantly or consistently to be ignoring recommendations, probation officers should refrain from cloaking what is happening by the preparation of reports.[17] There must also be much more forceful monitoring of the new and harsher penal regimes: in the first twenty-two months after the 'short, sharp shock' detention centre was reintroduced in June 1980, 188 young offenders had to be transferred out for physical or mental problems, and two died.[18] Walker and Beaumont also advocate resistance to the use of probation officers as direct instruments of control in the community.

Unfortunately, many of the most important injunctions for socialists in social work have to be negative because our position in the state structure places us at the executive end of social policy, and few of us have a great deal of room for initiatives outside national or local state guidelines. Furthermore, such initiatives should, as far as practicable, be created not by social workers but by clients and service users themselves. But it is depressing to be caught up in the mere politics of refusal, unless charged by the enthusiasm and determination of a genuine rebel movement; Cohen's manifesto for radicals of 1975, not itself particularly inspiring, is all the weaker for consisting almost entirely of 'Don'ts'.[19] There are positive means and goals in oppositional work, even on a small scale. Walker and Beaumont provide a useful checklist of criteria against which initiatives may be measured, and point out how many may well be couched in a wide enough form to gain support from liberals as well as radicals. Rightly they emphasise the development of useful services to which the state does not assign priority, including crèches, support for self-help groups, development of leisure skills for probationers instead of the outmoded work ethic, and community campaigning: something which might usefully be linked with Ian Taylor's advocacy of a much greater community accountability from the courts and police.[20] Within the agency, discussion of issues like open records not only uncover hidden prejudices but can provide the springboard for a much wider discussion and campaign about clients' rights. I have already suggested that it seems entirely legitimate for feminist work to be offered by social services, and socialists should give special emphasis to support feminist and anti-racist groups in influencing service provision. We also need to ensure access for clients to organisations countervailing the state bureaucracy. We would surely take it as axiomatic that any of our supervisees on Youth Opportunity Programmes (a Tory corruption of a liberal idea about work experience into a source of cheap labour, with few rights, and also a way to cook the unemployment statistics) should be informed of and encouraged to join the relevant union. For other client groups an active and non-bureaucratic trades council may provide the best link; for instance, in Sheffield there is a very lively Pensioners Action Group which is affiliated and presents regular reports.

There is, however, one central field where it seems imperative for socialists and radicals to take a firm oppositional stance: that of family policy. Social work has been used by the state to bolster up the nuclear family form; increasingly it is being used as a disciplinary structure, for example in the curfew proposals up for discussion for the 1982 Criminal Justice Bill. Ian Taylor, examining problems of juvenile justice, points out that although the family still provides essential support and emotional satisfaction for many people, there is increasing illogicality in concentrating social policy around the family form, when such thinking is increasingly inappropriate for the way many people are forced or choose to live, an absurdity symbolised by the misery caused to many by the traditional Christmas (my example not Taylor's!). Because social workers are the centre of the apparatus based upon family values, we must take all the more trouble not to force upon the family strains which it cannot handle, and to develop alternative models of care. We should support the case for state recognition of parenthood rather than marriage as a focus for financial and organisational measures. In our work with relatives of the elderly and disabled we should be seeking to avoid forcing them (especially the women) in the name of community care to take on more than they can handle, as well as trying to prevent removal into institutions remote from either family or community. A committed exploration of this middle ground could have important pioneering functions so that these economically marginal groups could help chart ways for all of us to combine personal caring with universal rights and individual freedom. As Taylor observes, a partially democratised state still has to be the channel for such developments in any transition towards socialism.

The more we consider oppositional work, the clearer it becomes that the infusion of socialism into social work cannot just centre on the activities of individual practitioners, or even of teams which attempt a socialist orientation but must remain within the present system. Social and political change will be buttressed not by socialist social work but by the creation of socialist institutions that are resources to the working classes, whether for individuals, groups or the movement as a whole. Our approach would often need to be turned completely around; for example, we need centres for the unemployed which have a political connotation, rather than throwing all our resources into centres for those who become mentally ill because of the stresses of unemployment. Such centres (some have already been set up) would also be organisational bases, and, in addition, would try to find ways of helping to integrate personal and political understanding with each other and with the possibility of change. Now there are limits to such a strategy: islands of socialism (like the health collectives discussed above) rarely survive long without considerable compromise. But we do need experimental models; they should not be idealised, nor should we be too depressed if they fail. Instead we should learn by examining how they have responded to the contradictions of social and economic life, and what new problems they have delineated. I am not a great believer in the possibility of 'prefigurative' institutions as solid achievements, particularly within the state. But I do not underrate their importance as part of the ideological war against our conditioning towards capitalist structures of being and thought.

In the last analysis these structures will only be changed by workers' experience as they struggle against them and develop new forms within that struggle. For this reason socialists cannot afford to abandon their organisation, nor some of their traditional weapons. Some critics have argued that the trade unions themselves should become part of the change and develop prefigurative modes of resistance; the strike sanction, they consider, should be abjured, especially in the public sector, because it is 'irresponsible' and alienating to outsiders.

Such a strategy seems to me little different from surrender. The unions must be changed; and we need to develop a wider range of tactics. But withdrawing our labour is our most powerful threat. It is no accident that a part of the Tory offensive has been to weaken trade-union structure wherever it can, especially at shopfloor level. The history of the Lucas Aerospace Combine Committee should be a lesson to us all. This combine put a great deal of work in during the mid-1970s to develop suggestions for ways in which the Lucas factories and machines could be turned over to more socially useful production. Its report was widely circulated and admired. But it made little impact on Lucas management, who eventually succeeded not only in sacking one of the shop stewards most influential in drawing up the alternative plan, but also in closing down some of the factories and forcing redundancies. It seemed that the Lucas shop stewards had neglected their own defensive organisation (admittedly hard to maintain at a time of intense demoralisation for trade unionists in the West Midlands); more significantly, they had not been in a position themselves to influence the outside market sufficiently to make their plans viable, despite support from some Labour councils. Within social services the events of 1978–9 have taught us of the need to use the strike weapon carefully, but to abjure it would in the end leave us with nothing more powerful than moral blackmail; if passed, the 1982 Employment Bill will even prevent other workers from taking action in support. So alternative forms of organisation are not enough and, in any case, are usually the first to go if cuts are introduced. We may want to widen the scope of union business and make it more accessible, but we cannot afford to forget the need for self-defence.

I have suggested that some of the oppositional tactics on offer may get support from liberal social workers. I now want to step back and examine two of the most prominent professional responses to the need for change within social services and to offer some thoughts on what, if anything, they may have to offer to those who seek a more authentically socialist approach. First, I shall consider skill development; and second, the 'patch' system of organisation or 'going local'.

Skill development and socialist social work

The last few years have seen an increasing emphasis on identifying and establishing social work skills, both in response to outside criticism and to assist the professional lobby. Many social workers have welcomed such moves in so far as they feel more confident in what they have to offer to clients and can become more assertive within their agencies. But critics have argued strongly against any reassertion of social work expertise, especially in the economic climate of Thatcherism, on the grounds that not only is this an attempt to increase the technology of oppression, but that an emphasis on skills is likely to provide a distraction from action, which may be more difficult but is much more essential if clients are to be adequately protected. In such circumstances increasing a social worker's repertoire means finding more effective ways of denying material resources and may have the consequence of forcing people to internalise their problems. These arguments seem to me to be powerful but overdeterministic. If skills are to be used merely in an attempt to manage the client population better, then those who use them are, at best, misguided. However, most skills are in themselves, like most technology, neutral, though they may be more or less relevant. We should examine them against a checklist of questions similar to those proposed by Walker and Beaumont. I have, for example, always been suspicious of moves to introduce psychotherapy into social work because I feel that it is often inappropriate and isolates both clients and practitioners. However, within psychology and psychiatry, despite some similar reservations, the realistic introduction of psychotherapy has helped to challenge the medical model and to open up the whole question of patients' rights to choose and participate in their treatment. Socialists may find some forms of psychotherapy much more acceptable than others (and its power to harm should not be underestimated), but the different models should themselves be subject to assessments of goals and consequences.

The arguments over skill development are not limited to practitioner skills. The growing appropriation of the sphere of social functioning as a suitable area for social work intervention has led to more social workers introducing social skills training for their clients. Critics of this approach, both within psychology and outside, have asserted that all that is being learnt is the ability to be a good middle-class citizen who can accept the postponement of gratification. Walker and Beaumont appear to adopt this view, but go on to argue for disseminating a model radical approach to electricity boards in cases of arrears or other dissatisfaction. This is merely skills training with a different object. My view is that radicals should not fight shy of anything that helps people to augment their personal resources, both individual and collective, over the whole range of social activity, from dealing with officialdom to the expression of intense emotion. This is quite different from drilling in behavioural etiquette. But once again the learning of skills must not be a one-way process, even with unpromising clients. Only recently have the often deviant skills of withdrawn chronic schizophrenics been given recognition. One advantage of social skills and also of problem-solving groups is that those attending them often have a wealth of resources and models; rather than the leader teaching physical or verbal drills, the group needs to evaluate different tactics and experiment with different skills.

Of course, given my remarks in the Introduction about the lack of personal skills in the helping professions, we may hardly seem the best people to engage in this sort of activity, except as a joint exploration. In order to increase the self-awareness of others we must work on our own selves. We cannot, for example, justifiably engage in such intense activities as family therapy without having worked on, assimilated and transcended our own families' emotional legacy to us. We need to be able to understand and contain our own pain, as well as that thrust on by others, during our work. The growth of women's therapy groups and of techniques such as psychodrama (whose collective method and sharing of emotion does, if well handled, offer considerable scope for the socialist exploration of emotional themes and experience) are encouraging developments. The value of the latter, and of other techniques like problem-solving or cognitive therapy, is that they do not attempt to offer or impose answers, but rather to clarify feelings, thoughts, communications and objectives. There is also room for introducing co-counselling techniques both into work with clients and into supervision. One useful approach, developed by John Southgate and others, is an amalgam of co-counselling with the feminist and socially conscious school of analysis founded by Karen Horney. Developing these or similar techniques would assist social work to shed some of its authoritarian structure and also to understand more about personal risk-taking.[21]

I have said little in this book about training, partly for reasons of space. However, I think it is worth re-emphasising the need for an effective and demystifying training that will help social workers to function more effectively within their agencies. One of the reasons social work is often so depressing is that very often we have only ourselves to offer as immediate resources, and we are required to take the strain. Although there has been improvement in the content of many C.Q.S.W. courses, they are, in my view, still too shallow to enable people to function adequately and their existence enables agencies to minimise the need for intensive post-qualification training. The C.Q.S.W. has also come under attack from the Right; the sociological content is alleged to include the fomenting of Marxism. The Left's response has been to defend the C.Q.S.W. format, in particular the independence it maintains from the priorities of government and of individual social services departments. Yet this freedom is not untrammelled; students from courses with a radical reputation have found it difficult to obtain both placements and jobs. And the reduction in job opportunities and secondment has placed the existence of some C.Q.S.W. courses under threat. It is thus not surprising that the introduction of the new Certificate in Social Service (C.S.S.) has been regarded with hostility on the grounds that it is a second-rate and cheaper qualification, limiting the career developments of its holders, and rendering their training directly subject to agency ethos. These criticisms have a great deal of truth. C.S.S. holders have in general had a poor deal, both in recognition of the effort needed for the course, and in rewards after qualification. The course is based on a day-release system linked with colleges of further education where the academic input is often poor and the curriculum subject to agency agreement.

More disturbingly still, some authorities are reported to have withdrawn secondment funds for the C.Q.S.W. and to have supported the C.S.S. However, the changing job structure in social services is eventually going to mean that a different system of training will have to be introduced, and the C.S.S. model has more to commend it than many have allowed. Most of the above deficiencies could be remedied, and there is no reason to consider that the training departments of local authorities have to be less progressive than university or polytechnic departments. This would be still more true if efforts to democratise departments create pressure for more realistic training. Some at least of the curriculum should remain independent of the agencies. The disadvantage of a lack of variety of placements could be overcome by some sort of exchange system, and there would also have to be some provision for the support of those not directly employed by local authorities. But many of these problems would be balanced by the day-release system, which means that students can apply their learning directly to their jobs, and that most of them would be much better placed, as established workers, to achieve departmental change, than students who are merely guests of teams and much of whose energy after appointment is spent on becoming acculturated to their departments. There are strong arguments, which the Left should at least explore, for uniting the C.S.S. and the C.Q.S.W. with an initial core element based on the C.S.S. model, followed by development and divergence to meet different training needs. This would also increase the importance of what is now regarded as post-qualification training, to which agencies would have to become much more committed than they are now.

'Going local'

The latest social work fashion centres on systems of decentralisation which base social workers in small, locally orientated offices in order to achieve better access, community involvement and accountability.[22] It seems likely that 'patch' systems will be encouraged by the N.I.S.W. inquiry into social work. Many socialists, especially within Labour councils, support such reform. However, acceptance of 'patchwork' should not be uncritical; the idea is hardly a new one and, as presented by some advocates, seems to owe much to the heady days of the 'community' ideal of the 1960s.

As I have argued throughout, the case against the monolithic and bureaucratised delivery of social services is a strong one, supported, for different reasons, by Right, Left and even Centre. But each ideology had distinct suggestions for change; socialists need to hold to the principles of universality and transfer of both power and resources to workers and claimants. There are several reasons for questioning the ability of 'patch' systems to achieve such a transfer.

First, despite the genuine espousal of 'going local' by some socialist councils, it is no coincidence that there should be general moves throughout the country to restructure departments both for reasons of economy and to achieve a greater measure of control over the workforce by 'rationalising' decision-making. In some areas there has been an attempt to introduce a standardised service under direct 'H.Q. control'.[23] Elsewhere community care and the rebuilding of informal support systems have been all the rage, with many people seeming to have forgotten that communities and families have proved not to be strong enough to cope with modern social and economic pressures. Informal support systems need properly resourced back-up. But the remoteness of many services is caused precisely by the need to ration demand. There are also indications that the new 'patch' teams rely heavily on social work assistants and aides, as well as home helps. While radicals must recognise that the practical, direct and informal approach of these workers is often closer to the needs of clients than the style of the professional and middle-class social worker, the latter are usually called in because other workers find it hard to cope with the pain and stress of difficult or unusually demanding situations except in an emergency, because they lack consultation, support, training, experience and incentive. On the other hand, should they take such cases on board, they risk being exploited and given levels of responsibility by the state for which they are neither trained nor rewarded. Much of the discussion over this issue confuses those aspects of social work that represent services requested by clients, and those less acceptable functions that represent the watchful eye of the state; the question of responsibility is thus glossed over. And even for trained workers, there is no appropriate grading structure offered either to reflect new responsibilities or to keep workers in post and help stave off burn-out. It is no coincidence that advocates of 'patch' regard unionism as an enemy and fail to see why detailed job descriptions have evolved as protections for workers.

It may seem paradoxical, given some of the 'patch' aims of worker autonomy, to suggest that such a change may increase state control over workforce and community; nevertheless, this presents a real danger. A fragmented workforce may gain more local knowledge at the expense of a more general perspective. Small teams will find it much more difficult to influence central policy decisions unless they succeed in organising both together and with the local community; the sort of teams envisaged may in any case have more in common with traditional community-orientated services such as health visiting and be more relevant to maintenance functions than to social change. Favourable parallels with the 'community copper' have already been drawn in the professional literature. The need to maintain agency policy on, for instance, child-care decisions is likely to mean more effective central control, especially if middle-management tiers are reduced; ease of access to the directorate and some increase in delegated authority may not compensate. Lastly the information feedback by outposts to a central corporate management body is likely, as Cynthia Cockburn has warned, to increase local influence only at the cost of reinforcing central power.[24] The slightly different and more orthodox restructuring of a Fulham sub-office has been described by Bill Bennett in a model which overcomes some of the difficulties I have listed because of its size and the nature of that team's commitment.[25] However, it is still necessary to ask if this example does much more than to show that it is possible for an orthodox team to mesh effectively into other networks; it remains to be shown that the team is more of a resource to residents than to the local state.

The case for 'patch' teams is based on a reaction to bureaucracy and several unproven assumptions. It is no more a satisfactory blueprint for effective social services than any other of social work's magic technical solutions. But, despite these reservations, any such radical restructuring does offer opportunities for socialists, particularly if the hierarchy of authority can be challenged. Any move towards greater flexibility and responsiveness must be welcomed, but there must still be doubt about whether such reorganisation is really fundamental, and I want to suggest seven questions which socialists should ask themselves and management about any proposed schemes.

To start with we should ask about any new 'patch' scheme: does it represent a real transfer of resources to the area served, or is it merely a geographical rearrangement of services? An affirmative answer means that the agency is prepared to surrender some control over the use of budgets. Second, have the different communities, both of locality and of interest, been consulted before firm plans and costings have been reached? Third, does the team involved intend to adopt a collectivist approach to social problems instead of that normally defined by individual cases and caseloads? Fourth, is the agency prepared to rethink its attitude to issues such as child abuse, so that while the individuals involved are offered support and help, child care becomes recognised much more widely as a shared social obligation for individuals, neighbourhoods and the state? Fifth, are there flexible back-up resources with easy and non-stigmatising access? Sixth, is the team fully integrated in the agency with maximum delegated authority but full communication both vertically and horizontally, and with specialist work not being treated as an elite option? Finally, are the basic trade-union issues involving rewards and protection for workers adequately resolved? If these criteria can be even approximately met, then it may be possible to see locality and 'patch' teams as having some real potential for confronting the contradictions of welfare capitalism in a form which may herald an embryonic socialism. If, on the other hand, the criteria are disregarded, 'patch' teams will either become simply organs for service delivery, or, and this second alternative is perhaps more likely, they will become subject to massive bombardment of demand and will eventually disintegrate unless they can limit their tasks and divert the pressure.

Where do we go from here?

Ultimately the significance and future of social work depend upon the condition of capital, and socialists must presumably by definition be pessimistic about the ability of capital to stave off major social change. The Thatcherite assault on welfare is part of a desperate attempt to restore the rate of profit and to cope with the consequent massive increase in social casualties by means of law and order rather than by welfare. Resources for social services are declining at the very time that the need for them is growing, and even those social workers who regard their work as apolitical can no longer hide from what is happening, as nearly every new client brings fresh financial problems arising from unemployment, redundancy, huge fuel bills, rising rents and rates, or reductions in benefit.

Although I have argued that there are areas where social workers can be of specific help, we need to be much clearer about the limits of our usefulness. For instance, it may well be true that our safety-net role *vis-à-vis* the D.H.S.S. or the fuel boards saves those agencies from placing their own houses in order; I personally would be less optimistic about their motivation so to do, but the general advice and advocacy roles might well be better performed if split off from the other functions and even assigned to other bodies like advice bureaux; this would not excuse social workers from ensuring effective representation for their clients, but might make such assistance more widely accessible. Political activists will also consider that even individual change may be better achieved by taking part in mass events like the Right to Work Campaign or the People's March for Jobs than by intermediate treatment schemes. Socialists must not lose sight of the fact that signficant structural change which removes power from the dominant class will only take place successfully if the working and claimant classes develop their own structures through active participation in the struggles which are and will be necessary. On a more parochial level, we must also accept that, despite some reservations expressed in the section on 'patchwork', the best help is often given by members of peer groups and not by professionals. Part of our job as political activists is to spread the will and the ability to give such help. We should therefore be wary, even when faced with the current scale of welfare problems, of fighting simply to increase the social work establishment without being clear what that would achieve. Needs may well be met by the creation of posts with rather different job descriptions and by a more direct transfer of resources, though I still believe that social workers can, in the right setting, offer help which, even from a socialist point of view, is constructive rather than repressive.

Since social work is at best a flawed and limited way of helping people, and at worst descends to sheer deception, and since clients as a whole are neither organised nor possessed of much political weight, some Marxists have suggested that radicals should leave social work for other sectors of the economy. This position is the reverse of the belief that social work can alter the world and equally myopic. Within the employment opportunities which are open, social work seems as legitimate an occupation as many others provided that its limitations and contradictions are fully recognised. Moreover, it may matter a good deal to clients if they are dealing with someone committed to change as opposed to the *status quo*.

Neither social workers nor clients as a group wield much economic power, but we operate within the heartland of the ideological structure of capitalism. As social workers we have to engage in a continual struggle for reform by demanding that capitalism provides protective measures appropriate to the burdens it inflicts, but those of us who are revolutionaries have to keep a clear perspective that these reforms will never be sufficient. We have to prevent disillusion by stressing that a better life will depend only on far greater changes, and by suggesting and practising the means by which change can be achieved. Social workers are in a unique position to understand the way capitalist society works and to spread that understanding. We cannot, however, change that society without joining with all those who are exploited, in an organised mass movement within which we can begin to learn how individual expression, happiness and delight can be discovered, shared and extended without oppression.

Notes and references

Preface

1. Sheila Rowbotham, Lynne Segal and Hilary Wainwright, *Beyond the Fragments*, 1st edn (Newcastle Socialist Centre and Islington Community Press, 1979).
2. London–Edinburgh Weekend Return Group, *In and Against the State* (1st edn, London, 1979; 2nd edn, Pluto Press, 1981). See also Conference of Socialist Economists State Group, *Struggle over the State* (London, 1979).
3. Peter Leonard, 'Restructuring the Welfare State', *Marxism Today*, December 1979.
4. Peter Taylor-Gooby and Jennifer Dale, *Social Theory and Social Welfare* (London: Arnold, 1981).
5. Steve Bolger, Paul Corrigan, Jan Docking and Nick Frost, *Towards Socialist Welfare Work* (London: Macmillan, 1981).

Introduction

1. C. W. Mills, 'The Professional Ideology of Social Pathologists', *American Journal of Sociology*, vol. 49, no. 2 (1943) p. 171.

Chapter 1

1. *The Times*, 27 February 1970.
2. A. R. Crosland, *The Future of Socialism* (London: Cape, 1956).
3. Phoebe Hall, *Reforming the Welfare* (London: Heinemann, 1976).
4. P. Seed, *The Expansion of Social Work in Britain* (London: Routledge and Kegan Paul, 1973).
5. *Report of the Committee on Local Authority and Allied Personal Social Services* – the Seebohm Report (London: H. M. S. O., 1968) para 30.
6. Hall, *Reforming the Welfare*, pp. 27–8.
7. Seebohm Report, para 706.
8. Hall, *Reforming the Welfare*, pp. 122–3.

9. K. Sward, *The Legend of Henry Ford* (New York: Russell, 1948), quoted by H. Braverman, *Labour and Monopoly Capital* (New York: Monthly Review Press, 1974) p. 149.
10. Bill Jordan, *Poor Parents* (London: Routledge and Kegan Paul, 1974) pp. 113–14.
11. J. Cypher, 'Social Work and Social Reform', in H. Jones (ed.), *Towards a New Social Work* (London: Routledge and Kegan Paul, 1975) p. 21.
12. G. Pearson, 'Making Social Workers', in R. Bailey and M. Brake (eds), *Radical Social Work* (London: Arnold, 1975) p. 28.
13 L. Taylor and P. Walton, 'Industrial Sabotage: Motives and Meanings', in S. Cohen (ed.), *Images of Deviance* (Harmondsworth: Penguin, 1971) pp. 219–45.
14. *Community Care*, no. 171, 27 July 1977.

Chapter 2

1. Joel Handler, 'The Coercive Children's Officer', *New Society*, no. 314, 3 October 1968, documents this trend before reorganisation.
2. Bill Jordan, *Poor Parents* (London: Routledge and Kegan Paul, 1974) p. viii.
3. H. Specht, 'Disruptive Tactics', in R. Kramer and H. Specht (eds), *Readings in Community Organisation Practice* (New Jersey: Prentice-Hall, 1969) p. 384.
4. R. Miliband, 'The Problem of the Capitalist State', in R. Blackburn (ed.), *Ideology and the Social Sciences* (London: Fontana, 1972) p. 254.
5. P. Corrigan and P. Leonard, *Social Work Practice under Capitalism* (London: Macmillan, 1978).
6. V. I. Lenin, *The State and Revolution* (Moscow: Progress Publishers, 1969) pp. 8–9.
7. V. George and P. Wilding, *Ideology and Social Welfare* (London: Routledge and Kegan Paul, 1977) p. 90.
8. Quoted by R. Miliband in *The State in Capitalist Society* (London: Weidenfeld and Nicolson, 1969) p. 55.
9. Ibid., especially pp. 138–78.
10. S. Cohen, 'Manifestos for Action', in R. Bailey and M. Brake (eds), *Radical Social Work* (London: Arnold, 1975) p. 86.
11. Despite some inaccuracies, see M. Hewitt's discussion of the use of the welfare apparatus to assist the control of immigrants in *Case Con* 4, June 1971.
12. Corrigan and Leonard, *Social Work Practice under Capitalism*, ch. 9.
13. Lenin, *The State and Revolution*, pp. 15, 20.
14. *Limits of the Law* (London: Community Development Project, 1977).
15. K. Marx, 'Preface to A Contribution to the Critique of Political Economy', in *Marx and Engels, Selected Works* (London: Lawrence and Wishart, 1970) p. 181.

16. John Clarke, 'Critical Sociology and Radical Social Work', in N. Parry, M. Rustic, and C. Satyamurti, *Social Work, Welfare and the State* (London: Arnold, 1979).
17. G. Pearson, *The Deviant Imagination* (London: Macmillan, 1975) ch. 6. See also G. Stedman Jones, *Outcast London* (Oxford University Press, 1971).
18. London–Edinburgh Weekend Return Group, *In and Against the State* (London, 1979 and 1981).

Chapter 3

1. R. Williams, *The Long Revolution* (Harmondsworth: Penguin, 1965) ch. 3.
2. R. Pinker, *Social Theory and Social Policy* (London: Heinemann, 1971) p. 170.
3. The potential client population among children is delineated by P. Wedge and H. Prosser, *Born to Fail* (London: Arrow, 1973). Selwyn Smith found a higher incidence of non-accidental injury to children in working-class families; see his *The Battered Child Syndrome* (London: Butterworth, 1975) p. 198.
4. J. Packman, *Decisions in Child Care* (London: Allen and Unwin, 1969).
5. B. Davies, I. Barton, A. Macmillan, *Variations in Children's Services* (London: Bell, 1972).
6. Bill Jordan, *Poor Parents* (London: Routledge and Kegan Paul, 1974) chs 1, 2.
7. G. Konrad, *The Caseworker* (London: Heinemann, 1976) p. 16.
8. M. Simpkin, 'Clients in the Community', in R. Jenkins, M. Aldridge and R. Thorpe (eds), *Working in the Community*, Social Work Studies no. 1 (University of Nottingham, 1975) p. 94.
9. For a critical discussion of Bernstein's work, see H. Rosen, *Language and Class* (Bristol: Falling Wall Press, 1974).
10. Jim Slater, *Return to Go* (London: Weidenfeld and Nicolson, 1977) p. 228.
11. P. Janet, *La Force et faiblesse psychologique* (Paris: Maloine, 1932) p. 258.
12. I. Reid, *Social Class Differences in Britain* (London: Open Books, 1977).
13. *The Sunday Times Magazine*, 29 September 1976.
14. P. Kinnersley, *Hazards of Work* (London: Pluto Press, 1974).
15. *The Sunday Times*, 17 July 1977.
16. Factory Inspectorate, *Annual Report 1974* (London: H. M. S. O.). See also Dr G. Ffrench, *Occupational Health* (Lancaster: Medical and Technical Publications, 1973) pp. 62–4, who adds that many of the 7000 annual fatal accidents in the home can be attributed to poor design or cheap production.

17. P. Powell *et al.*, *2,000 Accidents: a shop-floor study of their causes* (London: National Institute of Industrial Psychology, 1971).
18. Health and Safety Executive, *The Explosion at the Appleby-Frodingham Steelworks, Scunthorpe, 4 November 1975* (London: H. M. S. O., 1976) p. 28.
19. P. Lomas *et al.*, *Poverty and Schizophrenia* (London: Psychiatric Rehabilitation Association, 1973).
20. E. M. Goldberg and S. L. Morrison, 'Schizophrenia and Social Class', *British Journal of Psychiatry*, no. 109, November 1963, pp. 785–802. See also R. Turner and M. Wagenfeld, 'Occupational Mobility and Schizophrenia', *American Sociological Review*, vol 32 (1967) pp. 104–13.
21. A summary of S. Michael and T. Langner, 'Psychiatric Symptoms and Social Class', *Diseases of the Nervous System*, vol 24 (1963) p. 128, by Myre Sim in his *A Guide to Psychiatry* (Edinburgh: Churchill Livingstone, 1974) p. 668.
22. G. Fielding (Bradford University), paper presented to the 27th Annual Conference of the International Communications Association, Berlin, 1977.
23. A. B. Hollingshead and F. C. Redlich, *Social Class and Mental Illness* (New York: Wiley, 1958).
24. J. Myers and L. Bean, *A Decade Later* (New York: Wiley, 1968).
25. Goldberg and Morrison, 'Schizophrenia and Social Class', p. 801.
26. V. Kral, 'Stress and Senile Psychosis', in *Proceedings of 5th World Congress of Psychiatrists, 1971* (Excerpta Medica Amsterdam International Congress) series 274, Psychiatry, part I.
27. G. W. Brown, T. Harris and J. R. Copeland, 'Depression and Loss', *British Journal of Psychiatry*, no. 130, January 1977, pp. 1–18.
28. *Profits against Houses* (London: Community Development Project, 1977) p. 33.
29. J. Westergaard and H. Resler, *Class in a Capitalist Society* (Harmondsworth: Penguin, 1976).
30. The information in this paragraph is taken from *Royal Commission on the Distribution of Income and Wealth, Report no. 1* (London: H. M. S. O., 1975).
31. Ibid., para. 171.
32. Westergaard and Resler, *Class in a Capitalist Society*, p. 68.
33. *Racism* (London: Counter Information Services, 1976) p. 34.
34. *Social Work Today*, vol. 8, no. 5, 3 May 1977.
35. G. Fiegehen, P. Lansley and G. Smith, *Poverty and Progress in Britain 1953–73* (Cambridge University Press, 1977).
36. M. Seeman, 'On the Meaning of Alienation', *American Sociological Review*, vol. 24 (1959) p. 784.

Chapter 4

1. G. Pearson, 'The Politics of Uncertainty', in H. Jones (ed.), *Towards a*

New Social Work (London: Routledge and Kegan Paul, 1975) p. 46.
2. G. Pearson, 'Making Social Workers', in R. Bailey and M. Brake (eds), *Radical Social Work* (London: Arnold, 1975).
3. P. Blau, *The Nature of Organisations* (New York: Wiley, 1974).
4. H. Prins, 'Motivation in Social Work', *Social Work Today*, vol. 5, no. 2, 18 April 1974.
5. G. Stedman Jones, *Outcast London* (Oxford University Press, 1971) pp. 251–2, citing M. Mauss, *The Gift* (London: Cohen and West, 1966) p. 15; see also p. 63.
6. P. Halmos, *The Faith of the Counsellors* (London: Constable, 1965) p. 5.
7. W. B. Yeats, 'Crazy Jane talks to the Bishop', in *Collected Poems* (London: Macmillan, 1971) pp. 294–5.
8. *Case Con* 15 (Women's Issue) Spring 1974.
9. N. Kay, 'A Systematic Approach to Selecting Foster Parents', *Case Conference*, vol. 13, no. 2, June 1966.
10. The same syndrome is reported from across the Atlantic by Esther Stanton, *Clients Come Last* (Beverly Hills: Sage, 1970).
11. See Bill Jordan, *Client–Worker Transactions* (London: Routledge and Kegan Paul, 1970).
12. Quoted by P. Blau and W. Scott, *Formal Organisations* (London: Routledge and Kegan Paul, 1963) p. 82.
13. See J. Packman, *The Child's Generation*, (Oxford: Blackwell, 1975).
14. For a striking documentation of the way in which personal and political speculation were used by senior management in a hospital setting to discredit vital and well-founded criticism, see *The Report of the Committee of Inquiry into St. Augustine's Hospital, Canterbury* (London: H. M. S. O. 1976) especially paras 4.57–4.80.
15. G. Pearson, 'Social Work: a Privatised Solution to Public Ills', *British Journal of Social Work*, vol. 3, no. 2, Summer 1973, pp. 209–25.

Chapter 5

1. See Zofia Butrym, *The Nature of Social Work* (London: Macmillan, 1976), and Bill Jordan, *Poor Parents* (London: Routledge and Kegan Paul, 1974); also Jordan, *Freedom and the Welfare State* (London: Routledge and Kegan Paul, 1976).
2. Butrym, *The Nature of Social Work*, p. 150.
3. Ibid., p. 111.
4. Ibid., p. 95.
5. M. Simpkin, 'Clients in the Community' in R. Jenkins, M. Aldridge and R. Thorpe (eds), *Working in the Community*, Social Work Studies no. 1 (University of Nottingham, 1975).
6. J. Mayer and N. Timms, *The Client Speaks* (London: Routledge and Kegan Paul, 1970).
7. Bob Deacon, *Case Con* 17, Autumn 1974, p. 31.

8. Home Office Research Unit, *Workloads in Children's Departments* (London: H. M. S. O., 1969).
9. J. Benington, *Local Government Becomes Big Business* (Coventry: Community Development Project Occasional Paper no. 11, 1975).
10. P. Corrigan and P. Leonard, *Social Work Practice under Capitalism* (London: Macmillan, 1978) p. 45.
11. H. Braverman, *Labour and Monopoly Capital* (New York: Monthly Review Press, 1974).
12. A. Macintyre, *A Short History of Ethics* (London: Routledge and Kegan Paul, 1967).
13. Best read in H. J. Paton, *The Moral Law* (London: Hutchinson, 1966).
14. B. Rodgers and J. Dixon, *A Portrait of Social Work* (Oxford University Press, 1960), quoted by P. Halmos, *The Faith of the Counsellors* (London: Constable, 1965) p. 149.
15. C. S. Lewis, *The Four Loves* (London: Fontana, 1963) p. 121.
16. Butrym, *The Nature of Social Work*, ch. 3.
17. R. Pinker, *Social Theory and Social Policy* (London: Heinemann, 1971) p. 151.
18. Tom Hart, *A Walk with Alan* (London: Quartet, 1973).
19. Halmos, *The Faith of the Counsellors*, p. 189.
20. Jordan, *Freedom and the Welfare State*, p. 166.
21. Hart, *A Walk with Alan*.
22. Halmos, *The Faith of the Counsellors*, p. 189.
23. Quoted by Ernst Fischer, *Marx in his Own Words* (Harmondsworth: Penguin, 1973).
24. P. Ariès, *Centuries of Childhood* (Harmondsworth: Penguin, 1973) p. 393.
25. Quoted by E. Zaretsky, *Capitalism, the Family and Personal Life* (London: Pluto Press, 1976). See also S. Rowbotham, *Woman's Consciousness, Man's World* (Harmondsworth: Penguin, 1973).
26. E. Fromm, *The Art of Loving* (London: Allen and Unwin, 1970).
27. I. Mészáros, *Marx's Theory of Alienation* (London: Merlin Press, 1972) p. 269.
28. Ibid., p. 289.
29. Pinker. *Social Theory and Social Policy*, p. 170.
30. Butrym, *The Nature of Social Work*, p. 119.
31. Quoted by H. F. Ellenberger, *The Discovery of the Unconscious* (London: Allen Lane, 1970) p. 190.
32. Ibid., p. 73.

Chapter 6

1. Brunel Institute of Organisational and Social Studies, *Social Services Departments* (1974) p. 42.
2. Ibid., p. 27.

3. Rosemary Stewart, quoted by A. Gatherer and M. Warren, *Management and the Health Services* (Oxford: Pergamon, 1971) p. 30.
4. R. G. S. Brown, 'Policy Analysis and the Welfare State', in W. D. Reekie and N. C. Hunt (eds), *Management in the Social and Safety Services* (London: Tavistock, 1974) p. 180.
5. Ibid., p. 183.
6. Cf. F. McDermott, *Self Determination in Social Work* (London: Routledge and Kegan Paul, 1975).
7. *The Report of the Committee of Inquiry into St. Augustine's Hospital, Canterbury* (London: H. M. S. O., 1976) para 6.43.
8. T. Johnson, *Professions and Power* (London: Macmillan, 1972) p. 45. Much of this account is drawn from Johnson's analysis.
9. J. H. Galper, *The Politics of Social Services* (New Jersey: Prentice-Hall, 1975) p. 60.
10. E. M. Goldberg, *Helping the Aged* (London: Allen and Unwin, 1970). See the correspondence in *Community Care*, April to July 1977.
11. Scott Briar, 'Is Casework Effective?', *Social Work* (U. S. A.) January 1973. See also A. Skinner and R. Castle, *78 Battered Children* (London: N. S. P. C. C., 1969); and M. Blenkner, M. Bloom and M. Nielsen, 'A Research and Demonstration Project on Protective Services', *Social Casework*, October 1971.
12. Bill Jordan, *Poor Parents* (London: Routledge and Kegan Paul, 1974) p. 150.
13. J. Packman, *Decisions in Child Care* (London: Allen and Unwin, 1969); B. Davies, I. Barton, A. Macmillan, *Variations in Children's Services* (London: Bell, 1972).
14. V. George, *Foster Care* (London: Routledge and Kegan Paul, 1970) p. 141.
15. A. Billingsley, 'Bureaucratic and Professional Orientation Patterns', *Social Service Review*, December 1964.
16. Johnson, *Professions and Power*, p. 53.
17. *Social Work Today*, vol. 3, no. 3, 4 May 1972, 'BASW News', p. II. The same point is made by A. Rowe, 'Some Implications of the Career Structure for Social Workers', in Reekie and Hunt (eds), *Management in the Social and Safety Services*.
18. Johnson, *Professions and Power*, p. 78.
19. J. H. Skolnick and J. R. Woodworth, 'Bureaucracy, Information and Social Control', in D. J. Bodua (ed.), *The Police, Six Sociological Essays* (London: Wiley, 1967); quoted by M. Cain, 'On the Beat', in S. Cohen (ed.), *Images of Deviance* (Harmondsworth: Penguin, 1971) p. 74.
20. Z. Butrym, *The Nature of Social Work* (London: Macmillan, 1976) p. 146.
21. Kay McDougall, Obligations of a Profession', *Social Work Today*, vol. 1, no. 6, September 1970, p. 20.

Chapter 7

1. This topic is discussed, all too briefly, by Eric Hobsbawm in the essay 'Revolution and Sex', in Hobsbawm, *Revolutionaries* (London: Quartet, 1977).
2. See the discussion in G. Pearson, *The Deviant Imagination* (London: Macmillan, 1975) ch. 3.
3. *The Guardian*, 26 May 1977.
4. Pearson, *The Deviant Imagination*, p. 46.
5. R. D. Laing, *The Politics of Experience* (Harmondsworth: Penguin, 1967) p. 102.
6. Ibid., p. 11.
7. Ed Conduit, 'Marxism and Madness', *Case Con* 12, July 1973.
8. For a brief English account, see *Case Con* 9 or *Red Rat* 5, both 1972. The S. P. K.'s own publications are *S. P. K. – Aus der Krankheit eine Waffe Machen* (Munich: Trikont, 1972); and *Dokumentation*, parts I and II (Heidelberg: Prolit-Buchvertrieb, 1972).
9. F. Kitson, *Low Intensity Operations* (London: Faber, 1971); see also J. McCuen, *The Art of Counter-Revolutionary Warfare* (London: Faber, 1966).
10. Ted Clark and Dennis T. Jaffe, *Towards a Radical Therapy* (New York: Gordon and Breach, 1973).
11. Crescy Cannan, 'Welfare Rights and Wrongs', in R. Bailey and M. Brake (eds), *Radical Social Work* (London: Arnold, 1975).
12. Ron Bailey, *The Squatters* (Harmondsworth: Penguin, 1973). See also Mike Downing, 'The Ideal Homes Myth', *Case Con* 11, April 1973.
13. R. Bryant, 'Professionals in the Firing Line', *British Journal of Social Work*, vol. 3, no. 2, Summer 1973, p. 173.
14. M. Ciacci, 'Psychiatric Control', in H. Bianchi, M. Simondi, I. Taylor (eds), *Deviance and Control in Europe* (London: Wiley, 1975).
15. See J. Barter and D. Carter, 'Climbing off the Fence', *Social Work Today*, vol. 3, no. 10, 10 August 1972; A. Power, 'Homes and Squatters', *New Society*, no. 510, 6 July 1972; *Inside Story*, no. 5, September 1972; *Case Con* 8, July 1972, and 9, October 1972.
16. For a simple but essential critical account of NALGO's structure and the Whitley Council negotiating system, see Barry White, *Whitleyism or Rank and File Action*? (London: NALGO Action Group, 1975).
17. Z. Butrym, *The Nature of Social Work* (London: Macmillan, 1976) p. 60.

Chapter 8

1. Kay McDougall, 'Obligations of a Profession', *Social Work Today* vol. 1, no. 6, September 1970.
2. Patricia Morgan, *Delinquent Fantasies* (London: Temple Smith

1978); Colin Brewer and June Lait, *Can Social Work Survive?* (London: Temple Smith, 1980).

3. Paul Halmos, *The Personal and the Political* (London: Hutchinson, 1978); Martin Davies, *The Essential Social Worker* (London: Heinemann/Community Care, 1981).
4. Allison Morris, Henri Giller, Elizabeth Szwed and Hugh Geach, *Justice for Children* (London: Macmillan, 1980).
5. George Smith (ed.), *Educational Priority, Vol. 4: The West Riding Project*, DES (London: H.M.S.O., 1975) ch. 13.
6. Michael Rustin, 'Social Work and the Family', in N. Parry, M. Rustin and C. Satyamurti (eds), *Social Work, Welfare and the State* (London: Arnold, 1979).
7. Steve Bolger, Paul Corrigan, Jan Docking and Nick Frost, *Towards Socialist Welfare Work* (London: Macmillan, 1981).
8. Ron Bailey, 'Social Workers: Pawns, Police or Agitators?', in Mike Brake and Roy Bailey (eds), *Radical Social Work and Practice* (London: Arnold, 1981).
9. *Forum for the Discussion of New Trends in Education*, vol. 22, no. 1, Autumn 1979; Tony Becker and Stuart Maclure (eds), *Accountability in Education* (London: Social Science Research Council, Educational Research Board, 1979).
10. Hilary Walker and Bill Beaumont, *Probation Work, Critical Theory and Socialist Practice* (Oxford: Basil Blackwell, 1981).
11. John Berger, *A Fortunate Man* (Harmondsworth, Penguin, 1969) esp. pp. 68–77.
12. Bill Jordan, *Freedom and the Welfare State* (London: Routledge and Kegan Paul, 1976).
13. Paolo Freire, *Pedagogy of the Oppressed* (Harmondsworth: Penguin, 1972).
14. Myra Garrett, 'The Problem with Authority', in Bailey and Brake (eds), *Radical Social Work and Practice*.
15. *The Guardian*, 30 November 1981.
16. Ian Taylor, 'Client Refusal', *Case Con* 7, April 1972.
17. Ian Wilson, 'A Dissatisfying and Reactionary Practice', *Community Care*, 26 November 1981.
18. *The Guardian*, 1 April 1982.
19. Stan Cohen, 'It's All Right for You to Talk', in R. Bailey and M. Brake (eds), *Radical Social Work* (London: Arnold, 1975) pp. 94–5.
20. Ian Taylor, *Law and Order: Arguments for Socialism* (London: Macmillan, 1981).
21. John Southgate, Rosemary Randall and Frances Tomlinson, *The Barefoot Psychoanalyst*, 2nd edn (London: Association of Karen Harvey Psychoanalytic Counsellors, 1978) and Rosemary Randall,

John Southgate and Frances Tomlinson, *Co-operative and Community Group Dynamics . . . or youth meetings needn't be so appalling* (London: Barefoot Books, 1980). For a philosophical account, see Nick Ragg, *People Not Cases* (London: Routledge and Kegan Paul, 1977).

22. Roger Hadley and Stephen Hatch, *Social Welfare and Failure of the State* (London: Allen and Unwin, 1981); Roger Hadley and Morag McGrath (eds), *Going Local* (London: Bedford Square Press, 1980). See also *Community Care*, October–November 1981, *passim*.
23. Mike Stein, 'Personal Social Services under the Conservatives', *Critical Social Policy*, vol. 1, no. 3, Spring 1982.
24. Cynthia Cockburn, *The Local State* (London: Pluto Press, 1977).
25. Bill Bennett, 'The Sub-Office: a Team Approach to Local Authority Fieldwork Practice', in Brake and Bailey (eds), *Radical Social Work and Practice*.

ALSO PUBLISHED BY MACMILLAN

Critical Texts in Social Work and the Welfare State

General Editor: Peter Leonard

Published

Pete Alcock and Phil Harris
WELFARE LAW AND ORDER

Steve Bolger, Paul Corrigan, Jan Docking and Nick Frost
TOWARDS SOCIALIST WELFARE WORK: WORKING IN THE STATE

Paul Corrigan and Peter Leonard
SOCIAL WORK PRACTICE UNDER CAPITALISM: A MARXIST APPROACH

Norman Ginsburg
CLASS, CAPITAL AND SOCIAL POLICY

Ian Gough
THE POLITICAL ECONOMY OF THE WELFARE STATE

Chris Jones
STATE SOCIAL WORK AND THE WORKING CLASS

Chris Phillipson
CAPITALISM AND THE CONSTRUCTION OF OLD AGE